A LOYAL OPPOSITION
IN TIME OF WAR

A LOYAL OPPOSITION IN TIME OF WAR

THE REPUBLICAN PARTY AND THE POLITICS OF FOREIGN POLICY FROM PEARL HARBOR TO YALTA

RICHARD E. DARILEK

CONTRIBUTIONS IN AMERICAN HISTORY, NUMBER 49

GREENWOOD PRESS

WESTPORT, CONNECTICUT ● LONDON, ENGLAND

Darilek, Richard E.
   A loyal opposition in time of war.

   (Contributions in American history; no. 49)
   A revision of the author's thesis, Princeton University.
   Bibliography: p.
   Includes index.
   1. United States—Politics and government—1933-1945.
   2. United States—Foreign relations—1933-1945.
   3. World War, 1939-1945—Diplomatic history.
   4. Republican Party. I. Title.
E806.D35   1976   320.9'73'0917   75-44655
ISBN 0-8371-8773-7

Library of Congress Catalog Card Number: 75-44655

ISBN 0-8371-8773-7

First published in 1976

Greenwood Press, a division of Williamhouse-Regency Inc.
51 Riverside Avenue, Westport, Connecticut 06880

Printed in the United States of America

Brief extracts appear in the book that are taken from *The Private Papers
of Senator Vandenberg*. Copyright 1952 by Arthur H. Vandenberg, Jr.
Reprinted by permission of the publisher, Houghton Mifflin Company
and by permission of Harold Matson Company, Inc.

To my students,
To my parents,
and
To Joyce

CONTENTS

ACKNOWLEDGMENTS

I wish to express my grateful appreciation to the following individuals and institutions which, at various times and in different ways, helped me in the preparation of this work; I hope that none of them will regret the result:

Francis L. Loewenheim of Rice University, for first sparking my interest in the historical study of foreign policy and suggesting this topic as a challenging one to pursue.

Richard D. Challener and Arthur S. Link of Princeton University, for alternately directing and inspiring this work in an earlier form as a dissertation, and Arno J. Mayer of that same institution, for useful criticism.

Sandra Jean Coyner and Mrs. Emily Lawyer, for providing much needed assistance at critical moments in the preparation of my dissertation.

Jon M. Wakelyn, the editor of this series, for encouraging me from the start to revise the dissertation for publication.

My colleagues in the History Department of Herbert H. Lehman College, the City University of New York; especially Davis R. B. Ross and G. Wylie Sypher, who are currently there, and Charles M. Radding and Alan Schaffer, formerly of that department, for most helpful comments and wise counsel during the process of revision.

Mary and Robert Eaton Kelley, Barrie and Georgette Peterson, Karen Sagstetter, Peter Lloyd-Davies, Daniel Park Teter, and Orville Vernon Burton, for invaluable aid and advice.

The Shelby Cullom Davis Center for Historical Studies of Princeton University, for a semester's leave from teaching and a fellowship which made completion of the revision possible.

The George N. Shuster Fellowship Award Committee of Lehman College, for material assistance during preparation of the final draft.

My typists in this endeavor, Mrs. James Farrell, Valerie Waite, Mrs. Helen Waite, and Kathy Dahlberg, for grace under pressure.

The staff members of the governmental and university repositories listed in the bibliography, for their obliging service and unfailing kindness.

Finally, but most important, my students at Lehman College, my parents, Doris M. and Louis J. Darilek, and my wife, Joyce, for their stimulation, encouragement, and ever-constant support during the writing of this book. To them, it is affectionately dedicated.

A vital element in the balanced operation of democracy is a strong, alert and watchful opposition. That is our task for the next four years. We must constitute ourselves a vigorous, loyal and public-spirited opposition party. . . .

Let us not, therefore, fall into the partisan error of opposing things just for the sake of opposition. Ours must not be an opposition against— it must be an opposition for—an opposition for a strong America, a productive America. For only the productive can be strong and only the strong can be free.

Wendell L. Willkie
New York Times
November 11, 1940

To me "bipartisan foreign policy" means a mutual effort, under our indispensable two-Party system, to unite our official voice at the water's edge so that America speaks with maximum authority against those who would divide and conquer us and the free world. It does not involve the remotest surrender of free debate in determining our position. On the contrary, frank cooperation and free debate are indispensable to ultimate unity. In a word, it simply seeks national security ahead of partisan advantage. Every foreign policy must be *totally* debated (and I think the record proves it has been) and the "loyal opposition" is under special obligation to see that this occurs.

Arthur H. Vandenberg
*The Private Papers of
Senator Vandenberg,*
552-553.
January 5, 1950

1 INTRODUCTION

This study derives from and combines a variety of interests, of which American politics, government, and foreign policy in the twentieth century are the most general. Certain more specific concerns, however, have combined here to give the work a focus on the Republican party during World War II. One of these is the wartime era itself, a period no longer being viewed by historians of the United States simply in terms of victory or defeat, of this country's supposed conversion from isolationism to internationalism, or even, simply, of the origins of the cold war. Increasingly, historians as well as other scholars have begun to concern themselves with aspects of World War II that profoundly altered long-established conditions of international relations.[1]

The war leveled what was left of the system of nation-state rivalries, with its delicate balance of power, that Western Europe had developed for itself and the world in the late nineteenth century and had already begun to undermine in World War I. In addition to laying waste the old, moreover, World War II also played midwife to the new: it brought forth, or released, a host of revolutionary ambitions throughout the world, thereby giving birth to all sorts of future problems and policies in international affairs. It is this revolutionary aspect of the conflict and of its era that is of principal interest here. World War II provoked revolution in many areas, including the United States. It profoundly altered long-standing traditions of American government and politics. Indeed, it is hard to underestimate the effect of the war in this regard. As one historian of the period, Richard Polenberg, has aptly put it, "World War II radically altered the character of American society and challenged its most durable values." It "redefined the relationship of government to the individual and of individuals to each other, and it posed questions about the relationship between civilians and the military, between liberty and security, and between special interests and national purpose which continue to perplex Americans. Pearl Harbor marked more than the passing of a decade; it signified the end of an old era and the beginning of a new."[2]

During this new era, a radical alteration sparked by the war also took place in terms of the relationship between the Congress and the president. World War II precipitated a sharp decline in the power of the former vis-à-vis that of the latter. In no area was this decline more marked than in foreign affairs. Prior to World War II the Congress, jealous of its traditional powers, had kept a relatively tight rein on the executive and had maintained firm control over the course of foreign policy, having weathered the most serious challenge to that control by defeating Woodrow Wilson's proposal for entry of the United States into the League of Nations following World War I. After that defeat, throughout the 1920s and 1930s, Republican and Democratic administrations alike felt compelled to remain aloof from the League of Nations. Franklin D. Roosevelt's administration, moreover, felt constrained to accept neutrality legislation with which it disagreed because of successful congressional pressure. In fact, a convincing case could perhaps be made that Congress, which appeared to be abdicating its powers in domestic affairs to the president at the beginning of the New Deal, took as its price for such an abdication—up to the outbreak of war in Europe in 1939—increased supervision of the nation's foreign policy. Certainly it worked the other way around: the Roosevelt administration to 1939 surrendered on matters of foreign policy, like the neutrality laws, in order to maintain support in Congress for domestic legislation.[3]

The onset and aftermath of World War II, however, worked a change in this pattern. The role of Congress in contrast to that of the president in foreign policy began to decline. The effectiveness of congressional checks on the executive in foreign affairs gradually but relentlessly weakened. Such milestones of American foreign policy in the post-war years as the Truman Doctrine, the Eisenhower Doctrine on the Middle East, and the Gulf of Tonkin Resolution, whatever one thinks of their justification or necessity at the time, represented ever more open-ended grants of power by Congress to the executive. One could even argue that this successive surrender of power continued into the 1960s and led to such tragedies of foreign policy as the Bay of Pigs invasion and United States involvement in Vietnam. Presumably, events of the later Johnson and Nixon administrations have revived, temporarily at least, stagnating congressional energies. Nevertheless, the decline of congressional versus presidential power in foreign affairs during the twenty years following World War II stands in marked contrast to the disposition of that power during the twenty years preceding that conflict. The change has profoundly altered the conditions of American politics and foreign policy.

Within Congress itself, a principal reason for this change has been a corresponding decline in the role of the opposition party in the making of foreign policy. That party plays an important part in determining what opposition, if any, Congress has to offer in the realm of foreign affairs. Writing on opposition parties in general, Charles O. Jones has observed that in this country "there is an identifiable minority party most of the time, and more than any other institution of its size, it offers opposition, criticism, and alternatives. If not *the* opposition on all issues and at all levels of government, it is certainly one major source of opposition." Or, as Robert A. Dahl has put it, whenever there is opposition in the United States on matters of policy, the opposition party is usually its source.[4]

Extrapolating from such scholarly considerations, one might reasonably conclude that an opposition party in the United States both works within and helps to create a climate of opinion with respect to foreign policy among the public at large and in the legislative and executive branches of government. Sometimes it does so by direct action in formulating alternatives; sometimes, by inaction—by refusing to formulate any alternatives at all; and sometimes, too, by consciously joining in support of the administration's foreign policy. Thus, an opposition party by its potential as well as its actual power in the governing structure of the United States plays a significant role at all times in the process of foreign policy formulation. During World War II the opposition party, at that time the Republican, faced anew the question of what role to adopt in view of the conflict. Other wars had raised the same question for opposition parties in the past, so the question itself was not new. What was new was the way *that* party during the course of *that* war chose to answer the question, for the Republicans in the end opted for formal bipartisanship as the proper role for their party in opposition during World War II. And thereby, as they say, hangs a tale—for two succeeding decades, at least, of American foreign policy.

The mere mention of bipartisanship and of an opposition party's role in matters of foreign policy raises certain long-standing questions of political theory and civic principle. How should that party conduct itself in such matters? Should it strive to provide alternatives to those of the majority party? Or should politics stop at the water's edge and yield there to some form of cooperation? Such questions have often arisen in the United States, particularly in times of international crisis. Scholars, among others, have then attempted to answer them. H. Bradford Westerfield, for example, writing in the 1950s and reflecting the dominant view of that cold war period, concluded that it was both valuable and necessary to maintain an effective bipartisan approach to foreign policy.[5] Not every scholar agreed with Westerfield, however. Somewhat earlier in the same decade, James MacGregor Burns defended the opposite point of view. The formulation of alternatives (rather than bipartisanship), he contended, was not only the function but the duty of an opposition party in the United States.[6] Burns's view, however, failed to gain general acceptance in this country until the late 1960s when widespread disillusionment with the war in Vietnam began to set in.

In the forum of contemporary politics in times of crisis, the question of bipartisan foreign policy has also, understandably, been a source of special and extreme concern to the opposition party, for that party confronts a very real dilemma at such times. On the one hand, as Norman Graebner has pointed out, the party has a built-in tendency to want to expand its power by any available means, but on the other, political necessity requires it to take into account "national limitations" and "responsible alternatives."[7] As the opposition party faced with this dilemma and the necessity for choice during World War II, the Republican party is a particularly apt subject. The G.O.P. has been in opposition (at least in the technical sense of lacking control of either Congress or the White House) during all the major conflicts—World Wars I and II, Korea, and Vietnam—in which the United States has engaged in the twentieth century.

Not only that, but the Republican party, which was the opposition party in Congress during Wilson's presidency as well as during Roosevelt's, was significantly responsible for the strong stands taken by Congress on foreign policy in both administrations. During and after World War II, Congress and the opposition party in it (again, for the most part, Republican) gradually abandoned the practice of active opposition in foreign policy and moved toward the greener political pastures of a cooperative, bipartisan approach which has since become a paragon of practice for legislators, executives, commentators, and scholars alike. Acting as a "loyal" opposition and encouraging this trend, Republicans, particularly those in Congress, bear a great deal of responsibility—whether for good or ill—for the development of bipartisanship, the diminution of the power of Congress, and the growth of the power of the presidency in foreign affairs.

An opposition party, of course, consists of more than simply its representatives in Congress, although when the party loses control of the

White House, its congressional delegation is likely to prove its most prominent part. In addition to senators and representatives, former or prospective presidential nominees who are not themselves members of Congress may constitute a highly influential or articulate source of the party's opposition in the area of foreign policy. The party organization, in particular its national committee, may serve as a center for formulating such policy or governors or other state party officials may play important roles.

Historian and political scientist James MacGregor Burns has provided some distinctions that may prove helpful in conceptualizing the elements that make up an American political party. He maintains "that to see the pattern of power at the national level only in terms of two parties is grossly misleading."[8] Whether in opposition or not, Burns contends, each major party can be seen as divided into presidential and congressional wings "that are virtually separate parties in themselves. They are separate parties in that each has its own ideology, organization, and leadership." The congressional party operates through its congressional chieftains, the campaign committees in both houses, and the congressional committee system with its seniority rule. The presidential party, on the other hand, operates through the national committee, the national convention, and the political organization under them.[9]

Any one of the four "parties," therefore, "can—and does—coalesce with any one of the others. We take for granted the coalition of the Democratic presidential and congressional parties," Burns argues, "and of the two Republican parties—though often we should not."[10] One important difference between the two wings in both major parties, a characteristic that helps distinguish between them in fact, relates to foreign policy: "both presidential parties are more liberal and internationalist than both congressional parties."[11] Both "presidential parties seem to have a more European orientation, the congressional parties, especially the Republican, a more Asiatic or Oriental" one.[12]

Burns's conceptual framework, with its postulate of relative presidential versus congressional internationalism, would appear to account for certain inconsistencies in the history of the Republican party's relationship to United States foreign policy. On the one hand, Republicans have been closely associated with various economic, political, and ideological positions generally considered to be touchstones of internationalism in foreign affairs. Beginning with the very first Republican administration, that of Abraham Lincoln and William H. Seward, the party's presidents and secretaries of state have invariably worked to expand the country's interests abroad in terms of trade, territory, or potential influence. Seward's purchase of Alaska, Ulysses S. Grant's lobbying for acquisition of the Virgin Islands, James G. Blaine's push for reciprocal trade agreements, Benjamin Harrison's support for American incorporation of Hawaii, and William McKinley's approval of war with Spain, annexation of the Philippines, and "open door" notes on China, to name but a few examples, all serve to illustrate aspects of Republican internationalism in the nineteenth century.

In the twentieth century, the party's most colorful leader, Theodore Roosevelt, launched the United States on a new path to world power and glory in conscious emulation of European imperial diplomacy. Roosevelt, his secretary of state, Elihu Root, and his successor in office, William Howard Taft, deeply affected the course of internationalist activities in the United States, from gunboat diplomacy in Panama to dollar diplomacy in China and the Far East and from conferences on international law at The Hague to proposals for a League to Enforce Peace after World War I.

Following the Great War, Republican administrations of the 1920s and 1930s did not abandon their party's internationalist traditions. Warren G. Harding's secretary of state, Charles Evans Hughes, called the Washington Disarmament Conference, which defined a new order for international interests in the Far East as well as limited capital ship construction among the major naval powers. Frank B. Kellogg, secretary of state under Calvin Coolidge, was responsible for the signing of a number of treaties between the United States and other nations pledging the signatories never to war against each other. Herbert Hoover and his secretary of state, Henry L. Stimson, both of whom were active in various internationalist endeavors during preceding Republican administrations, took stands against Japanese occupation of Manchuria in 1932 and cooperated with the League in the matter despite a long-standing aversion to the latter in the United States and the existence of a great depression which rendered the use of force against the Japanese difficult to contemplate. Hoover, in his approach to the depression itself, constantly advocated international efforts to solve its problems, in contrast to the nationalistic approach put forward by his opponent in the 1932 presidential campaign, Franklin D. Roosevelt.

On the other hand, despite such strong evidence of internationalism, the Republican party has also been closely associated with isolationism in the history of United States foreign policy, especially in the twentieth century. Isolationism itself has been variously defined: antipathy toward Europe and things European (particularly military alliances, power politics, and wars), belief in the invulnerability and suzerainty of the United States in the Western Hemisphere, a fervidly nationalistic desire to preserve American freedom of action; all have figured prominently in most historical definitions of isolationism.[13] Historically, too, this isolationism has cut across party lines in the United States. In the twentieth century, however, the Republicans as a party have been more closely linked with the phenomenon than the Democrats, largely because of their prominent role in events relating to the involvement of the United States in World Wars I and II.

In connection with World War I, Republicans are remembered for the defeat of Woodrow Wilson's bid to obtain membership of the United States in the League of Nations. Led by Senator Henry Cabot Lodge of Massachusetts, Republicans and irreconcilables in the Senate tacked on numerous isolationist reservations to Senate acceptance of the League Covenant. In general, the reservations called for guarantees of American sovereignty, of United States interests in the Western Hemisphere via the Monroe Doctrine, and of congressional approval in advance of any commitment of the nation's forces to a peace-keeping action by the League. In the end, Wilson and his Democratic faithful found the reservations unacceptable and the prospects of United States participation in the League of Nations died, for the Republicans refused even to deal with the League after they took control of the White House in 1921.[14] Furthermore, the United States under the Republicans during the 1920s negotiated separate peace treaties with its former enemies in World War I, instituted the highest protective tariff in the nation's history, demanded repayment of the Allied war debts, and, in general, refused to become involved in any political arrangements aimed at increasing the security of the postwar status quo in Western Europe.

The Republican party is also linked closely with isolationism in connection with opposition to American entry into World War II. Party members are regularly identified with the drive, in the years immediately prior to United States involvement in the fighting, to legislate against a possible recurrence of the circumstances that had led to entry into World War I. In the Senate, the Nye Committee was established to investigate the munitions, banking, and shipping industries' economic interests in World War I and their responsibility for involving the United States in that conflict; the committee, though established by a Democratic Congress, was named after its Republican chairman, Gerald P. Nye of North Dakota. Most Republicans in Congress supported the Nye Committee's investigations as well as neutrality legislation designed to keep the United States out of future wars by avoiding trade with belligerents. They also opposed repealing such legislation when war in Europe broke out again in the late 1930s. Relying on isolationist concepts of a fortress America, moreover, the majority of Republicans in Congress opposed

the Lend-Lease Bill to aid Great Britain and objected to the establishment
of a selective service system in the United States on the eve of the nation's
entry into its second world conflict.[15]

When applied directly, therefore, Burns's framework for analysis helps
to explain the apparent contradiction between isolationism and internationalism in the Republican party. On the one hand, by postulating a congressional wing of a party that is more isolationist than its presidential
counterpart, it suggests that the isolationist side of the Republican legacy
in foreign policy derives from the party's representation in Congress. Indeed, during periods from which evidence of this isolationism is most often taken—immediately after World War I and immediately before World
War II—Republicans in Congress played key roles in shaping American
foreign policy and the party's relation to it. During both of these periods,
congressional Republicans were the party's principal representatives in
national government.

On the other hand, by postulating a presidential wing more internationalist than the congressional, Burns's model also takes into account
the internationalist side of the Republican past. Internationalism surfaced
mainly in periods when Republican presidents and secretaries of state,
then representing the party more directly than congressmen, conducted
the foreign policy of the United States. Accordingly, internationalism may
actually be alive and thriving in the presidential wing of a party when that
party is not in control of the White House. A supposedly isolationist Republican party, therefore, could nominate in 1940 (on the strength of the
internationalist sentiment within its presidential wing) a candidate who
was relatively unknown in the party's congressional circles and an outspoken internationist, Wendell L. Willkie, to oppose Franklin Roosevelt's
bid for a third term. Finally, isolationist and internationalist elements
might both be present in the party and in government at the same time—
as in fact they were in the 1920s when Republicans controlled both the
White House and Congress—thus explaining some of the contradictions
in the party's historical image in regard to foreign policy.

Several problems arise, however, in trying to account for isolationism and internationalism in the history of the Republican party
this way. In the first place, an individual can at the same time be a member of both the congressional and presidential wings of the party. This
was obviously the case in the period under consideration, for Joseph W.
Martin, Jr., of Massachusetts, the minority leader of the House of Representatives, in 1941 became chairman of the Republican National Committee as well. Second, isolationists can be found in both wings of the
party, not just the congressional, and internationalists are also present in
Congress. Warren R. Austin of Vermont and Joseph H. Ball of Minnesota

in the Senate and Charles A. Eaton of New Jersey in the House are
examples during World War II of prominent Republican advocates of
internationalist positions and views. In the presidential wing of the party
at that time, prominent prewar isolationists, like Colonel Robert R.
McCormick of the *Chicago Tribune* and General Robert E. Wood of
Sears, Roebuck and Company, brushed shoulders with such avowed internationalists as Wendell Willkie and Harold E. Stassen.

Furthermore, difficulties arise in using the concepts of isolationism
and internationalism themselves. There are limits to the explanatory power
of these terms when they are used to describe different historical situations. In addition to transcending party lines, they lack precise definition
and must always be considered relatively, in terms of positions taken on
foreign policy at any given time. Congressional Republicans, for example,
are considered isolationist both for blocking Wilson's League of Nations
after World War I and for voting in favor of neutrality legislation in the
late 1930s. To a significant extent, however, the vote against the League
was a manifestation of a number of Republicans' personal animosity toward Wilson as well as a power struggle over executive versus legislative
prerogatives in foreign affairs; it was not simply the emanation of some
innate congressional isolationism.[16]

In the late thirties, moveover, the overwhelming electoral triumphs
of Franklin Roosevelt and his fellow Democrats had the effect of in-
stalling many Democrats in formerly Republican internationalist seats
in Congress, particularly from states on the East Coast. Republican representation in Congress was thus reduced to a small, hard core of basically
middle western isolationists whose positions on foreign policy were not
necessarily representative of the party as a whole.[17] Understanding specific historical situations, therefore, might lead to serious qualification
of the contention that the presidential wing of a party is more internationalist than the congressional.

The distinction between presidential and congressional branches itself needs to be questioned. There are, of course, certain very real differences within a party along these lines. One such difference, a fairly
obvious one, is that the offices around which the two branches center
serve different functions of government in the American constitutional
system. Congressmen have a unique responsibility for legislation, particularly in domestic affairs, whether or not their party's nominee is
president. Presidential party members may be concerned with specific
issues and bills while out of power, but final responsibility for legislation resides in Congress. The president, on the other hand, has responsibility for initiating legislation, particularly in the field of foreign policy,
as well as for executing laws once they are passed. In such circumstances,

congressional party members often find their options limited to approval, disapproval, or attempted modification of what has been proposed to them. Such differing functions and responsibilities dictate different interests.

Another fundamental distinction between a party's congressional and presidential branches lies in the nature of the United States electoral system. Each wing of a party, in fact, normally arises from and appeals to different constituencies. Presidential leaders, for example, have to deal with a national electorate that is much more broadly based than the regional or local electorates on which congressmen depend. The necessity for a broad-based appeal by these leaders is obvious, particularly during a presidential compaign or when the party controls the White House; at such times presidential leadership generally directs its stand on issues toward finding a common denominator of support in the national electorate in order to obtain or remain in power.

Members of Congress, on the other hand, depend upon essentially local or, at best, regional constituencies that are not necessarily microcosms of the national electorate. Given an adverse reaction in his or her constituency, a person in Congress may wind up at odds with the majority of the party on an issue and with a majority of the party's Congressional members. In fact, at least five different levels of possible allegiance can be delineated for a party member in Congress. In addition to loyalty to a constituency, a party, or fellow members of that party in Congress, a legislator may identify most strongly with a particular committee or, perhaps, with the Congress as a whole—with its traditions and responsibilities as an independent branch of government.

Because of such varying electoral forces, constituencies, and allegiances, therefore, not all members of Congress can properly be considered members of a congressional "party." Congressional representatives can be found who lean more toward presidential than congressional leaders in the party and who belong, logically, more with the presidential wing of their party than with the congressional. Burns even argues that there is a presidential wing "in each party in Congress, but it lacks strength and stability because its numbers keep getting decimated."[18] The congressional wing thus consists of those legislators who come to Congress from the safer electoral districts and who have seniority and influence in Congress. It also may contain those who cluster around these legislators, taking their cues from them and perhaps expecting to gain influence and seniority for themselves eventually. At bottom, however, the established party leaders in Congress define its congressional wing, or "party."

This definition of a congressional party as consisting in essence of "the regulars from the safer seats" points to the need for further qualification.[19] To talk of a congressional party in terms of the senior members of that party in Congress is to talk more of individuals, of leadership—of an "elite," if you will—than of an institution or the kind of structured organization that the word "party" suggests. A certain kind of leadership or individual defines a party as much as, if not more than, a party itself defines the individuals in it. That is precisely why Burns has to postulate the somewhat awkward device of a presidential wing inside the congressional in the first place—to take care of those individuals in Congress who do not appear to take their cues from the congressional leadership at all. With few exceptions, the same qualification holds true for the notion of a presidential party. Here again, the kind of leadership that that wing of a party chooses to follow in areas like foreign policy as much defines its separate existence from the congressional wing as any institutional distinctions, especially when a member of the party occupies the White House (and those distinctions become even less clear).[20]

When their party lacks control of the White House, congressional members of that party tend to be "drawn into the vortex of the senior leaders."[21] A struggle often ensues, moreover, between these leaders and those in the presidential wing for control of the party as a whole. "There has long been a question of jurisdiction when we have been the party in opposition," wrote Charles D. Hilles (a Republican national chairman in the 1930s) during World War II, "and there have been jurisdictional jealousies in consequence." These jealousies have often been "capitalized," he added, "by a few ambitious men."[22] Such men in Congress may become active in the party's presidential wing out of a desire to run for president. Republican senators Robert A. Taft of Ohio and Arthur H. Vandenberg of Michigan, for example, both candidates for their party's nomination in 1940, remained potential candidates (off and on) for quite a while after that and played most active roles, as this work will demonstrate, in matters related to the presidential wing. Apart from any ambitions they may have for presidential office, however, leaders of a party's congressional wing rarely bypass an opportunity to secure their own congressional interests and positions in depth. In the wake of an election year defeat, therefore, they can often get their grip on the National Committee, elect one of their own as national chairman, and "penetrate the machinery of the national convention."[23] Again, Representative Joseph W. Martin, Jr., serving simultaneously as Republican national chairman and minority leader of the House, is an excellent case in point from the period under discussion here.

The primacy of individual leadership is particularly noteworthy in the area of foreign policy. Republican association with isolationism in 1918-1920 and in the late 1930s, for example, might best be understood in terms of the relative isolationism of prominent congressional Republican leaders and their greater degree of visibility and importance in the party at those times. In both cases, the party confronted Democratic administrations moving in what were, by contemporary standards, definitely internationalist directions toward participation by the United States in a League of Nations in the one case and toward American involvement in World War II in the other. Prominent congressional Republican leaders opposed those objectives. Because they did so and because they either dominated or overshadowed members of the presidential wing of their party during these periods, these congressional Republicans fashioned for themselves and for their party as a whole, a reputation—or an image, if you will—of isolationism, one that lingered on in historical consciousness.

That image may or may not have conformed in all cases to reality. While some Republicans, like senators Hiram W. Johnson of California and William E. Borah of Idaho after World War I and Arthur Vandenberg and Gerald Nye prior to World War II, may be considered isolationists by almost any standard, others, like Senator Lodge, who led the fight against Wilson's League, were internationalists by all but the most relative standard: a general willingness to place domestic considerations ahead of personal views on foreign policy. Such willingness, on the other hand, may be more endemic among congressional leaders than presidential ones. Members of the former tend to be more concerned in the long run with safeguarding their own seniority in Congress, and the American electorate, on which that seniority ultimately depends, has on the whole shown a marked propensity over time to concentrate its attention on domestic issues rather than on matters of foreign policy.[24] In terms of this relative definition of isolationism, therefore, the image of congressional isolationism does not lack substance. That image, moreover, together with the image of isolationism in the Republican party derived from it, was and is a real image, as Burns's own reliance on it in constructing his theory serves to indicate. The image itself was, both historically and politically, an important legacy for the Republican party to have to deal with in foreign policy, especially during World War II.

But what of the World War II period itself, the time of a presumed "conversion" of the Republican party and the nation from isolationism to internationalism?[25] Was the same relative degree of congressional Republican isolationism operating during the war as before? These are some of the questions which this work seeks to answer.

An even more important question, however, relates to when, how, and why the Republicans, as the opposition party at the time, opted for bipartisanship in foreign policy during and after World War II. To what extent did that choice represent an actual decline of oppositionism in foreign affairs, with whatever far-reaching effects that that decline may have had in terms of the cold war, the war in Vietnam, and the decline of Congress's ability to check the president in foreign affairs? Donald R. McCoy has argued that bipartisanship began during World War II and "was to a considerable extent, a result of Republican opposition, not acquiescence." It was a "covert weapon of opposition," he contends, finally "wrung from the administration" in 1944 "by Republicans and by those Democrats in Congress who also felt left out in the making of decisions"; it was "as much a device to express opposition views as it was to gain support for government policy."[26] Is this judgment correct?

The requirements of answering such questions have set certain boundaries to the scope of this work. In the first place, as one might have anticipated from the foregoing discussion, it will focus on Republican congressional and presidential leaders (as opposed to "parties"), and upon issues of foreign policy during World War II as perceived and dealt with by those leaders in turn. Thus, Chapter 2 identifies the G.O.P. leaders in Congress on foreign policy and recounts initial reactions to Pearl Harbor. Chapter 3, after similarly identifying the leadership on foreign policy in the presidential wing of the party, carries the account of that group's activities through the mid-term elections of 1942. Congressional Republican unrest following those elections through the summer of 1943 is the subject of Chapter 4, while Chapter 5 covers activities in the party's presidential wing up to and including the unusual party conference on post war foreign policy held at Mackinac Island, Michigan, during September 1943. In Chapter 6, discussion centers around moves by congressional Republicans under the leadership of Senator Arthur Vandenberg to neutralize foreign policy as an issue in the 1944 election campaign and to fashion a bipartisan approach to that subject. Chapter 7 traces similar activities being carried on at the same time by presidential Republicans under the leadership of John Foster Dulles and Thomas E. Dewey. Finally, Chapter 8 concludes the work with an assessment of Republican foreign policy in the elections of 1944, an account of the new relationship between the presidential and congressional wings of the party worked out by Vandenberg and Dulles during the campaign, and—in an attempt to answer the main questions to which this work is addressed—an evaluation of the meaning of this new relationship in terms of the party's past and future history in the area of foreign affairs.

A second limit to the scope of this work, one that should be apparent from the sketch of the chapters just presented, is that its account of events

and of politics during World War II is confined largely to the period of the
Roosevelt administration. It stops just short of the changeover from the
Roosevelt to the Truman administration and avoids a detailed discussion
of the many historical arguments and problems attendant upon that change
itself. The wisdom of such a limitation is admittedly questionable. The
issues, however, change somewhat with the change of leadership; problems
with the Russians in connection with the proposed United Nations, for
example, or with the Russians in general, for that matter, become more
prominent in the later period. Furthermore, the change in administrations and especially the loss of President Roosevelt from the scene after
so many years significantly changed other political conditions that had
been operating for an unusually long time. In the end, limiting analysis
to the one cohesive period makes sense in light of the conclusion of
this work that, by the time Roosevelt died, the basic contours of a bipartisan foreign policy which was to endure for two to three decades
had already been established.

A final boundary of this work is that it deals for the most part with
how issues of foreign policy during World War II affected the Republican party rather than with how Republicans affected foreign policy.
The concern here will be more with what happened within the party
itself, with the choices in foreign policy its leaders made and with what
happened to the party in American politics because of those choices,
than with the extent to which the party directly influenced the course
of United States foreign policy. This limitation does not mean that
the importance of the party's role in the formulation of foreign policy—
the role of the opposition party discussed earlier—is being minimized
or ignored. Rather, it reflects a belief that one has to understand the
dynamics of foreign policy issues within a party first, in order to understand why the party at any given time elects to pose alternatives,
remain silent, or cooperate with an administration on foreign policy—
the principal ways in which a political party expresses its opposition
in the United States. This work, in other words, which contends in effect that the framework of domestic politics in this country furnishes
a kind of structural imperative to the making of foreign policy, does so
only after that political framework has been thoroughly investigated.

In the end, this study purports to show that Republican party
leaders during World War II chose to express their opposition in foreign
policy more by silence and selective cooperation with the administration
than by actively formulating alternatives. Their choices eventually culminated in the celebrated bipartisan approach to foreign policy that has
thus far been distinctive of the post-World War II era. More important,
however, the work contends that Republicans arrived at that approach

not because of a basic change in ideology or personal conviction—by undergoing some great "conversion" in foreign policy, as has been supposed—but rather because party leaders came to see it as a strategic political solution to some basically political problems. Thus, the word "politics" in the title of this work cuts two ways. In one sense, it refers to the usual competition over issues and office between Republicans and Democrats—the structural or institutional imperatives of both as parties. In the other sense, "politics" here also applies to the struggle for influence over issues of foreign policy within the Republican party itself.

CONGRESSIONAL
2 REPUBLICANS RECOVER
FROM PEARL HARBOR

On Sunday, December 7, 1941, the day that would "live in infamy" for many Americans, Senator Harold H. Burton of Ohio was dining at Union Station in Washington, D.C. There he first heard news of a Japanese attack on Pearl Harbor. Arming himself with a portable radio, Burton quickly repaired to his office on Capitol Hill to await developments.[1]

As was often his custom on such Sunday afternoons, Burton's colleague, Senator Arthur H. Vandenberg of Michigan, was leisurely annotating his scrapbook, bringing up-to-date the record of his long battle against what he regarded as President Roosevelt's steps toward participation in the war against the Axis Powers, when word reached him of the bombing. Later Vandenberg would claim that his "convictions regarding international cooperation and collective security for peace took firm form on the afternoon of the Pearl Harbor attack" and that that day "ended isolationism for any realist." For the moment, however, he confined his thoughts and activities to noting the event in his journal, telephoning his support for action against Japan to the White House and explaining in a press release that, despite differences with President Roosevelt "on other things," prewar noninterventionists like himself "were ready to 'go along'—making it plain that we were not deserting our beliefs, but that we were postponing all further argument over policy until the battle forced upon us by Japan is *won*."[2]

Burton and Vandenberg are examples among Republicans of the different types of individual James MacGregor Burns had in mind when he distinguished between party members in Congress who lean strongly toward the party's presidential wing and those whose loyalties ultimately lie with its congressional counterpart.[3] Burns's distinction, it will be recalled, was grounded in part on differences in outlook on foreign policy, presidential Republicans presumably being more internationalist than their congressional counterparts. Senator Burton belongs in the presidential internationalist camp. He was elected to the Senate for the first time in 1940, the year in which Wendell Willkie, an avowed internationalist, captured the Republican presidential nomination from Burton's fellow Senator from Ohio, Robert A. Taft, and the year too in which Franklin Roosevelt, along with Burton, carried that state. During 1941 Burton voted in favor of Lend-Lease and of legislation empowering the president to extend selective service, in contrast to the majority of his congressional Republican colleagues. He later became President Harry S. Truman's first appointee to the United States Supreme Court.

Allied with Burton on foreign policy in the Senate was another Republican figure who shared an orientation toward the presidential wing of the party in this period, Joseph H. Ball of Minnesota. Appointed to his position in 1940 by Harold Stassen, the governor of Minnesota who became known during the war years as an advocate of postwar international organization and as a potential Republican presidential nominee, Ball soon made a name for himself as an outspoken advocate of internationalist causes. He was an ardent supporter of Wendell Willkie during the war years and, after Willkie's death in 1944, he endorsed Roosevelt for reelection that year because of the stand the president took in favor of postwar world organization. Two other Republican senators who shared the internationalist but not necessarily the presidential leanings of senators Burton and Ball were Warren R. Austin of Vermont and Wallace H. White, Jr., of Maine. The assistant minority leader, Austin was a consistent supporter of the administration's foreign policy and a legislator of ten years' experience in the Senate by 1941; he became a member of the Foreign Relations Committee in 1944 and was appointed United States ambassador to the United Nations in 1946. Senator White also voted with the Democrats more often than not in matters of foreign policy and served on the Foreign Relations Committee; in 1944 he became for a time the Senate's minority leader.

Senator Vandenberg, on the other hand, was more to be identified with the congressional and isolationist camps of his party in Congress. A veteran in 1941 of more than two terms and many noninterventionist battles in the Senate, Vandenberg was at that time not the top ranking but perhaps the leading Republican on the Foreign Relations Committee. Both Hiram Johnson of California, the old irreconcilable from the days of Woodrow Wilson and the fight over the League, and Arthur Capper of Kansas outranked Vandenberg on the committee, but of the three, Vandenberg took the most active role in the committee's deliberations. He was seconded in his efforts there by Gerald Nye of North Dakota, well-known for his own special Senate committee's investigations into the or-

igins of World War I and for his labors in behalf of the isolationist America
First organization. Furthermore, Robert M. LaFollette, Jr., an independent
Progressive from Wisconsin who carried on his famous father's opposition
to war, consistently allied himself on the Senate floor and in the Foreign
Relations Committee with noninterventionist Republicans like Vanden-
berg and Nye against the administration's prewar foreign policy.

In this period, Republican Senator Robert Taft of Ohio also oriented
himself toward the congressional wing of his party and its isolationist
positions in foreign policy. Following an unsuccessful attempt to capture
the Republican presidential nomination in 1940, Taft devoted more and
more time to his role in Congress and to rallying opposition there against
the New Deal. He voted regularly with noninterventionist Republican colleagues against administration foreign as well as domestic policy. Over the
entire group in the Senate stood Charles L. McNary of Oregon, the Minority Leader and Republican nominee for vice-president in 1940. McNary,
who died in 1944 and was succeeded as minority leader by Wallace White,
was a noninterventionist before the war; he had been placed on the ticket
in 1940 as a congressional, isolationist counterweight to Wendell Willkie
and his interventionist views.

To complete the picture of congressional Republican leadership on foreign policy in 1941, mention must be made of the House of Representatives, which had less responsibility, constitutionally, for the conduct of
foreign policy than the Senate but was similarly divided in terms of con-
gressional-presidential, isolationist-internationalist loyalties. On the one
hand, there were congressionally oriented isolationist Republicans like
Representative Hamilton Fish in the House. A member of Congress since
1919 and the ranking Republican on the House Foreign Affairs Committee,
Fish was a prime mover in the America First organization and, ironically,
the representative of President Roosevelt's home district in New York. On
the other hand, there were internationalist Republicans like Representative Charles Eaton of New Jersey, the second ranking Republican on the
Foreign Affairs Committee. Eaton was the Republican on the committee
with whom the administration preferred to deal; he consistently supported
it on foreign policy. Meanwhile, presiding over the 165 Republicans in
the House as minority leader in 1941 was Representative Joseph Martin
of Massachusetts, an individual with roots in both wings of the party and
both camps on foreign policy. Martin at that time was also chairman of
the Republican National Committee. Although he had supported Wendell
Willkie for the party's presidential nomination in 1940, Martin had nevertheless remained a kind of study in political ambiguity, for he had maintained a noninterventionist voting record both before and after that.[4]

The unexpected Japanese attack on Pearl Harbor created a dangerous situation not only for the United States but also for congressional Republicans like Martin, Taft, and Vandenberg, who had previously advocated policies aimed at the noninvolvement of Americans in the growing conflict in Europe. These policies, generally termed "isolationist," had included opposition to Lend-Lease, selective service, and the repeal of neutrality legislation. They had depended to a considerable extent upon a deep-seated aversion in America to war (particularly wars of European origin like World War I) and a long-standing confidence in the invulnerablility of the United States to transoceanic attack.

Events of December 7, 1941, however, had dealt the isolationist position a startling blow which later reports of enemy planes and submarines, sighted in the areas of Los Angeles and San Francisco, did little to soften.[5] A favorite isolationist concept—that of a "fortress America" situated strategically behind two great oceans and practically invulnerable to attack—was no longer trustworthy, either in fact or in rhetoric. Interventionists could now take the Japanese attack and the reported sightings on the coast as proof positive of error in the antiwar, noninterventionist positions against which they had been arguing all along. Given this situation, the possibility of an adverse public reaction in the months ahead to the prewar noninterventionism, or isolationism, of most congressional Republicans increased and posed a serious political threat to the fortunes of the party in 1942, a congressional election year.

The image of prewar isolationism, however, was not the only historical circumstance that threatened Republican senators and representatives now that the United States was finally involved in the conflict. Another area in which they soon began to feel politically vulnerable centered around a longer-standing historical image of isolationism and concerned the degree to which Republicans in general, but congressional Republicans in particular, were to be held responsible for the defeat of Woodrow Wilson's League of Nations in the United States after World War I. To what extent, in other words, were Republicans going to be held responsible for the occurrence of a second world conflict?

Even before Pearl Harbor, internationalists of all political persuasions had argued that the outbreak of war in Europe had vindicated Wilson's arguments in 1919 and 1920. The war might have been avoided, they suggested, had the United States only accepted the blueprint for collective security and international organization that Wilson had advanced. After Pearl Harbor, the argument was pressed further. Internationalists were increasingly drawn to the conclusion that Wilson had failed "because some men, in pursuit of office only, and to satisfy a partisan malice, were ready again to gamble on the crucifixion of mankind."[6]

Who were these men? The answer more often than not came back,

in increasingly undiscriminating rhetoric, that they were "Republicans."[7]
Located for the most part in the Senate, these Republicans, the accusa-
tion ran, had rejected the League and destroyed Wilson's dream of world
peace in order to humble the president and gain selfish political advantage for themselves. The appropriate corollary invariably followed: if
these Republicans had not sacrificed the League on the altar of partisanship and political hatred, the international organization might have
saved the world and the United States from the cataclysm of World
War II.[8] In the aftermath of Pearl Harbor, therefore, Republicans in Congress had ample reason to fear political disaster ahead.

Shortly after the Japanese attack—that same evening, in fact—Roosevelt summoned both Democratic and Republican congressional leaders
to the White House. Together with the president and his cabinet, they
assessed the situation in the Pacific and discussed what Roosevelt should
say to a rapidly assembling Congress the next day. According to one of
the participants, Senator Austin, who was impressed that the president
could be so considerate of "minor personal conveniences" in the midst
of the "stupendous pressure" of events, Roosevelt had provided a table
of drinks and food for the leaders, anticipating that their meeting would
probably last into the night. The president "appeared well and vigorous,"
Austin noted, but "his hands disclosed how much he was actually disturbed. They not merely shook, they fluttered, when he undertook to
light a cigarette." Describing the course of events leading to the attack
as well as his and Secretary of State Hull's efforts to preserve peace with
Japan, Roosevelt angrily compared that country's onslaught at Pearl
Harbor to the "perfidy" of Hitler's invasion of the neutral countries of
Western Europe.[9]

After their meeting with the president and his cabinet, the Republican
leaders of both houses issued statements assuring the country of their own
and their party's awareness of the need for national unity in that hour of
crisis. "There is only one party when it comes to the integrity and honor
of the country," Representative Martin of Massachusetts proclaimed. His
counterpart in the Senate, Charles McNary of Oregon, was somewhat more
specific. "The Republicans," McNary ventured, "will all go along, in my
opinion, with whatever is done."[10]

On Monday, December 8, President Roosevelt appeared briefly before
a joint session of Congress and asked for a declaration of war against Japan. In the Senate, following the president's address, Democratic floor
leader Tom Connally of Texas, who had made known in advance a desire
to dispense with speechmaking on the resolution in view of the state of
emergency, rose to call for a vote. To his distress, Connally was inter-
rupted by Senator Vandenberg asking for the floor. As the Michigan Re-

publican insisted upon his desire "to make the record clear," Connally reluctantly yielded to him.

Vandenberg then explained that he felt compelled to make a brief statement "lest there be any lingering misapprehension in any furtive mind that previous internal disagreements regarding the wisdom of our policies may encourage the despicable hope that we may weaken from within." Repeating the statement he had already made to the press regarding the attack, Vandenberg castigated the Japanese once more for Pearl Harbor and pledged the support of noninterventionists like himself for war against them. He also recalled the previous positions of noninterventionists in opposing United States involvement in war and contended that "though America still hates war, America fights when she is violated and fights until victory is conclusive. God helping her, she can do no other."[11]

After that, Senator Connally called for a vote on the war resolution. The Senate responded unanimously in favor of it. The House followed suit, with one exception. Republican Representative Jeannette Rankin of Montana, a pacifist who had voted against participation by the United States in World War I—during the only term, apart from this one, that she ever served in Congress—again said no to war.[12]

Obviously excited by Republican promises of support like Vandenberg's as well as by the degree of unanimity achieved on the war declaration, the *New York Times* editorialized the following day:

> Congress has spoken—no, thundered—its answer to the madmen of Japan. With a swiftness of action never before achieved in the whole history of this country and a unanimity of mind and spirit which for all practical purposes is complete, the challenge of the treacherous friend that now becomes the mortal foe has been accepted. Gone is every sign of partisanship in the Capitol of the United States. Gone is every trace of hesitancy and indecision. There are no party lines today in Congress. There are no blocs, no cliques, no factions. The house-divided within itself has ceased to exist in Washington. In its place there arises an assembly of American patriots whose single thought and passionate concern are the safety of our people.[13]

At first glance, indeed, this judgment of nonpartisanship by the *Times* appeared to be justified. Soon after its publication, the Senate's Republican conference adopted a resolution suggested by Henry Cabot Lodge, Jr., of Massachusetts, drafted by Taft of Ohio, and reported to the Senate as a whole by Minority Leader McNary, pledging the conference to "unanimous support" of the president "in the vigorous and efficient prosecution of the war."[14] The Senate then proceeded to vote, again unanimously, on the president's request for a declaration of war on Germany and Italy. In the House—with the exception once more of Representative Rankin (who this time voted "present")—the outcome on the second declaration was the same.[15]

Many former Republican critics of the Roosevelt administration's foreign policy rushed to line up behind their party's leaders in Congress after Pearl Harbor and pledge their support to the president, the country, and the war effort. Focusing on the need for national unity now provided them with an opportunity to direct attention away from potentially detrimental records of prewar isolationism. Republicans so concerned could now argue that postmortems on those records during wartime would only reintroduce an old disunity at the worst possible time and ought at least to be postponed until, in the words of Vandenberg, "we have rebuilt our inadequate defenses to a point of total victory."[16]

Together with other members of Congress, G.O.P. legislators reacted unanimously in favor of President Roosevelt's war message on January 6, 1942, "no member" reportedly permitting "anything like outright criticism to go into quotes after his name."[17] Significantly, a special Senate subcommittee responsible for inquiring into alleged interventionist propaganda in the nation's movie industry soon disbanded. Established through the efforts of the prominent Republican isolationist, Senator Nye, supported by the America First Committee, and staffed by members who were active foes of the administration's foreign policy, the committee announced a suspension of its investigation "in the interest of national unity."[18]

Aside from pleas for wartime unity, another early response to the problem of former isolationism common to congressional Republicans was to offer, as, for example, Representative Fish and Senator Lodge did on hearing of the Pearl Harbor attack, to resign from Congress and seek a combat position in the armed forces or some other activity related more directly to the war effort. Senator Vandenberg also pointedly volunteered his services in this manner, but in his case as in others, the president's policy was to urge the legislator to remain in Congress and work for nonpartisan unity there and in the country at large.[19] In general, what Arthur Krock concluded as a result of talking to six former critics of the administration's prewar foreign policy just after the attack on Pearl Harbor seemed true for virtually all: they were now "agreed that obviously there never had been a chance for honorable appeasement of Japan."[20]

The appearance of unanimity between the administration and congressional Republicans on the war issue, however, was deceptive, as Senator Ball soon pointed out in an article depicting his colleagues after Pearl Harbor. While "the Japanese attack united America in our war effort," he observed, "it did not by any means settle the basic foreign policy issue that dominated the national political scene and Congress during 1940 and 1941."[21] Some congressional Republicans in fact preferred to concentrate on this issue—the question of whether the administration's foreign policy had been leading to war all along—rather than bury it beneath pledges of wartime unity. In a speech delivered in Pittsburgh the day of Pearl Harbor, for example, Senator Nye accused the administration of having provoked, and the British of having planned, an attack of the kind the Japanese had just launched.[22]

Although Nye's remarks were virtually lost amidst the flood of statements issued that day in support of the war effort, the lack of complete congressional unity on the issue broke into the open on December 11, the day the war declaration on Italy and Germany was passed. In the Senate that day, Republican Charles W. Tobey of New Hampshire demanded that American losses at Pearl Harbor be made public immediately and in detail. Tobey, moreover, called for a complete congressional investigation of the attack and for the removal of Secretary of the Navy Frank Knox, the Republican internationalist who had accepted service in Roosevelt's wartime cabinet prior to American involvement in the conflict.[23]

The morning after Pearl Harbor, Tobey had complained about a lack of specific information from the Navy Department regarding the amount of damage resulting from the attack. After having requested an investigation from Democratic Senator David Walsh, chairman of the Senate Naval Affairs Committee, Tobey and other interested colleagues had been instructed to await the president's speech to the nation that evening for the information they desired.[24] The speech had failed to satisfy Tobey, a ready speaker at America First Committee meetings before Pearl Harbor, a propagator of the belief that the administration's foreign policy was furthering a gigantic conspiracy to drive the American people toward war, and the sponsor of an unsuccessful anticonvoy resolution in 1941 intended to unmask this conspiracy. He decided to press his case on the Senate floor.[25] Thus on December 11 he had insisted that Congress had the right and duty to "demand that those who may be called upon to make the supreme sacrifice shall not make that sacrifice because of inefficiency" and "that the Navy Department be administered by a Secretary of the Navy who is responsible, who stands for efficiency . . . and who has in his heart a great single purpose—to prosecute this war successfully no matter what the cost."[26]

A chorus of Democratic countercharges greeted these demands. On the Monday of Tobey's initial request for information, Emanuel Celler of New York had demanded in the House that such isolationists as the New Hampshire Republican apologize to F.D.R. for their prewar positions, while in the Senate, Millard Tydings of Maryland had defended the administration's silence on losses in the Pacific as essential to keeping the knowledge from the Japanese.[27] After Tobey's later complaints, however, Senator Scott W. Lucas of Illinois, another administration supporter, took the floor to subject Tobey to "a public castigation such as rarely has been administered by one member of Congress to another."[28]

Lucas was enraged that the Republican senator should rail about lack of information so soon after the attack, while at the same time—and in the absence of such information—accusing Secretary Knox and the administration of inefficiency. He "dares condemn the negligence of someone out in the Pacific without any facts," Lucas complained of Tobey. "I say to the Senator from New Hampshire, 'in so far as negligence is concerned, look at your own record from the standpoint of national defense.' Ah! Shame on you for saying at this hour, only 96 hours, practically, after the occurrence of those sad events, 'No details, no details.' "[29]

Pleas for national unity in wartime had failed to bury the hatchet. The outburst over responsibility for Pearl Harbor rekindled passions and brought back bitter memories of the controversy over intervention versus non-intervention that had been fought right up to the outbreak of hostilities. Senator Ball put his finger on the nerve of this continuing controversy in his article describing Congress during the first weeks of the war:

> Perhaps, so far as the people are concerned, this issue was decided against isolation by Pearl Harbor. But so far as the political leaders of the people in Congress are concerned, there is plenty of evidence that isolation is not a dead issue but merely on the shelf until a more opportune time to argue it. The tendency of isolationist leaders in Congress to blame the Pearl Harbor disaster on the lend-lease policy indicates they still cling to the isolationist position basically, refusing to recognize the worldwide aims of the Axis. So far as this writer has noticed, no isolationist leader has publicly, or even privately, admitted he or she was in error, and plenty of them privately argue that the interventionist policy was responsible for Japan's attack.[30]

An excellent case in point demonstrating the accuracy of Ball's observation was that of Senator Vandenberg, himself a leading isolationist before the war, a former member of the Nye Committee to investigate the origins of World War I, and a noninterventionist candidate for the Republican presidential nomination in 1940. The "war mongers," complained Vandenberg, indignant at renewed attacks by administration supporters on the prewar positions in foreign policy that he had avowed, are doing "the very best they can to try to make it appear that the 'non-interventionists' are in some way responsible for our lack of preparedness not only in Pearl

Harbor but everywhere else." Against this idea, Vandenberg argued that
the noninterventionists had "almost to a man" been "scrupulously careful to support all national defense appropriations" for which the administration had asked, that the administration had *"never asked for one that
it did not get,"* and that if the administration did not get enough, fault
lay "in the asking." According to Vandenberg, the truth of the matter
was "that it was the 'interventionists' (from the President down) who
were constantly saying to the country 'this way lies peace': and it was
the non-interventionists who were constantly saying to the country 'this
way lies a war for which you are totally unprepared.'"[31]

Citing the Democratic national platform in 1940 and Roosevelt's
speeches during the campaign as proof, Vandenberg also argued on behalf
of Republicans that "the Democrats themselves were officially 'non-interventionists'" (which, he contended, was "the *correct* term to be used
rather than 'isolationist'") before Pearl Harbor, advancing policies like
Lend-Lease and the repeal of neutrality legislation on the premise that
they would keep the country out of war.[32] In private, the Michigan senator recalled that Republican noninterventionists had insisted at the time
that those policies would ultimately lead to war. To one constituent, in
fact, he advanced the very argument that Ball had reported in his article,
namely, that the administration's "final ultimatum to Japan two weeks
ahead of Pearl Harbor (culminating these policies) made a Japanese attack inevitable."[33]

Republican "'non-interventionists' could—if they pleased," Vandenberg contended, "shout from every housetop 'we told you so!'"; instead they had been "content to shout 'Let's win the war!'"[34] Senator
Robert M. LaFollette, Jr., nominally a Progressive but a faithful congressional associate of Republican isolationists before the war, joined
Vandenberg in calling down blame on those "trying to peddle the false-
hood that the United States is ill-prepared for war because of the noninterventionists," particularly "former enthusiastic interventionist pub-
licists" looking for "scapegoats" now that Japan was proving a tougher
opponent than anticipated.[35]

Other noninterventionist Republicans, as disturbed by attacks on
their prewar positions as Vandenberg and La Follette were, began to
echo Senator Tobey's original complaint against the administration's
handling of Pearl Harbor both before and after the attack. They joined
in his assault upon Roosevelt's Republican secretary of the navy, Frank
Knox, charging him with over-optimism in his assessments of the ade-
quacy of defenses in the Pacific and, thus, with a failure of responsibility in regard to the country's preparedness for war in that region.[36]

Pleas for national bipartisan unity had failed to obviate questions of
past or future Republican responsibility for the war entirely. It remained,

therefore, for Senator Taft to articulate more fully the emerging conception among congressional Republicans of their party's role in opposition
during wartime. In a speech delivered to the Executive Club of Chicago on
December 19, Taft addressed himself to this subject and to the question
faced by members of the minority party in Congress of "whether they
should criticize the administration of the war—either the legislative measures proposed or the actual conduct of the war itself."

As "a matter of general principle," Taft proclaimed, there could be no
doubt that criticism of the administration in time of war was "essential
to the maintenance of any kind of democratic government." He voiced
a common fear among his congressional associates, however, by noting
that there would be "newspapers and others" in his constituency who
would attack him unless he accepted "the leadership and recommendations of the President on every issue." Nevertheless, Taft could not find
"any authority for such a course."

> The duties imposed by the Constitution on Senators and Congress-
> men certainly require that they exercise their own judgment on ques-
> tions relating to the conduct of the war. They require that they do
> not grant to the President every power that is requested unless that
> power has some relation to the conduct of the war. They require
> that they exercise their own judgment on questions or appropriations
> to determine whether the projects recommended have a real necessity
> for the success of the war.

Even President Wilson, Taft noted, had once said "that criticism in time
of war was even more necessary than in time of peace."

Congress, therefore, was responsible for "reasonable criticism," according to Taft, and such criticism included, by the senator's definition
of reasonableness, the question of the administration's culpability in the
matter of Pearl Harbor.

> The surprise at Hawaii should, in my opinion, be investigated by com-
> mittees of Congress, and not left entirely to the Executive Department.
> We might well investigate whether Secretary Hull told Secretary Knox
> the contents of the note which he submitted to the Japanese Govern-
> ment ten days before, requiring them to withdraw from China, and
> which was not published until after the attack on Hawaii. Did Secre-
> tary Knox communicate to the admiral [at Pearl Harbor] that we had
> sent an ultimatum to Japan which in all probability they would not
> accept? Perhaps the fault at Hawaii was not entirely on the admirals
> and generals.

On the other hand, in regard to any questions of congressional or Republican culpability resulting from prewar noninterventionism, Taft ruled that they had already been settled:

> It may be an interesting theoretical discussion today as to who was right and who was wrong, but we can and we should adjourn that discussion and leave it to history to decide. The position of interventionists and non-interventionists alike was always consistent with 100 per cent support of any war which did occur. Past differences are forgotten by 95 per cent of the people. They should be forgotten by all.[37]

After the Japanese attack, then, congressional Republicans like Taft and Vandenberg were willing—to a degree and in public—to let bygones be bygones in foreign policy. Their willingness to do so, however, did not stem from any kind of conversion experience in that area. On the contrary, as Vandenberg noted in the passage quoted above, noninterventionists like himself could, "if they pleased," have shouted "from every housetop 'we told you so!'" And Taft also remarked in his speech of December 19 that he had "always felt confident" and still felt confident that the United States "could stand against the entire world and resist any attempt to invade this country."[38]

That is not to say, however, that the vulnerability of America to attack which Pearl Harbor and its aftermath had demonstrated failed to register on these Republican isolationists. Taft said in the same speech that "this has been a war of surprises. No one could have predicted any feature of it six months in advance."[39] He and others undoubtedly felt, for the first time, a sense of immediate physical danger to the United States. The war had, after all, come in a manner and from a direction they had not anticipated, concerned as they were to prevent American involvement in the conflict in Europe. As Ball had observed in his article after Pearl Harbor, "In all the discussions of how America might be drawn into World War II, both on and off the floor of Congress, no one (except the Japs) apparently ever considered seriously the possibility of what actually occurred."[40]

To some extent, therefore, men like Taft meant exactly what they said when they called for 100 percent support of the war effort, particularly in view of their prewar positions regarding the country's being substantially unprepared for any conflict. To a greater extent, however, they shared a sense of immediate political danger. Noninterventionist congressional Republicans were now, more than ever before, politically vulnerable to charges by their opponents that they had failed to foresee the necessity of United States involvement in the war and had thus contributed directly to the difficulties of the moment. The Democrats were also politically vulnerable in 1942. They too inherited a kind of natural disadvantage from Pearl Harbor: they became politically responsible for the running of a war which, given the dearth of Allied successes in its early phases and the general lack of preparedness for it by the United States, was not going very well. Republicans in Congress were able to make greater and greater use of this disadvantage as the year 1942 progressed.

Taking their cue from Senator Taft, congressional Republicans were soon able to depart from purely defensive positions in foreign policy and begin scoring more positive gains by holding the administration, in Senator Vandenberg's phrase, to "strict accountability" for effective and efficient results in its prosecution of the war.[41] G.O.P. members in Congress, sensing what they believed to be strong public support for criticism in this area, cast themselves in the role of watchdogs over the administration's conduct of the war and played that role by stepping up attacks on executive personnel and organization. In addition to Secretary Knox, Secretary of War Henry L. Stimson (formerly secretary of state in the Hoover administration) and his running of the War Department, Secretary of Labor Frances Perkins, and Mrs. Roosevelt, who was working in the Office of Civil Defense, drew criticism for either incompetence or lack of effectiveness in managing their various war-related activities.[42]

President Roosevelt himself, of course, headed the list. At the outset, however, Republican critics of the administration tended to keep their attacks on him private, so as not to appear to be undercutting their commander-in-chief—and their own professions of unity and service—during wartime. Senator Vandenberg, for example, complained to his wife: "Roosevelt . . . hasn't demobilized a single one of his old 'social revolution' units . . . . The country is getting ugly—and I don't blame 'em—*so am I*. Even we in the Senate can't find out what is going on. This is Roosevelt's private war! He sends out troops where he pleases—all over the map."[43]

One early attempt to fix the conduct-of-the-war issue at the forefront of public discussion, thus distracting attention from the issue of isolationism, is particularly worth noting. It was also an attempt to rectify the difficulties with the president that Vandenberg had pointed to above and was of obvious interest to Congress (and to the opposition party in Congress) in terms of its role in foreign policy vis-à-vis the Executive. Soon after Pearl Harbor, Vandenberg proposed establishing a joint congressional committee on war cooperation, a single committee to work as liaison between the Executive and the Congress on the war—"an organization somewhat like the Committee on the Conduct of the War during the days of the Civil War."[44] Vandenberg's proposal became a significant and recurrent one in Congress during the war. In view of the historical precedent he had cited, recalling as it did Abraham Lincoln's problems with a similar committee, one can appreciate why the proposal might appear highly ominous to the administration.[45]

Various congressional committees or their chairmen during World War II could, and often did, summon administration officials before them or went themselves to administration officials for information on specific aspects of the war. Senator Connally, for example, who was chairman of the Foreign Relations Committee on which Vandenberg sat, arranged for a representative from the State Department, Assistant Secretary Breckinridge Long, to meet with the committee once a week and provide it with diplomatic information on the progress of the war. Vandenberg was nevertheless dissatisfied with the overall pattern of these "present 'consultations.'" For him they were too "few and far between," and they usually consisted of "the President's own political leaders in Congress." The arrangement did not fulfill "the all-out liaison" function, "regardless of politics or parties," that Vandenberg believed the situation required.[46]

Vandenberg's proposal of a single liaison committee was by no means unrelated to calculations of party interest or to his prewar positions on foreign policy. He was admittedly looking by way of such a committee for some "kind of formula for collaboration between the Administration and Opposition without requiring the Opposition to agree with everything the President did."[47] Moreover, Vandenberg linked the proposal to the issue of his own prewar isolationism by recalling that he had first tried to establish such a committee two years before when the country was making its first appropriations for national defense.[48]

The Senate had in fact established in March 1941 a Special Committee to Investigate the National Defense Program, popularly called the Truman Committee for its Democratic chairman (the future president), Harry S. Truman of Missouri. The committee conducted investigations "on almost all phases of the war effort except those matters having to do with military strategy and tactics," and Republican senators Burton and Ball were both members of it.[49] During the course of its investigations from March 1, 1941 to April 28, 1948, the committee unearthed sufficient evidence of waste, corruption, and mismanagement in the defense industry to lend credence to Republican charges during the war that the same thing was happening in government.

As Vandenberg was quick to point out, however, his wartime proposal of a congressional-executive liaison committee envisioned something new and different, bearing implications for Congress far beyond those of mere partisan or personal advantage. He believed that the committee, without interfering "with the President's prerogative of conducting the war," could "very well be a meeting place for satisfying the sense of responsibility which members of Congress inevitably feel, which may not otherwise be too easily satisfied unless there is some such official instrumentality" linking the two and their mutual responsibilities together. Rather than rely on the already existing but disparate committee system for that purpose, Vandenberg proposed the one committee to streamline congressional consultation and control during wartime. This committee, he maintained, would still allow for unified military command.[50]

Although he found considerable enthusiasm for his proposal outside of Congress, Vandenberg found too little within that body to make the idea work. Members were as jealous of their individual privileges and powers as of their congressional responsibilities.[51] Eventually Vandenberg himself became disillusioned with the proposal and with the lack of congressional support for it. He stopped pressing the idea for the time being, but not without declaring that "there must be a broader sharing of vital responsibility" during the war at some point. For the moment, however, heralding the new note of retrenchment among former isolationists, Vandenberg surmised that before such sharing of responsibility could be had, "Congress and the country must be brought very much closer to the *realities* of this war."[52]

Concern with such "realities" led to an avowed desire on the part of many Republican isolationists that the principal military and naval efforts of the United States be directed against the Japanese in the Pacific rather than the Germans in Europe. Secretary Knox was once again taken to task, this time for advocating in a January speech that the navy clear up the Atlantic before all else.[53] "It is a sound principle of war," the *Chicago Tribune* proclaimed in response, "to concentrate on the principal and proximate enemy." For the United States, that enemy was Japan. Playing upon long-standing fears it had itself helped establish, that clarion of prewar isolationism warned its readers: "If we scatter our strength in a dozen trifling expeditions all over the world, we may succeed only in giving the Japanese the opportunity to strike us at home."[54]

Republicans in Congress were drawn to this concentration upon the Pacific phase of the war for more than simply motives of protection and defense against the Japanese threat. Reminiscent of the spirit of Senator Nye's remarks the day of Pearl Harbor, some of them feared, in one of the oldest traditions of isolationism, nefarious British interests in the Far East. They foresaw the sacrifice of American concerns in that region to Great Britain, should Europe and not the Pacific be made the principal combat area. For such reasons, in the early stages of the war, Pacific-minded isolationists among Republicans were highly wary of Winston Churchill's visits to the United States and his meetings with Roosevelt. They feared the British prime minister's presumed influence over the president in matters of military strategy and saw in the appointment of General Sir Archibald Wavell of Great Britain as Supreme Commander of Allied forces in the Far East proof of this influence, as well as of a supposed tendency to favor British interests in that region over American and Dutch.[55]

To the extent that they could commit themselves on the matter without calling unfavorable attention to their prewar records, Republicans in Congress also began predicting longer timetables for the war than administration plans envisioned. Arguing that Japan could not be attacked successfully until a "two-ocean Navy" and a "three-ocean air force" were ready, Senator Taft concluded that since that was "not likely to be before 1945," it was difficult to see how the United States could "transfer a great Army to Europe and begin an attack on Germany itself until 1945." In Taft's view, if everything went well and according to plan, "five years" would not be "an unreasonable time" for the war to last.[56] Such an argument was not necessarily inconsistent with a noninterventionist's defense of his record on preparedness prior to Pearl Harbor. The longer it took the United States to arm itself during the war, he could claim, the greater the reason for avoiding the conflict initially.

A concerted Republican attack upon the administration encompassing all of these various interests—military preparedness, concentration upon the Pacific front, and "strict accountability" for efficient conduct of the war—was launched early in 1942 over the plight of General Douglas MacArthur and his troops under siege by the Japanese in the Philippines. The overt issue was whether or not the administration was doing all it could to reinforce MacArthur and his men. Much more was at stake, however, than simply the loss of an island fortress on Corregidor. The longer MacArthur held out there, the more attention he drew away from Europe to the Far East and the inadequacy of American military capabilities in the Pacific; the more, too, did his and Republican political capital rise vis-à-vis the White House.

MacArthur's own press releases, stressing his belief in the importance of the Pacific war area as well as his lack of air power, contributed greatly to maintaining both Republican and national focus upon him. Communications coming to Washington from all over the country following these releases urged leaders to have the general and his gallant men reinforced.[57] Resolutions were passed by various state legislatures lauding MacArthur. In the House, praise for his continued stand in the Pacific against hopeless odds resulted in one member's recommending him for president, which sparked a burst of applause. In the midst of this swelling tide of emotion, Congress even changed the name of a road in the District of Columbia to MacArthur Boulevard in his honor.[58]

Besides serving as a focal point for opposition to the administration, support for the new-found national hero also became a kind of outlet for pent-up noninterventionist sentiments. Senator LaFollette sponsored a resolution that was subsequently passed designating June 13, 1942, the forty-third anniversary of the appointment of MacArthur to West Point, as "Douglas MacArthur Day."[59] Even Wendell Willkie, certainly no Asia-first isolationist, responded to this general effusion of sentiment, anxiety, and support by proposing that MacArthur be brought home and placed in absolute control of all war operations.[60]

Needless to say, the political significance of such ferment was not lost upon the executive branch of the government. It constituted an immediate and unignorable pressure to devote more attention to the Pacific at the same time that the administration was trying to assure its European allies of a primary commitment to their theater of the war. Nor for that matter did MacArthur's press releases, often independent of his reports to the War Department, increase his popularity in Democratic circles. There was even speculation in Washington that his capture by the Japanese might not be looked upon in some circles as a completely unmitigated disaster.[61]

In any event, President Roosevelt certainly appreciated that MacArthur's capture or surrender would provoke bitter criticism of his administration at home; he ordered the general to remove himself from Corregidor to Australia and there succeed Britain's General Wavell as commander-in-chief in the Far East. The president thus solved for the time being the problem of whether or not to bring MacArthur back to the United States where he would be all too readily available to run as the Republican candidate for president in 1944.[62] Furthermore, given the nature of the new MacArthur appointment, Roosevelt temporarily allayed fears of increasing British and declining American influence in the Pacific area.

The focus on MacArthur, however, had already proved a boon to many Republicans in Congress, providing another politically advantageous way out of the dilemma occasioned by their prewar non-interventionist positions. They could read in the rise of public concern over the conduct of the war, which had been accelerated by the plight of the General and his men, omens of a successful political future for themselves. As early as January 1942, Senator Taft was using his own sense of the public's dissatisfaction over the war issue to assess Republican chances in the fall elections. In his opinion, popular impatience with the lack of progress in the fighting would be most helpful come November in reelecting and expanding the number of Republican representatives and senators, none of whom, Taft believed, was likely to be defeated because of a noninterventionist record in foreign policy.[63] If it had not been exactly proved yet, as Senator C. Wayland Brooks, favorite candidate of the *Chicago Tribune* claimed during his April primary campaign for reelection in Illinois, that prewar isolationism was a dead issue in congressional politics (that it had been "sunk at Pearl Harbor"), it was evident by spring 1942 that the issue had been eclipsed in importance by more immediate concerns.[64]

While diverting attention from the prewar isolationism of many congressmen, the conduct-of-the-war issue, as it took greater hold on the public, also freed Republicans in Congress to renew their attacks on a favorite target, the New Deal; it even provided them with a new basis for these attacks. Phrased in a general sense by Herbert Hoover (still the favorite intellectually, if no longer politically, of many congressional Republicans), the Republican argument against the New Deal in 1942 was that incapacity and inefficiency in domestic affairs could be "obscured and got away with by politics, propaganda, lies and oratory" in times of peace but that such failures could not be tolerated during wartime. "A government that is incapable in peace will be licked in war," Hoover warned. "Events thus created by the enemy will sooner or later make domestic policies."[65]

Taking heed of such warnings, Republicans and others in Congress began supporting Senator Taft's call at the outset of war for cuts in nondefense spending and for the elimination of such New Deal agencies as the Civilian Conservation Corps, the Farm Security Administration, the Farm Tenant Program, the National Youth Administration, and the Works Projects Administration.[66] By April, Taft had drafted a resolution to be presented to the Republican National Committee, scheduled to meet that month in Chicago, which called upon the party to oppose all administration efforts to use the war as an excuse for unsound domestic panaceas. The resolution, which also pledged the party to preserve free and private enterprise as well as equal opportunity for all, was accepted unconditionally at the meeting.[67]

A second resolution introduced by Taft at the April meeting related to the question of American responsibility for postwar world order. Republican spokesmen had been eying the postwar objectives announced by President Roosevelt in such proclamations as the Atlantic Charter and the Four Freedoms with a good deal of unease. To them they smacked of attempts by the administration to have the United States guarantee worldwide social and economic freedoms after World War II, in addition to the primarily political freedoms Woodrow Wilson had hoped to establish after World War I.[68] Many Republicans in Congress in early 1942 intended to thwart this presumed drive by Roosevelt for a new social-economic world order—an international New Deal—just as their predecessors in 1919 and 1920 had frustrated Wilson's objectives. Such a purpose, in fact, lay behind Taft's second resolution for the National Committee. That resolution, about which more will be said in the next chapter, called for concentration upon victory in the war above all else and urged avoidance of questions of postwar world order until that victory was assured. Both of Taft's resolutions, however, represented more than the face value of their statements and, by way of conclusion to this chapter and introduction to the problems of the next, their broader purposes deserve to be indicated.

As a politically vulnerable group casting about in the wake of Pearl Harbor for leadership and for acceptable issues in foreign policy, congressional Republicans had found themselves in considerable disarray. By spring 1942, they had still not solved the problem of leadership. Were prewar interventionists like senators Burton, Ball, or possibly Austin now going to carry the day and swing their party in Congress into line behind the administration and a new internationalism? Or were the former noninterventionists, fearing the effects of such a course—senators like Taft and Vandenberg and members of the House like Representative Fish—going to be able to rally their troops and have the final say? In either case, whose particular approach and guidance on foreign policy were most likely to prevail? By spring 1942, the noninterventionists seemed to hold the edge, but the question of leadership among them had yet to be decided. A bid for that leadership, in fact, was one of the broader purposes behind Taft's resolutions.

In terms of issues early in 1942, congressional Republicans like Taft had been successful in defending themselves against opposition attacks on their prewar records in foreign policy—more successful, in fact, than they had dared to hope at the beginning of the year. What they had been looking for above all was "some plan to rationalize," as one source put it, the antiadministration stand of many of them on war measures prior to December 7, 1941.[69] For as Taft himself had written a little more than a week before Pearl Harbor, "Nine years out of ten the fundamental issue is one of domestic policy and we ought not to permit the breaking up of a party on any question of foreign policy."[70] They had come up with the strategy of focusing their own and the public's attention on the administration's conduct of the war. Thus they could argue, whenever the need arose, that the country's lack of adequate preparation was one of the reasons for their opposition to intervention in World War II at an earlier date.

These same congressional Republicans, however, wanted to insure that the party as a whole, but especially the internationalists located largely within the presidential wing, adopted the same strategy. 1942 was a congressional election year, and many Republican members of Congress were wary of eliminating one threat only to find a new one cropping up in their own backyards. Hence, among congressional Republicans in 1942, there was a strong desire to lead and control the presidential wing of the party as well as their own. Taft's resolutions for the April meeting of the Republican National Committee also represented a move in this direction.

PRESIDENTIAL
3 REPUBLICANS AND THE ELECTIONS OF 1942

Within the presidential wing of the Republican party, initial reactions to the news of Pearl Harbor paralleled reactions just witnessed in Congress. Previous discord quickly submerged and supposedly drowned in a sea of fixed purpose as Republican and Democratic party members alike throughout the land joined in pledging their support to the president in that hour of national crisis.

The past three Republican contenders for Franklin Roosevelt's office—Herbert Hoover, Alfred M. Landon, and Wendell Willkie—assured Roosevelt of their and the country's unified support for declarations of war. The nation's governors, of whom thirteen were Republicans in 1941, joined with leaders of business, labor, and farm organizations in eschewing "all personal, political, sectional or group interests not compatible with a maximum defense effort."[1] They signed a pledge to that effect and presented it to the president. The country's most prominent isolationist organization, the America First Committee, which numbered many Republicans among its supporters, issued an appeal to its members to support the war effort and disbanded immediately.[2] Even the *Chicago Tribune*, Colonel Robert McCormick's sounding board of midwestern and Republican isolationism, fell into line.[3]

The chairmen of both national political parties exchanged unity telegrams with each other and with the president. Democratic Chairman Edward J. Flynn suggested that the party organizations be combined and made available immediately for civil defense work and for such war-related activities as the sale of bonds and stamps. His Republican counterpart, Joseph W. Martin, Jr., did not go quite so far. In fact, he undercut Flynn's suggestion somewhat by noting that many members of the Republican party were already performing such services, but he did pledge that his party would eagerly answer any call to service and would not

permit politics to endanger national defense. The Democratic National
Committee chose to interpret the chairmen's exchange as "the most complete adjournment of domestic politics since the formation of the two
party system."[4]

President Roosevelt reflected the views of his party in his replies to
both chairmen. Roosevelt echoed Flynn in suggesting that the party organizations could best be of service in civil defense. In thanking the
chairmen for the "patriotic action" of their parties "in eschewing partisan politics" and thus promoting unity, the president claimed that in
wartime there could be no such politics and concluded that a "political
truce" would be in effect "for the period of the emergency."[5]

Despite its greater size and number of clearly definable officers and
levels of organization, the presidential wing of the Republican party,
like its congressional counterpart, looked to its national leadership to define party positions on pressing national issues.[6] This was especially the
case after Pearl Harbor, when, for obvious reasons, issues of national
survival and foreign affairs became particularly acute. Who then were
the leaders of the Republican presidential wing on these issues?

In the first place, they were the party's immediate past presidential
contenders, Willkie, Landon, and Hoover. In the second, they were potential Republican presidential nominees. Here again, Willkie's name
heads the list. In fact, according to a survey in late 1941 of 9,554 G.O.P.
county chairmen, women leaders and Young Republicans conducted by
a party organ, *The Republican*, 42 percent of those polled indicated a
presidential preference for the former Republican nominee, the highest
percentage for any potential candidate listed. Hoover also made that list
with 6 percent in his favor, but a greater number, 15 percent, inclined
toward the young prosecuting attorney (soon to be governor) of New
York, Thomas E. Dewey. Other Republican governors, or about-to-be
governors, should be included in this category: Harold E. Stassen of
Minnesota (with 2 percent in the *Republican*'s poll), John W. Bricker of
Ohio, and Earl Warren of California.[7]

In addition, there were party congressional leaders who took an active
interest in the presidency, or the presidential wing of the party, or both.
Senator Robert Taft's name would have to head this list. Having received
19 percent of the support of local leaders in the 1941 poll, he was runner-
up to Willkie in that presidential test, just as he had been at the Republican National Convention in 1940. Senator Arthur Vandenberg, another
also-ran in 1940, should be included in this group, he received a 3 percent rating in the poll. So too did Representative Joseph Martin, the Republican national chairman, who presided over this motley crew in the
presidential wing of the party as well as over Republicans in the House as

minority leader. It was Martin who had pledged his party's support in the war effort to President Roosevelt and Democratic National Chairman Flynn.[8]

Among presidential Republicans, the reactions of Wendell Willkie to the Pearl Harbor attack were most interesting. In that hour of vindication for his prewar support of Roosevelt's foreign policy, the former Republican standard-bearer went one step further than the president in extending the olive branch to his opponents. Willkie proclaimed the past debate over participation in the war ended and asked that previous differences over international affairs be forgotten. He then urged the administration to appoint isolationists to wartime posts of responsibility in preference to others who had been "all-out, pre-war supporter[s] of the President's foreign policy."[9]

Willkie's conception of national unity, unlike that of the Democrats, did not require "that politics be adjourned," at least not in the sense that "the government function without an opposition group in Congress." In an interview published one week to the day after Pearl Harbor, Willkie championed criticism, "in war as in peace," to bring out "mistakes of policy and management" and "to steady the confidence of a war-worried people in their leadership."[10] Following his loss to Roosevelt in 1940, Willkie had advised fellow Republicans to assay the role of a "loyal opposition" in American politics: not to be "an opposition against," opposing for the sake of opposing, but to be "an opposition for—an opposition for a strong America, a productive America."[11] Now, much as Senator Taft had for the congressional wing of the party, Willkie defined such opposition and the proper role of Republicans during wartime simply yet broadly as "doing nothing that would give aid or comfort to the enemy."[12]

Willkie praised President Roosevelt's announced program for arms production in 1942 and 1943 as "magnificent," whereas Taft and others doubted its sufficiency. He tempered his praise, however, by voicing a hope that Roosevelt would immediately reorganize "his government and policies to the end that these accomplishments may be made possible. They cannot be brought about by his present organization and administrative methods."[13] After the outbreak of war, Roosevelt offered Willkie a position on the War Labor Board comparable to the post held under the Wilson Administration in World War I by former Republican President William Howard Taft. Willkie declined the job, letting it be known in the process that he would respond to any genuine call from the president to be of service, but that he and his associates viewed the post of arbitrator in industrial disputes "as an act of 'trickery' intended to still the clamor for new faces in the defense picture without taking any of the basic control out of the hands of the New Dealers."[14]

Willkie was not the only leader in the Republican presidential wing
to advocate a strong minority role for party members during the war.
Chairman Martin himself, upon hearing of the national emergency occasioned by Pearl Harbor, postponed a meeting of Republican state
chairmen and vice-chairmen which had been scheduled for January. He
made it quite clear at the same time, however, that the party expected
senatorial, congressional, and state elections to be held during 1942
and that it would fight to win them. "We must retain the two-party
system," he affirmed in response to persistent rumors that congressional elections would be suspended that year.[15] As if to emphasize the
point and at the same time take Willkie up on the idea of amnesty for
former isolationists, Martin on January 5, 1942, appointed Clarence Buddington Kelland executive publicity director of the Republican National
Committee.[16] A non-interventionist and member of the America First
Committee prior to the war, Kelland had supported Willkie in 1940 and had
served voluntarily as publicity director in the campaign. He had split with
the candidate afterwards over the latter's pro-interventionist views.

Kelland's appointment dissatisfied Willkie, who, although he had
suggested that amnesty and a helping hand be extended to former isolationists, was still unalterably opposed to their prewar noninterventionist
positions. Unlike Kelland, Martin, or Taft, Willkie believed (along with
many Democratic leaders) that isolationism in war or in peace must once
and for all be repudiated by the United States, and the sooner, the better.
In that interview conducted after Pearl Harbor in which he had championed the cause of partisan opposition during wartime, Willkie had also
urged his fellow Americans—especially the Republicans—not to forget
what they were fighting for. As he defined it, they were fighting for the
elimination from the world of narrow nationalism and isolationism, "which
are the breeders of war and of economic degradation and of poverty."[17]

To this end, Willkie began a concerted drive in 1942 to regain control
of the presidential wing of the party, which had reverted to such leaders
of the congressional wing as Chairman Martin after the loss to Roosevelt
in 1940. As the "first step" in this drive and "in organizing the Republican
front" for the year's congressional campaign, Willkie launched a movement
to replace Kelland.[18] Martin, however, stood firmly behind his publicity
director, whose attitude reflected the stance of the great majority of isolationist Republican senators and congressmen up for reelection that year.
Like them, Kelland supported vigorous prosecution of the war and considered politics indispensable in wartime. The hope of the world, he said
in a speech in Salt Lake City, lay in the ballot boxes of the United States;
it was now more than ever mandatory that each citizen engage vigorously
in politics.[19]

In response to Kelland's Salt Lake City speech, Democratic National

Chairman Flynn accused Republicans of dangerous partisanship and issued a warning against the election of a hostile (i.e., Republican) Congress
in 1941.[20] Aside from sounding a death knell to the hope for unity he had
voiced a month earlier, Flynn clearly recalled by his pronouncement Woodrow Wilson's disastrous plea in 1918 for a Democratic Congress to strenghten
his hand in wartime. So much did Flynn's action bring to mind the historical precedent, in fact, that President Roosevelt himself felt compelled to
respond to the chorus of Republican outrage and countercharges which
greeted Flynn's statement. In a news conference on February 6, Roosevelt in effect repudiated that statement by remarking that in wartime he
wanted congressmen, "regardless of party," with records of supporting
the government in the emergency.[21] Although the statement was ambiguous (what congressman had not supported the war effort since Pearl Harbor?), it was sufficient to arouse the ire of the president's fellow-Demo-
crats. Roosevelt conferred with Flynn at the White House over the incident on February 11 and planned a fireside chat for Washington's Birthday to counter in public the developing political backlash. In that talk,
the president indicated that pre-Pearl Harbor support of his efforts related to the war was the desired criterion, as far as he was concerned, for
continuance in congressional office. Thus he ostensibly shifted the issue
from partisanship to isolationism.[22]

    Meanwhile, Republicans sprang to the rostrum in response to the is-
sues raised by Roosevelt and Flynn. The occasion was Lincoln's Birthday
and the Republicans' annual Lincoln Day dinners throughout the country. Originally intended by Chairman Martin to be patriotic demonstra-
tions, they turned into the most partisan political gatherings of the war
to that point as Republicans throughout the nation indulged themselves
in speechmaking over Flynn's statement. Willkie in Boston, Kelland in
Indianapolis, and Dewey in New York, among others, responded to the
Democratic chieftain's remarks. Dewey, for example, spoke ominously
of "an American Cliveden set" in Washington and other cities "scheming
to end the war short of military victory." Willkie, on the other hand,
urged that the party not await such "inevitable reactions" of the war as
Flynn's but develop "an affirmative program," along lines he himself had
been advocating, right away.[23]

    Flynn's statement and the Republican reaction to it catapulted
the party into the 1942 election campaign and signified that the time of
political unity had definitely passed. It was "politics as usual" once
again between the two parties as well as within the Republican. Writing
in February, Raymond Moley concluded that the country at large, having taken "at face value" the statements about national unity coming
from every side in December, considered pre-Pearl Harbor issues of iso-

lationism and interventionism "as dead as mackerels." National party leaders, however, refused to bury these issues.[24] Roosevelt's response to Flynn's statement and the disagreement between Willkie and Martin over the appointment of Kelland revived the old prewar controversy over intervention versus nonintervention, or, as generally phrased, isolationism versus "internationalism." Within the Republican party itself, moreover, a struggle for control over the presidential wing was already taking place along these lines.

The basic antagonists in this struggle were Willkie and Taft. Representing the extreme of prewar interventionism, Willkie demanded that the G.O.P. repudiate any vestiges of former isolationism. He was seeking to renew his control over the party on the basis of that issue. Taft, on the other hand, spoke for the prewar isolationist faction located primarily within the party's congressional wing. In 1942 that faction wanted above all to protect itself in the congressional elections against attacks on its members' prewar positions in foreign policy, attacks of the kind that Wendell Willkie, for one, was getting set to launch. In line with their prewar positions, many congressional Republicans also wanted to block Willkie's attempt to lead presidential Republicans, and the party as a whole, in advanced internationalist directions. They were, therefore, seeking control of the presidential wing of the party themselves.

The first test of strength for both sides in the Willkie-Taft conflict was scheduled to take place in the Illinois primary elections on April 14, 1942. These elections were also to be the first response to President Roosevelt's call for the selection of candidates who had a clear "record of support" of the administration on war-related issues. The question of prewar noninterventionism was sure to figure prominently in them. Senator C. Wayland Brooks and a majority of the sixteen Illinois Republican House members, most notable among them Representative Stephen A. Day of Chicago, had been strongly isolationist before Pearl Harbor. Brooks and Day were stoutly backed by the *Chicago Tribune.* Their renominations were opposed, however, by leading Republican interventionists, particularly Wendell Willkie and Frank Knox, a former owner of the *Chicago Daily News* and Roosevelt's Republican Secretary of the Navy, as well as by the president himself.[25]

A second test of strength in the struggle for control of the party was set to take place soon after the Illinois primary at a Republican National Committee meeting set for April 20 in Chicago. That meeting was going to have to deal not only with the issue of immediate prewar isolationism but also with another major problem in the history of the party and foreign policy: Republican association with the defeat of Woodrow Wilson's League of Nations. Soon after World War II began, in fact, this problem led to arguments within the presidential wing of the party over the desirability of establishing an international organization to insure postwar peace.

The United Nations Declaration of January 1, 1942, appeared to be a first step toward such an organization. With the announcement of the Declaration, the administration aimed to capitalize on bitter memories of Wilson's defeat and harness a potential groundswell of support for postwar world order to its side. Democratic partisans were already asking whether "the egotism and the jealousy" displayed by Republicans twenty-two years ago, "which ultimately rendered the covenant [of the League] worse than inoperative," would again prevail.[26] For this reason alone, Willkie warned his party, it would be political suicide for the Republicans to let the Democrats monopolize the internationalist issue. Although Republican Chairman Martin had responded enthusiastically to the United Nations Declaration, he had remained noncommittal about his party's hopes for the postwar world.[27] Martin and his colleagues were waiting for the April meeting in Chicago to begin dealing with the issue.

Senator Brooks and Representative Day won renomination in Illinois handily on April 14, and when the Republican National Committee convened in Chicago six days later, Brooks was the author of one of three competing resolutions which sought to define a position for the committee and for the party on the question of postwar world order. Willkie and Taft sponsored the others. Willkie's resolution demanded that the party shelve isolationism, oppose appeasement or compromise in the prosecution of the war, and favor worldwide cooperation to bring about a lasting peace. In a key passage, the Willkie resolution called upon the party "to undertake now and in the future whatever just and reasonable international responsibilities may be demanded in a modern world."[28] For the congressional faction of the party, Taft's resolution urged support of the war but avoided mention of postwar commitments, while Brooks's fifty-five-word statement called for all-out war, maintenance of the two-party system, and safeguarding of the Bill of Rights.[29]

Chairman Martin blocked full-scale debate on the resolutions by the entire National Committee and set up a special seven-man subcommittee, with power to write a substitute if necessary, to consider them. Contrary to the objectives of both Willkie and Taft, Martin was seeking to preserve the image of party unity on the issue by driving the dispute underground. The subcommittee surfaced with an 800-word compromise resolution calling for the conduct of the war under a unified command, an equitable distribution of the "tragic burdens" of the war, reduction of nonwar expenditures, and a safeguarding of constitutional rights. In place of the crucial passage in Willkie's draft, the subcommittee came up with a much more generalized statement on postwar responsibility. While affirming that the nation had "an obligation to assist in bringing about understanding, comity, and cooperation among the nations," the resolution simply said that after the war "the responsibility of the nation" would not be "circumscribed within the territorial limits of the United States."[30]

Although Senator Taft continued to maintain that the adoption of any statement regarding postwar commitments by the party at that time was a mistake, he did not view the end product as a surrender to Willkie's concept of postwar responsibility. To make that point clear, Taft called attention specifically to the deletion in the final statement of phrasing that had recalled the League of Nations in Willkie's original proposal.[31] Willkie, however, hailed the resulting resolution as an abandonment of isolation and a triumph. In that judgment, he was echoed by many supporters in the press. Even opponents like the *Chicago Tribune* joined in that assessment briefly and read Willkie and his internationalist views out of the party.[32]

There was little in the document itself, however, to support Willkie's conclusion. It was actually ambiguous enough to embrace all positions, including those of such diverse figures as Representative Hamilton Fish of New York, the embodiment of prewar Republican isolationism, and Democratic Secretary of State Cordell Hull, a lineal descendant of Wilsonian internationalism. Since it was an election year, many Republican noninterventionists voiced no disagreement in public with the conclusion that, by the passage of the April resolution, the party had repudiated isolationism, but they knew that nothing of the kind had taken place.[33] As Senator Arthur Vandenberg observed in private, he did not see how anybody could disagree with the statement. It did not require the United States to do more in terms of force, for example, than had previously been done. The idea of a Willkie victory in the committee resolution, therefore, was "sheer bunk."[34] To Herbert Hoover, pro-Willkie reactions to the April statement were about the same. "The humor of these Republican resolutions," he wrote a Republican friend and confidant shortly after the meeting, "is that ten or twelve days ago I wrote the critical paragraph on post-war relations and gave it to two committeemen in Chicago. It is a long way from Willkie's draft."[35]

Given these differing interpretations of the compromise statement arrived at by the Republican National Committee in Chicago, it seems fair to conclude that the only isolationism officially abandoned by the party in April was isolationism of word, not of belief. The resolution clearly had not, as one observer claimed, vindicated Woodrow Wilson in the high council of Republicanism.[36] Following closely on the heels of the victories of Brooks and Day in the Illinois primaries, however, the April resolution and public reaction to it had helped change the isolationist image, if not the reality, of the party in foreign policy and diverted attention from that potentially dangerous specter in a wartime election year.

The national chairmanship and Representative Martin's possession of it had also been a bone of contention between the Willkie and Taft factions prior to the Chicago meeting. Martin had originally acquired the chairmanship, despite his congressional responsibilities as minority leader in the House of Representatives, because he was one of the few candidates available who was generally acceptable to both camps. By April 1942, in their battle for control of the party's presidential wing, each group was looking to replace him with a chairman more closely associated with its particular views.[37] As in the case of the resolution on postwar foreign policy adopted at the April meeting, however, voices of political moderation and compromise within the party again prevailed, and Martin was retained in the post. In fact, within more moderate circles of the party at this time there was even talk of having to get rid of both Taft and Willkie for the good of the party.[38]

The course of Republican politics later in 1942, particularly in the primaries and elections of that year, tends to support the conclusion that a successful shift away from the image of prewar isolationism and from the extremes of the Willkie and Taft positions took place. Apart from the April meeting and resolution, the main vehicle for this shift was a critical concentration by Republicans, in both the presidential and the congressional wings of the party, on the administration and its conduct of the war. Capitalizing on the growing public discontent over the Allies' failure to win significant victories, Republicans continued to turn charges of lack of preparedness for war back on the Democrats, either by criticizing the administration's prewar conduct of foreign policy for leading the United States toward war unprepared or by assigning lack of preparedness in general to the president's presumed concentration upon domestic social and economic reforms.

Former party standard-bearers Herbert Hoover and Alf Landon called attention to what they perceived as widespread and growing public dissatisfaction with the government's wartime activities. During a visit to the Midwest, Hoover wrote in May, he found deep suspicion of administration statements, great anxiety, and rampant skepticism.[39] Attributing these sentiments in the main to the absence of a great victory, Hoover also concluded that there was bewilderment over war objectives. People could not reconcile a crusade for liberty, he claimed, with acceptance of the Soviet Union and the British Empire as partners.[40] Landon wrote Senator Taft as early as February 1942 that he had noticed a recent increase in criticism of President Roosevelt in this connection, that it was coming open and above board, hot and heavy from both former friends and supporters of the president, and that, even to Landon's mind, it was "shocking." The country had lost the fine, fighting edge of unity it had possessed immediately after Pearl Harbor, according to Landon, and attempts by the administration and interventionist groups to throw blame on isolationists for the war had backfired. He concluded that a big year lay ahead for Republicans in 1942 and that political trends were decidedly going their way.[41]

Clearly President Roosevelt himself had public discontent with lack of progress in the fighting in mind when he agreed to the British proposal for an invasion of North Africa before the end of 1942. When hopes for the anticipated cross-channel invasion of Europe proved unattainable that year, the president for the most part resisted demands, even from his closest military advisers, for a greater war effort in the Pacific. Roosevelt was determined to involve American troops in action against the Germans somewhere in 1942. In this resolve, he evidenced an awareness of the public's concern with results; he set October 30 as the latest possible date for the invasion of North Africa and implored General Marshall: "Please make it before Election Day."[42]

So great did the public's preoccupation with this issue appear, in fact, that Republicans were induced to forget temporarily their clash with the administration over responsibility for Pearl Harbor. They were even able to relax pressures for a primary offensive against the Japanese. Greater possibilities seemed inherent in mounting popular support for the idea of appointing a single naval or military commander-in-chief to direct the war effort. Given the G.O.P.'s interest in General MacArthur, whom Wendell Willkie had first suggested for such a post, this idea was indeed, as one observer concluded, "not devoid of ulterior political purpose" among Republicans.[43]

In any event, there was a certain natural limit to the length to which charges of prewar isolationism could be carried in an election year, for otherwise, as Senator Vandenberg pointed out, "the electorate would have to repudiate *itself* and its own pre-Pearl Harbor attitudes."[44] That limit certainly appeared to hold for most Republicans in the primaries of 1942. Although internationalists Harold E. Stassen and Joseph H. Ball won the Republican nominations for governor and senator, respectively, in Minnesota over anti-interventionist opposition and isolationist Representative Oscar Youngdahl lost his Minneapolis district seat (to Dr. Walter H. Judd of later "China Lobby" fame), former isolationists won renominations in Illinois, Indiana, and South Dakota. Their isolationism did not harm them, reportedly, because of widespread dissatisfaction with administration mistakes in the war effort.[45] Although apathy was marked—in large measure due, no doubt, to military enlistments and war-time worker mobility—Republicans maintained that a definite political trend against the administration had been established and could be reversed in the remaining weeks before the election only by a smashing military or naval victory.[46]

As an extension of his bid for control of the party on the issue of postwar international organization, Willkie and some of his supporters had determined even before the April meeting to use whatever influence they could muster in the primaries to oppose Republican congressional candidates with prewar isolationist records.[47] If the primaries were any test, however, such influence proved minimal indeed. Following the victories of Brooks and Day in Illinois, former isolationists opposed by Willkie triumphed in Iowa and in Missouri, much to the delight of the *Chicago Tribune*.[48] That publication relished reporting the results of a questionnaire by the *Missouri Republican,* a semi-monthly newspaper circulated among party officials throughout Missouri, to which 764 of 765 respondents replied in the negative regarding Willkie's leadership and ability to speak for the party in that state.[49] The *Tribune* also reported that the state convention of Indiana Republicans had refused to accept for its platform a statement like the one issued by the National Committee in April but had adopted instead one that resembled the original Taft resolution.[50] In New York, moreover, Representative Hamilton Fish won renomination in the primary despite the concerted opposition of Willkie, Dewey (who won the nomination for governor in that same election), and Roosevelt.

Although Willkie had led in the presidential preference poll conducted by *The Republican* in late 1941 and had still seemed to be the front-runner at the time of the Chicago meeting, he had slipped to second place in a Gallup poll taken later during the primaries.[51] On that occasion, General MacArthur bettered him, doubtless indicating the surpassing strength of the conduct-of-the-war issue in Republican circles. Although a similar poll a month later showed Willkie still ahead of Dewey, his closest civilian rival, he could hardly have considered himself or his position on foreign policy in the party on the rise.[52]

Sensing a potential threat from Dewey in both areas, Willkie refrained initially from endorsing his rival's candidacy for governor of New York. He thought Dewey unnecessarily evasive in his views regarding the future international role of the United States.[53] Urged by supporters to oppose Dewey for the New York Republican gubernatorial nomination himself, Willkie declined but pointedly observed that this refusal did not affect any aspirations he might be harboring for the presidency.[54] Nevertheless, Willkie refused to endorse Dewey's candidacy for governor until just before the election in 1942.

For the issue of postwar international organization itself, the year 1942 was too soon to predict a fate. A poll taken in July showed 70 percent of the Republicans responding to be in favor of joining a league of nations after the war. Other polls taken at the same time, however, showed all such expressions of opinion to be at best vague and ill-defined.[55] A majority of the American people apparently preferred to concentrate on the conduct of the war during 1942 and to postpone specific thoughts about peace until victory was assured.

In line with his own anti-isolationism and the drive to lead the party toward commitment to a postwar organization, Willkie came out in August with a three-point pledge which he urged all Republican candidates for office to sign. The third and most telling point contained a call for international institutions after the war, including an international armed force.[56] He had no signers. This fact alone should serve to discredit claims of a Willkie victory at the April meeting, not to mention notions of any historic reversal of role in foreign policy effected there by the party.

From the opposite end of the party, Taft challenged Willkie on foreign policy in his own bailiwick, New York. Writing to Chester Colby, chairman of the Board of the General Foods Corporation there, Taft responded to a recommendation from Colby that the Republican party begin tailoring its stands on issues of foreign policy to the results of public opinion polls by remonstrating that the "very trouble with the Republican Party, to my mind, has been its constant compromising with what it guessed public opinion to be." Ordinarily, Taft argued as he had before Pearl Harbor, "foreign policy has not played much part in the division between the parties. There is no reason why it should play any great part at the present moment, because the only issue should be the aggressive prosecution of the war." Significantly, however, he predicted that "because of Mr. Willkie's statements, and in any event as we get closer to the end of the war it will again become dominant and may divide the party." His own belief was that "there should be no insistence on forcing that issue. A gradual and friendly discussion may enable us to agree on a moderate position of reasonable responsibility in other parts of the world. That should be the endeavor of Republican leaders today, rather than to insist upon any immediate declaration regarding the kind of peace to be set up after the war."[57]

During the summer of 1942, Willkie received a further challenge to his attempt to lead the party on the postwar issue when Herbert Hoover and Hugh Gibson published their opinions on that subject in *The Problems of Lasting Peace*.[58] Taking issue with a favorite internationalist theme, the former president and the retired Republican diplomat argued that the League had failed not because the United States had de-

clined to become a member but because Britain and France had abandoned it by reverting to their old, accustomed forms of power politics
during the interwar years. Hoover and Gibson did not object either to
the League or a balance of power among nations per se; but rather, they
wanted the problem of enforcing a future peace separated from the question of a postwar international organization. To that end, they suggested
that the wartime Allies, once victorious, should establish a permanent
military pact to disarm potential aggressors as well as a new league of
nations based on international law and moral opinion for the peaceful
settlement of international disputes.[59]

Given the Hoover-Gibson challenge in addition to his apparent in-
effectiveness in the primaries, Willkie needed some boost by the end
of the summer to restore his own sagging political fortunes and those of
his internationalist beliefs. Thus, when Roosevelt offered him an army
plane and the designation of personal representative of the president for
a trip around the world designed to dramatize the global nature of the
anti-Axis alliance, Willkie quickly seized the opportunity.[60] Actually, the
trip had a variety of propaganda purposes. By circumnavigating the globe
during wartime, Willkie was supposed to demonstrate Allied control of
the airways, the strength of the American industrial machine which gave
him the means to do so, and the unity and stamina of a political system
which was able to allow an opposition party leader to travel freely abroad
in times of crisis. Doubtless, as some Republicans suspected, the administration also hoped to gain political capital on the home front from this
last purpose.[61] Accompanied at his own request by correspondents
Gardner Cowles and Joseph Barnes, who were given leave from their duties in the Office of War Information to make the trip, and by an American
army crew, Willkie embarked in late August on the fifty-day, 31,000-mile
administration-sponsored junket.

If, however, the president had dreams of reaping immediate additional
support either at home or abroad from the trip, they were soon dashed.
After visiting Stalin in Moscow, Willkie was quick to echo the Soviet
leader's persistent call for a second front in Europe "at the earliest possible moment our military leaders will approve"—much to the chagrin of
Roosevelt and Churchill, who had all summer long been struggling to explain to the Russians why the first combined Anglo-American operation
against the Germans was going to take place in North Africa and not on
the European mainland.[62] Willkie had not been informed of the Medi-
terranean landings being planned in Washington before embarking on
his trip. He was still unaware of them when he made a further plea in
Moscow that "public prodding" be applied to Allied military leaders to
open a second front in Europe.[63] Later, upon arriving in China and con-

versing with Chiang Kai-shek, Willkie similarly endorsed Chiang's demands
for the China-Burma-India theater: immediate increases in aid to China,
an Allied offensive in Burma, and firm timetables for "an end to the empire of nations over other nations."[64]

Needless to say, Willkie's remarks created something of a stir in British and American governing circles. Shortly after hearing about them,
Churchill delivered himself of the famous remark that he had "not become the King's First Minister to preside at the liquidation of the British Empire."[65] In Congress, long-standing opponents of his political views
further attacked Willkie.[66] Finally, President Roosevelt, at a press conference, dismissed accounts of Willkie's statements and, by inference, his
views themselves as pure speculation.[67] Two days after the first reports
of Willkie's comments, however, Under Secretary of State Sumner Welles
began a move to secure final approval of a treaty repealing the extraterri-
torial rights of the United States in China, after years of inactivity on the
subject.[68]

Having learned while still abroad of the controversy stirred by his remarks, Willkie was angered by what he presumed to be Roosevelt's duplicity
and was quick to insist that his "understanding" with the president before
departure "had made it perfectly clear that he [Willkie] remained free to
state his own opinions in addition to carrying out the President's assign-
ments."[69] When he finally returned to the United States (and following
a somewhat heated report to the president), Willkie delivered a speech
over radio on October 26, one week before the elections, reporting the
results of his trip to an estimated thirty-six million listeners.

In that speech, Willkie again defended his position as a free agent on the
trip and reemphasized the themes he had previously enunciated. Calling
once more for a second front in Europe, an offensive against the Japanese
in Burma, a definite commitment to ending western imperialism around
the globe, and the winning of the peace as well as of the war, he also warned
Americans that in order to maintain a reservoir of good will for their
country throughout the world, they must play an active, constructive role
in freeing that world, both economically and politically, and in keeping it
at peace.[70] Willkie later recounted these conclusions, along with the high-
lights and impact of his trip, in a best-selling book, *One World.*[71]

Willkie's trip and the commentary upon it might have had an effect on
the Republican outcome in the 1942 elections. Current dissatisfaction with
the administration's conduct of the war was undoubtedly exacerbated by
Willkie's report. Neither the trip nor the speech, however, had fostered
that dissatisfaction originally, and many Republicans had both objected
to the presumption of Willkie's leadership of their party implied by the
trip and criticized him strongly for not having stayed in the country dur-

ing important weeks of the campaign to help promote G.O.P. candidates
for office.[72] The president's own activities, moreover, or those of his associates in office, were at least as important as (if not more than) those
of his Republican counterpart in influencing the outcome of the November
elections. Perhaps the most significant instance of such presidential activity
came in the New York race for governor. There Roosevelt objected
to the nominee of James Farley's state Democratic organization, John J.
Bennett, and threw his support behind a rival candidate, Senator James M.
Mead.[73] Much as the Dewey-Willkie squabble over the same office in New
York contained wider-ranging implications for Republicans, the Democratic quarrel involved broader considerations for the Roosevelt administration.

In the first place, by fostering the notion that rejection of his own
preferred candidate in New York was equivalent to repudiation of his
wartime leadership, Roosevelt and his supporters created a more or less
self-fulfilling prophecy. The Democratic organization in New York refused
to go along with the president's choice, and repudiation of Roosevelt is
exactly what was claimed and believed. Second, given the failure of his own
party members to heed his pleas for support during wartime, not only was
Republican criticism of Roosevelt's leadership amplified, but the White
House was deprived, according to one G.O.P. analyst, "of the right to ex-
pect support on the one ground that the independent element and parents of service men might have had difficulty in ignoring" despite im-
passes in the fighting: "the popular tradition of backing the President in
wartime."[74]

Finally, the Democratic fissure in New York State virtually guaranteed the election of Thomas E. Dewey as governor, thus assuring the Republican party and its brightest new star of an important base from which
to challenge the Democratic leadership for national office in 1944.[75]
Roosevelt was scored in party and press alike for his abortive intervention
in the New York race. Once more the "lesson" of Woodrow Wilson in
1918 was trotted out to confirm the folly of presidential intervention in
electoral politics during wartime.[76]

No such lessons were lost on the loyal opposition. Republicans united
against Roosevelt in the final election struggle, sensing a favorable trend
in their direction in the absence of military victories. Early October saw
the appearance of a ten-point manifesto aimed at assisting Republicans
running for Congress. Put together by Representative J. William Ditter
of Pennsylvania, chairman of the Republican Congressional Campaign
Committee, with the help of Representative Everett M. Dirksen of Illinois and approved by 115 Republican representatives, the list contained
criticisms of the administration's conduct of the war and of Roosevelt's

presumed preoccupation with politics instead of the fighting. In addition, the manifesto pledged that the party would oppose any attempt at a negotiated peace and would see to it that the nation's war effort continued unabated until "complete decisive victory was won." For these reasons, as well as for more specifically domestic ones, the manifesto urged preservation of the two-party system and an increase in its effectiveness (presumably by the election of Republicans on November 3); it also affirmed that "the United States has an obligation and responsibility to work with other nations to bring about a world understanding and cooperative spirit which will have for its supreme objective the continued maintenance of peace."[77] The *New York Times* chose to view this manifesto as it had the Republican National Committee's April resolution, namely, as another major party document repudiating isolationism.[78] As in the case of the April resolution, however, this judgment of the manifesto is difficult to accept. Forty Republican leaders found the statement on American postwar obligations too strong to endorse. The entire document, moreover, was admittedly only a general expression of party policy, issued solely for the purposes of the campaign; it hardly committed the party or even the signers themselves to anything specific.[79]

Twenty-six million Americans, 50 percent less than in 1940, went to the polls on November 3, 1942, five days before the first Allied landings in North Africa, and gave the Republicans forty-four additional seats in the House and nine in the Senate, the party's best showing in an election since the 1920s. Roosevelt's governing margin was slashed to the lowest point of his entire presidential career, and he only narrowly escaped the fate of Woodrow Wilson in 1918. In the House, the number of Republicans increased from 165 to 209, a scant seven members short of control, and included prominent isolationist Hamilton Fish, the only candidate in the campaign against whom Roosevelt had personally spoken out. In the Senate, G.O.P. strength rose to thirty-seven seats, continuing a steady growth begun in 1937; this strength, moreover, pointedly did not include the only candidate in the campaign the president had specifically endorsed, independent Republican George W. Norris of Nebraska, who was defeated for reelection by party regular Kenneth S. Wherry. Republicans also scored important gains in state government. Apart from Dewey in New York, Earl Warren was elected governor in California; Harold E. Stassen, in Minnesota; John W. Bricker, in Ohio; and Leverett Saltonstall, in Massachusetts. These results promised the national party a new base, both of power and of popular appeal, for the presidential elections in 1944.

As with most general elections in the United States, it is extremely difficult to measure the outcome of the 1942 contests in terms of a single critical or overriding issue. Perhaps one gauge of the meaning of these

elections, however, may lie in what the two parties, in taking stock of
the results, thought they meant. Initially, the Democrats attributed their
losses in the elections to the low voter turnout and believed that many of
their regular supporters were ineligible to vote either because they were
serving in the armed forces or because they were moving to new wartime
jobs and lacking in minimum residency requirements.[80]

In this assessment, the Democrats were seconded to a degree by pro-
fessional analysts of public opinion. Even their own pollsters, however,
pointed out that among traditionally Democratic low-income groups
not particularly affected by wartime service or occupational requirements, there had also been marked disinterest in the elections.[81] The
results of one canvass of Democratic candidates for House and Senate
in forty-three states showed that 44.7 percent of the respondents believed that resentment against the conduct of the war had dominated
the thinking of their constituents. Replies cited in evidence the belief
that the United States should have been able to defeat Japan easily but
had not yet done so. Some volunteered the opinion that if news of the
North African campaign had preceded rather than followed the elections, the results would have been different.[82] Stephen Early, Roosevelt's
press secretary, shared this view; he himself first learned of the Mediter-
ranean invasion shortly before it began and exclaimed at the news, "Je-
sus Christ . . . why couldn't the Army have done this before the election!"[83]

The report to Roosevelt on this canvass of Democratic candidates in
1942 concluded emphatically that isolationism was not dead. Particularly
in the Midwest, it observed, except for districts dominated by the Polish-
Slav vote, every reply had indicated that isolationism was at least as strong
as ever.[84] Additional Democratic postmortems on the election tended to
corroborate this judgment and to concur in the belief that without a re-
form within the administration, a marked change for the better in the
war, and a clearer definition of Allied peace aims, the next election would
prove a real catastrophe for the party.[85]

In analyzing their victories in the elections, Republicans likewise concluded that the conduct-of-the-war issue had been decisively important
in producing the outcome. They linked this issue more closely, however,
with their own continuing charges of executive inefficiency and doubts
about the competence of the high command. As another major factor
in their success, Republican analysts noted the marked discontent in the
Midwest over agricultural price controls. On the whole, they believed, the
election results had been a favorable response to the kind of increased
partisanship that the G.O.P. had been practicing, the prospects for the
future of which looked bright indeed.[86]

"It would be absurd to say that 'isolationism' was not an issue in the election," a writer for the party organ, *The Republican*, proclaimed in triumph following the elections. Recalling that President Roosevelt himself had "injected the issue into the campaign with a bang when he called on the voters to return senators and representatives who had been for his foreign policy before Pearl Harbor" and that the "New Deal's national chairman, Ed Flynn, further pointed up the issue by declaring, in almost so many words, that a Republican victory would be equivalent to a great military victory for the Axis," *The Republican*'s analyst noted that " 'isolationism,' or failure to support the Administration's foreign policy before Pearl Harbor, occupied a major place in the campaigns waged against more than 100 House members and perhaps a dozen senators seeking re-election!" He also recalled that isolationism had been a widely used issue in many Republican primary battles. "But, as an issue either in the primaries or the final elections," he concluded, " 'isolationism' laid a very large egg." . . . Of "115 members of the House of Representatives who survived the primaries and who were selected for purging by 'interventionist' groups, 110 were re-elected and only 5 were defeated."[87]

Furthermore, the writer for *The Republican* observed, the "issue of 'isolationism' vs. 'interventionism,' as it affects the post-war role of the Republican party" was not setfled in the November 3 elections. "It is true, as some New Dealish commentators have gleefully pointed out, that the elections have tended to sharpen the outlines of 'isolationist' and 'interventionist' groups within the Republican ranks. There does not appear to be any reason to believe, however, as the same commentators are hoping, that this will lead to a serious and lasting rift within the party. When the time comes, the issue will be decided within the Republican party."[88]

Within the party itself, an important effect of the election was to discredit even further both the Willkie and Taft extremes on the question of prewar isolationism. Viewed strictly in terms of the foreign policy issue, the outcome in 1942 was a smashing success for the moderate, or cautious, approach to the problem. Many Republicans entered the campaign in that first year of direct American involvement in World War II with some potentially fatal handicaps deriving from their prewar records and views on foreign policy. More than the Democrats, they and their party bore the recently discredited image of isolationism. Simply by avoiding the political pitfalls inherent in that image, Republicans, particularly those in the congressional wing of the party, celebrated a kind of triumph in 1942, one whose significance reached beyond the additional seats gained by their party in the House and Senate.

The election results themselves had shown the political liability of the short-run, or immediate prewar, isolationist problems of the party to be minimal, given the public's concentration upon the course and conduct of the war. Indeed, it seems reasonable to conclude, as the election analyst for *The Republican* did, that the charge of prewar isolationism failed as a campaign issue "because it was a direct attack on the patriotism, not only of the senators and representatives at whom it was aimed, but also of the millions of citizens whose pre-Pearl Harbor attitude toward the Administration's foreign policy had been accurately mirrored by the congressmen who were now under attack." This factor "may be assumed to have held the votes at least of the citizens whose pre-war opinions had been 'isolationistic.' Pre-war 'interventionists,' it may be assumed, were not disposed to punish members of Congress for their pre-war views, so long as they now showed every inclination to support vigorous prosecution of the war, and were presumably further influenced by such factors as Wendell Willkie's report, a week before the election, on his trip around the world."[89]

On the other hand, the elections, had indicated little or nothing about the party's long-run isolationist problem: its connection with the defeat of Wilson's League of Nations. That specter had yet to make the power of its presence fully known. The 1942 election results, however, had demonstrated to Republicans the advantages of temporizing on the issue of future participation by the United States in an international organization and had encouraged them to refrain from formulating definite positions of their own on that subject. The elections served in an immediate sense, therefore, to retard development of both a new image for the party and a thorough debate on foreign policy in the United States.

So widespread among Republicans was belief in the efficacy of caution and delay following the elections, in fact, that National Chairman Martin felt able to resign his position as head of the presidential wing of the party (and mediator between the Willkie and Taft factions) and call for the election of his successor. Growing consensus on what should constitute appropriate strategy for the party in foreign policy, however, was not the only consideration behind Martin's announcement. His resignation was also symbolic of a significant development in the struggle between presidential and congressional factions of the G.O.P. for control of the presidential wing. The congressional faction was obviously strengthened after the elections in 1942, but so too was the presidential, as the increased number of Republican governors elected demonstrated. Martin's resignation reflected in part a movement away from the congressional leadership's domination of the presidential wing of the party toward control by

new leadership within the presidential wing itself. Such a shift was further indicated in late 1942 by the announcements of senators Taft and
Vandenberg, both of whom had been candidates for the Republican
presidential nomination in 1940, that neither would seek the office in
1944.

4 CONGRESSIONAL REPUBLICANS RISE UP IN 1943

The elections of 1942 had yielded several important results for Republicans in Congress. First of all, the outcome had strengthened their hand considerably as the opposition party in Congress. They had gained nine new seats in the Senate to bring their total there to 37, higher than at any time since the beginning of the New Deal. By the middle of 1943, with the addition of three seats following the regular elections, they had increased their representation in the House to 212, as compared to 216 for the Democrats and 4 for third-party candidates—again, a greater number than at any time since 1932. In terms of formal party alignments, therefore, the Republicans were almost equal in number to the Democrats in the House, while in the Senate, whose powers in foreign affairs were broader and more jealously guarded by tradition, they commanded on paper more than the one-third number of votes necessary to withhold consent from any treaties the Roosevelt administration might negotiate in the next two years. With the possibility that such negotiations might include a treaty of peace and the memories of Woodrow Wilson's experiences in this connection growing fresher in everyone's mind, the added Republican strength in the Senate looked impressive indeed.[1]

The real increase of Republican strength in Congress, however, was not to be found on paper alone or in total numbers of votes. It was also reflected in the extra seats on committees to which Republicans in both Houses found themselves entitled as a result of their election victories. In the House, they gained 173 new positions on 47 standing committees. In the Senate, they picked up 70 seats on 33 committees, increasing their ratio from one Republican to two Democrats on most committees in 1942 to a two-to-three relationship in 1943. Republicans became entitled, for example, to two new posts on the Senate Foreign Relations Committee, which would take a first look at any treaty legislation the

administration might propose. As for the Democrats, they suffered not
only a loss of seats on committees after the elections but a loss of commanding majorities on some, which meant among other things that fewer
Democrats could afford to be absent in the future when crucial votes
were being taken. More important, however, the conservative coalition of
Republicans and Southern Democrats that had been formed before the
war to oppose the administration on domestic legislation was further
advanced. In the process, the power of Congress and of Republicans in
it was materially strengthened at the expense of the president and of his
Democratic supporters.

An awareness of their increased strength soon began to grow among
opposition party members in Congress. The immediate effect was to renew
and intensify their demands for more direct congressional participation
in the conduct of the war. These demands had reappeared during the
election campaign itself in connection with Republican charges of administration misconduct in the war effort. Further fuel had been added to
these changes by the evidence of waste and mismanagement in the nation's
defense program that the special Senate investigating committee chaired
by a Democrat, Harry Truman, kept turning up. Republicans Everett
Dirksen of Illinois and Melvin J. Maas of Minnesota had both come forward in October with proposals in the House for legislative participation
in the running of the war. Representative Maas, a critic in particular of the
conduct of the war in the Pacific, had urged that the military and naval
committees in Congress be consolidated, while Dirksen had introduced
a resolution to establish a congressional high command, a joint House-
Senate committee, on war and postwar problems.[3]

Following the elections, Arthur Vandenberg renewed his call in the
Senate for "strict accountability" of the Executive to Congress, decry-
ing what he considered to be the "complete and total lack of authentic
liaison between the White House and Congress in respect to war responsibilities," and reaffirming a congressional responsibility for the conduct
of the war. Vandenberg declared that the "people themselves are pro-
gressively insisting upon the recognition of this Congressional responsibility" and he repeated his long-standing demand for a joint congressional-
executive committee.[4] His demand was seconded by minority leader
Joseph Martin in the House.[5]

At the same time, Wisconsin Republican Senator Alexander Wiley
proposed the establishment of a Foreign Relations Advisory Council, "in
the thought that the creation of such a Council can materially aid in eliminating the friction between the Executive and the Legislative branches
which has frequently characterized the presentation and ratification of
treaties in the past."[6] In a letter to Secretary of State Hull, Wiley com-

plained that personal contact between members of key committees in Congress and the administration, an arrangement which the secretary and others in the administration preferred, was an inadequate means of consulting with Congress during wartime. Ominously, he warned that American history was "studded with the sad stories of Secretaries of State who apparently were not blessed with your congressional friendships. American history and the history of your predecessors, which I need not review here, indicates [*sic*] conclusively that the presentation to the Senate Foreign Relations Committee of a treaty which is virtually a *fait accompli* or which has at best had only the informal 'advice' of the Secretary's personal friends, may meet with a disastrous emasculation or rejection."[7]

Much less ominously, Senator Vandenberg called for the establishment of a "victory coalition" of Republicans and Democrats with partisan politics and "New Dealism" ruled out for the war's duration.[8] To this end, Vandenberg announced, he supported a resolution submitted by Democratic Senator Francis Maloney of Connecticut proposing a consolidation of congressional committees on the war along the lines of the Maas resolution.[9] For its part, the administration moved through Secretary Hull to head off such proposals. Hull agreed to increase his department's contact and consultation with the standing committees which regularly dealt with matters of war and foreign policy; other departments did the same.[10] In the end, Republicans in Congress decided to live with this state of affairs. Their accession, however, derived as much from rival committees' jealousies of long-standing prerogatives and, perhaps, the increased Republican strength on these committees as from any conscious diminution of political partisanship in foreign affairs.

In fact, partisanship was very much in evidence. Congressional Republicans went into an uproar over President Roosevelt's nomination of their party's old nemesis, Democratic National Chairman Edward Flynn, as minister to Australia and special ambassador of the president in the Southwest Pacific. The move seemed to them to be a blatant act of political partisanship, especially in view of Flynn's statement in 1942 challenging their fitness for office during wartime. Senator Taft and other Republicans threatened a full Senate inquiry into the circumstances surrounding the nomination if Flynn should be approved by the Foreign Relations Committee.[11] Some suggested that the reason the president wanted Flynn to go to the South Pacific was to have a politically experienced friend there to keep an eye on General MacArthur, whom Roosevelt expected the Republicans to nominate for president in 1944.[12] Although the Foreign Relations Committee, following a review of Flynn's Bronx political connections, ultimately approved the Democratic chairman for the post, his name was withdrawn by the administration in order to allow the political storm to subside.

The outburst over the Flynn nomination, as well as over congressional participation in the conduct of the war, indicated that noninterventionist Republicans like senators Taft and Vandenberg were interpreting the 1942 election results in a most favorable light. The results convinced them that Republican prewar isolationism, the image and record of which were particularly associated with party members in Congress, was not as serious a political liability as at first it had appeared. This interpretation of the election, combined with their party's increase in strength as a result, reinvigorated congressional Republican isolationists in 1943. They now felt safe enough to resurrect issues derived from prewar days but glimpsed only briefly in 1942. Vandenberg, for example, could charge in response to the administration's refusal to establish a liaison committee with Congress that a recently published State Department White Paper on American entry into the war proved that Congress had not been informed as it should have "of the international realities . . . in policies and events for six critical months preceding Pearl Harbor."[13]

One form which this isolationist upsurge in the new Congress took was a drive by noninterventionist Republicans in the Senate to remove Warren R. Austin of Vermont from the position he had held there since 1939 as assistant minority leader. According to a rule adopted by the Senate's Republican Conference in January 1935, no assistant leader or whip was to be elected by Republicans, but the chairman of the conference was authorized "to appoint Senators from time to time to assist him in taking charge of the interests of the Minority."[14] The chairman of the conference in 1935 and afterwards was Charles McNary, the floor leader of the minority, who in 1939 and again in 1941 had named Austin to look after party matters in his absence. This designation had not set well with certain of Austin's isolationist colleagues, like Vandenberg and Nye, who opposed him as assistant leader because of his consistent support of the administration's foreign policy, his connections with Wendell Willkie in the presidential wing of the party, and his generally outspoken internationalist positions and views.

In October 1939 Austin had been one of the first Republicans on Capitol Hill to call for total repeal of the Neutrality Act and in 1941 had helped to sponsor an amendment to that effect. He had been vociferous in favor of Lend-Lease, voting for it as well as for selective service legislation before the outbreak of war at Pearl Harbor. As recently as December 30, 1942, in a nationwide radio broadcast, he had called upon the United States to begin negotiations immediately with its allies "to determine the vital and controversial questions of the future peace."[15] Shortly after the broadcast, according to Austin, his internationalist colleague and friend, Wallace White of Maine, had confided to him that the "isolationists

don't want you for Assistant Leader; they have nothing against you personally, but they say you don't represent their views; they are in a majority of Republicans, having about 20 votes, and they want a man who rep-
resents their views for Assistant Leader."[16] That man was reportedly
Senator John A. Danaher of Connecticut, who had voted against every
interventionist measure which Austin had approved.[17]

Reporters sympathetic to the internationalist cause got wind of the
anti-Austin campaign in the Senate and variously portrayed it in the press
as "renewed evidence of the deep division in foreign policy within the
ranks of the Republicans," as one more sign that once the war had been
won there would be "wide differences of opinion as to the part the United
States should play in international affairs," and as an indication that
the isolationists were interpreting the November elections as a victory.
Strong pressure was reportedly being brought to bear upon McNary to
prevent Austin from continuing as assistant leader, the pressure being de-
picted as but a preliminary skirmish in the isolationist-internationalist
struggle among Republicans that had yet to be resolved.[18] Linking the
controversy to the April meeting of the Republican National Committee
and the postwar resolution adopted then, one writer contended that "if
the isolationist members of the Party cannot commit the Party definitely
to their viewpoint, they want to make sure that it is not committed to
any form of internationalism. Thus they want to avoid Senator Austin's
internationalism, just as the National Committee . . . wants to avoid the Chicago *Tribune*'s isolationism."[19] Wendell Willkie, asked to comment on reports that the isolationists were out to get Austin, replied that he hoped
that they were inaccurate since there could be "no greater tragedy than
for the United States Senate to repeat its action of 1920 in preventing
the United States from assuming its obligations toward the establishment
and maintenance of world order."[20]

Leaders among the Senate's Republican isolationists quickly denied
reports that a plot was afoot to unseat Austin. Nye, for example, disclaimed any knowledge of such a campaign, not to mention any complic-
ity in it on his part. Observing that he had heard occasionally an "expressed wish that we should have a leadership that would be reflective of
the majority of Republican sentiment," Nye commented that there never
had been "an approach to it."[21] In the meantime, McNary moved to play
down accounts of a battle among Senate Republicans and to shift their
emphasis. He indicated to Austin that the entire matter was "a tempest in
a teapot" and remarked to a reporter that it looked to him as though an
effort was being made by "some persons" to stir up the isolationist issue
and thereby cause friction among Republicans in the Senate. McNary implied that the fires were being stirred by interventionists like Willkie, not

the isolationists, and intimated that Austin would continue to serve as assistant leader.[22]

Austin himself noted the reports and the comment by Willkie with approval, but he did so in private. Publicly he remained silent, "in spite of many temptations to speak" and "many requests for information," remarking only to reporters that he did not want to say anything about the situation except that he regretted "very much" that it had occurred.[23] To one sympathetic correspondent, however, he did comment that "this Isolationist maneuver has prompted an outpouring of evidence to its authors which ought to convince them of their misjudgment of the last election. I feel sure that it will weaken their position in spite of the fact that they have a majority in number at the present time on the Republican side of the Senate. It may even have the effect of converting some of the new men to our cause."[24] He also observed that soon after the controversy had erupted, he began receiving messages from various isolationist senators indicating that they would support him.

When the Republican Conference met on January 8 to organize formally for the new session, "the harmony was so thick," according to McNary, that it "ran down my cheeks." The question of an assistant leader was not even mentioned and the old rule was left intact, permitting McNary to appoint an assistant when and if he chose. Questioned by a reporter after the meeting about how he would fill the post, McNary replied rather sharply, "I appoint someone to fill in when I'm not there and I'll do that when I get ready."[25] A month later, the position still had not been filled.

More than anyone, Austin remained aware of the vacancy. Privately, he noted that McNary had acted surprised to see him at a White House meeting of congressional leaders to which Austin had been invited for a report by the president on his recently concluded conference at Casablanca. He also recorded that Vandenberg, upon being informed of his presence at the White House gathering, had sworn with an oath, "Well, that settles it!" According to Austin, Vandenberg had spent half an hour at an informal Republican gathering criticizing him for attending the report to leaders of Congress and objecting to the assumption that Austin was one of the leaders.[26]

Toward the end of February, when McNary was absent from the Senate, Wallace White, not Austin, took over as minority leader, a position that White was to acquire in his own right following McNary's death in 1944. The move appeared to confirm speculation in some quarters that "perhaps the isolationists had in the end exerted more power than was originally realized."[27] A more accurate interpretation is probably that McNary himself had moved to dampen further controversy in the matter by appointing a

more moderate internationalist as assistant leader than Austin, thus preventing either side in the dispute from claiming a victory or registering a defeat.
McNary had already attempted to mollify Austin by urging him in January
to accept a seat on the Senate Foreign Relations Committee. At the time,
it appeared that Republicans would gain two additional seats on the committee as a result of their electoral triumphs. Seniority dictated that one of
them should go to Senator James J. Davis of Pennsylvania, a former noninterventionist. McNary himself was entitled to the other by the same principl
In asking Austin, who was next in line, to serve on the committee instead,
McNary commented that although certain isolationists had requested him
to apply for the position, it would not be good "for the Republican Party
to have it said that it 'packed' the Foreign Relations Committee with Isolationists."[28]

Austin was not particularly excited by McNary's offer, even though he
had applied for a seat on the committee in every session of Congress since
he had been there. He remarked to McNary that he knew the "color of the
Committee" and that, except for White, its minority members (Johnson,
Capper, LaFollette, Vandenberg, Shipstead, Nye, and Davis) were all isolationists. Indeed, when the final allocation of seats on the committee resulted
in the Republicans gaining only one instead of the expected two, Austin was
neither bitter about the outcome nor cynical about assurances that the
next available seat would be his. He "felt badly," he recorded, about the
effect on the internationalist cause for which he was fighting, fearing that
on a close controversial question relating to a treaty of peace, the committee, counting the number of isolationist Democrats on it, might be opposed to collaboration by the United States in the postwar world. On the
other hand, he considered that he might be more free, not being on the
committee, "to continue the activity (in which I have been engaged from
the beginning) for a more vigorous prosecution of the war on the home
front, and for the preparation of public opinion to support a peace in
which the United States recognizes its responsibility, and takes its proper
leadership in the new world." If he were on the Foreign Relations Committee, he might be limited by "the natural loyalty" which he would feel
to his fellow members on the committee.[29]

Austin was most unhappy, however, about McNary's failure to reappoint him assistant leader, although he apparently bore no malice toward
the minority leader in that regard. He did attribute evil motives in the
matter to Senators Vandenberg, Danaher, and Rufus C. Holman of Oregon,
particularly after a conversation with Senator Danaher had revealed to
him that an isolationist "cabal" formed by the three had been conspiring
against him as early as 1939 and had even gone so far as to tinker with the
record of the Republican Conference in 1941 which had confirmed McNary's

previous appointment of him as assistant leader. This discovery, combined with Vandenberg's recent propaganda against him, hardened Austin's attitude toward his isolationist colleagues, though not so much as to make him violate his sense of "natural loyalty" and speak out against fellow congressional Republicans.[30] While still hoping that the Senate would not "lead the way back to disastrous Isolationism" and that if public opinion proved "strong enough, these so-called Isolationists would reverse themselves," Austin nevertheless warned that the "impossible situation" which men such as Vandenberg were creating would have to be resolved in some way.[31] If not, he predicted, then senators like himself, who were "interested in the cause of the war, including attainment of its objectives," were quite likely to "start something."[32]

Meanwhile, Republican isolationists like Senator Vandenberg were having a field day early in 1943 attacking the administration's wartime foreign policy from a variety of prewar perspectives. Nowhere was their renewal of old familiar charges more clearly in evidence than in debate over Lend-Lease, opposition to which had provided a tell-tale rallying point for prewar isolationist sentiments. It came up for congressional renewal in 1943. Isolationist Republican leaders like Vandenberg, Taft, and Nye had opposed Lend-Lease in 1941 because its passage then had seemed to them likely to involve the United States in the war in Europe. In 1943, however, there was never much doubt that extension of Lend-Lease as an instrument of the wartime alliance would be approved, even by its former opponents. Public opinion was highly in favor of renewing the provisions of the act, particularly following victories in North Africa and the Pacific and the need to supply Allied forces there.[33] Vandenberg in fact now labeled Lend-Lease the "king-link in the chain of international cooperation for victory."[34]

It soon became obvious, however, that Republicans in Congress, in line with Vandenberg's objective of holding the administration to "strict accountability," intended to scrutinize the Lend-Lease program in detail prior to approving it. Their hope was to weaken the Executive's powers over the program while at the same time strengthening Congress's control over its expenditures. Led by Hugh A. Butler of Nebraska, the Republicans began their drive in the Senate in January, amidst the furor over Flynn's nomination, by demanding a complete congressional investigation of Lend-Lease. Butler criticized it for being based on "the dole" and likened the program to a worldwide W.P.A. He contended that it would eventually wreck the American treasury and contribute to the spread of communism at home and abroad.[35]

Butler's wide-ranging charges were picked up by other Republicans in Congress and spread to specific areas of interest within the Lend-Lease program. In spite of a $500 million loan to China authorized by Congress the preceding year, Republicans accused the administration of slighting China in the Lend-Lease appropriation and demanded an increase in supplies to Chiang Kai-shek under the proposal. With equal fervor they maintained that China should be raised from a subservient status and placed on an equal protocol basis with the Soviet Union in terms of the original bill. Principle united with expediency in this case as Republicans with a personal or professional interest in the Chinese, like representatives John M. Vorys of Ohio and The Reverend Walter H. Judd of Minnesota, combined with others of their party more directly desirous of harassing the administration or the Soviet allies. Here lay seeds of the Republican romance with China and Chiang Kai-shek that were to grow into the political marriage of the later forties and fifties.[36]

Another channel into which isolationist Republican objections to the administration could flow in 1943 was an amendment to the Lend-Lease extension bill proposed by Vorys in the House. The amendment sought to protect Congress's powers to make any settlement or "final determination of benefits" under the program. It arose from a general apprehension among congressional Republican isolationists that Roosevelt might use the Lend-Lease authorization to involve the nation in postwar commitments, to effect some sort of internationalist *fait accompli* in line with his own as yet unannounced plans for postwar world order. More specifically, Republicans like Vorys feared that the president might employ his powers under Lend-Lease to change tariffs or make agreements regarding commercial aviation and military bases. Thus Vandenberg, while acclaiming Lend-Lease as the "king-link" in the victory chain, insisted with equal, if not surpassing, force that it was an instrument for wartime use only. He made it quite clear (and helped see to it that the Senate Foreign Relations Committee did likewise) that the Lend-Lease master agreements were not to be considered binding on the Senate in any future determination of the peace.[37]

Congressional isolationists also attacked alleged concealment and misuse by Great Britain and the Soviet Union of American aid under the program. Republican Representative Hamilton Fish charged, for example, that the British were selling Lend-Lease material to their own people, depositing the proceeds in the royal exchequer, "and not returning one cent to us for the goods."[38] Such charges immediately prompted the administration's Lend-Lease chief, Edward R. Stettinius, Jr., to supply the Democratic floor leaders of the bill, Tom Connally in the Senate and Sol Bloom in the House, with evidence that "large quantities of supplies . . . were being used effectively in combat."[39] In the end, the Vorys amendment was defeated and the Lend-Lease extension bill proceeded to pass both houses of Congress with ease; many Republican opponents of the original measure, including Vandenberg, Vorys, Nye, and Taft, voted for it.[40]

The Republican isolationists' concern over advance postwar commitments and infringements on the powers of Congress surfaced also in debates over the Trade Agreements Act of 1934 which, like Lend-Lease, came up for renewal in 1943. As with Lend-Lease in 1941, most Republicans had voted against the trade agreements program when it had appeared before Congress in 1940.[41] In 1943, however, wartime political expedience again dictated that Republicans not oppose such a measure on its face. Arguments for it in the House centered around the need to extend the act as evidence of a willingness on the part of the United States to pursue policies geared toward international cooperation in the postwar era. Thus, a majority report of the House Ways and Means Committee had called, in the interests of wartime unity and future peace, for a large bipartisan vote to demonstrate an absence of partisanship on the question of postwar international cooperation. A minority report filed by nine Republicans on the committee, however, had rejected the majority's argument.[42]

G.O.P. critics of the bill objected much less to its substance, which aimed at lower reciprocal tariffs, than to its method of operation. In the Senate especially, attention was devoted to the question of congressional participation in the making of future trade agreements. Many in that body, jealous of its traditional powers in foreign affairs, protested that the administration was keeping Congress from participating in future trade agreements as a first step toward barring congressional participation in future peace negotiations. Taft charged that the State Department had demonstrated "an intention by executive agreement, without consulting Congress, of doing everything it can to write the provisions of the peace as it thinks they should be formulated."[43] The attitude of the administration, Senator Brooks of Illinois warned, was "reminiscent of the fact that President Wilson failed to take Congress in as a partner in his determination of the future course of the world at the conclusion of the last world war."[44] McNary proposed to include Congress in the trade treaty negotiations by giving it a vote on arrangements which it considered injurious to the national interest.[45] Ultimately, a majority of Republicans in both houses voted to extend the Trade Agreements Act as it stood, but they did so only after an amendment sponsored by Senator Danaher had shortened the period for renewal from three years to two. In the House, Republicans favored extension almost three to one—145 to 52 votes; in the Senate, the vote was much closer—18 to 15.[46]

The decisive issue for those voting in the majority appeared to be the argument that the trade agreements program should not be disturbed during wartime in order to keep unity at a maximum between the United

States and its allies.[47] "Psychologically," observed Austin, a consistent supporter of the program, it was "a positive benefit," even though the wartime situation had both confused and prevented chances to test its "real effect."[48] Taft agreed with him, remarking that since the whole issue was "academic" during the war anyway, opponents of it did not like to speak out.[49] Vandenberg, who professed on the one hand to have "a deep conviction that this Act is unconstitutional because it permits the President to make treaties without Senate ratification," had, on the other, "an equally deep feeling that *none* of our relationships with our Allies should be disturbed during the progress of this war."[50] He favored renewal of the trade agreements, but he also supported an amendment declaring them subject to termination six months after the war. "America must maintain," Vandenberg contended, the present "fraternity of battle—without any interruptions by pre-victory arguments or premature peace quarrels between us" until the war was "unconditionally" won.[51]

In general, the fear of hidden postwar commitments was distinctive among isolationist congressional Republicans like Vandenberg. Prewar beliefs and positions predisposed them to suspect any moves by the administration or former interventionists that might tend to commit the United States to a role of far-reaching participation in postwar foreign affairs. A principal defense against this possibility was to elaborate traditional constitutional arguments on the need for prior congressional, and especially Senate, approval of wartime arrangements with postwar implications. In late 1942, for example, Vandenberg had taken a stand against a joint resolution appropriating money to Panama in gratitude for Panama's making 100 military sites available to the United States without cost. Once again the objection was not to the substance of the resolution but to its form. To Vandenberg it smacked of the idea, increasingly being suggested to avoid the post-World War I experience, of making future commitments by executive agreement instead of by treaty. Such agreements might then be approved by a joint resolution, a procedure requiring a majority vote in both houses of Congress; the traditional treaty process necessitated a two-thirds vote of approval in the Senate alone. Fearing a United States commitment by executive agreement to some unlimited internationalist scheme for world order, Vandenberg opposed tampering with the traditions of Congress in foreign affairs and was able to draw to his side many like-minded legislators, not all of them Republicans or former isolationists.[52]

Republican reaction to the Panama resolution, extension of trade agreements, and renewal of Lend-Lease all indicated that a general strategy of caution and studied delay on the question of a future peace had evolved within the isolationist faction of the party in Congress. Publicly, this strategy was justified on the grounds that there were definite limits abroad to the distance that immediate postwar planning could go. As Vandenberg put it, the voice of the United States would "not be the *only* voice" at any future peace conference:

> Mr. Josef Stalin will be a very powerful figure in that epical council. He has never even remotely indicated what his postwar objectives may be—indeed, he may not even allow our observers to visit his battlefront. . . . Again we do not yet know in any sort of *reality* what Mr. Winston Churchill has in mind respecting the British Empire when the time comes to write the formula of peace. He too will be a potent figure. Thus far he has spoken only in the vaguest generalities.
>
> Under such circumstances, it is a practical impossibility for America to lay out a postwar world or to write any sort of definitive specifications for our postwar context.[53]

More purely political considerations, however, also underlay isolationist Republican strategy on the postwar issue. The election results of 1942 had alleviated the short-term problem of the image of non-interventionist Republicans in Congress—the question of their responsibility for the outbreak of war at Pearl Harbor. But the elections had done nothing at all for their party's long-standing historical problem—its image of having sabotaged Woodrow Wilson's peace proposals after World War I and of having been responsible in a broader sense for the outbreak of World War II. As Vandenberg himself noted in private, "The United States' refusal to join in the League of Nations after World War I was strongly in the minds of Congressional leaders, and in the minds of the leaders of the other Allied nations, too. Nobody wanted another fiasco in the field of international collaboration for peace."[54] The fear that this image might rise up to haunt them in future elections plagued many Republicans in Congress, reinforcing their determination to move as slowly and carefully as possible on the subject of postwar planning.

The strategy of the congressional Republican isolationists, however, was not allowed to run its course. It soon faced a serious challenge not only from Democrats but also from other Republicans both within and outside of the party's congressional wing, a challenge which raised anew the fearful specter of the G.O.P.'s long-term historical image. Public opinion polls in late 1942 and early 1943 showed that American attitudes on the subject of a future peace were still largely unformed regarding specifics but definitely in favor of planning for that peace to begin immediately.[55] To some Republicans in the Senate, delay no longer seemed appropriate strategy to follow on the issue, given the public's attitude toward planning as well as their own internationalist beliefs. Many of these internationalists, encouraged by the November election victories of incumbent senators White, Ball, and Styles Bridges of New Hampshire, had gathered at a dinner given by Ball in late January to court new Republican senators and to honor Governor Stassen of Minnesota, who had been distinguishing himself in the presidential wing of the party by vigorously championing a program of immediate postwar planning. At that dinner they had coaxed from McNary a statement that he was in favor of such planning, but they wanted more. True to Austin's prediction at the time of McNary's failure to reappoint him as assistant leader, the internationalists soon moved to "start something."[56]

In March 1943, fellow members of the Senate's Truman Committee—Republicans Ball and Burton and Democrats Carl A. Hatch of New Mexico and Lister Hill of Alabama—joined together in a bipartisan attempt to bring the question of an international organization for peace directly before Congress. They introduced a resolution in the Senate calling upon the United States to request that the allied nations form a permanent international organization immediately. This organization was to coordinate administration of the war's military, political, and economic aspects, establish means for peaceful settlements of disputes between nations, "provide for the assembly and maintenance of a United Nations military force," and "suppress by immediate use of such force any future attempt at military aggression by any nation."[57]

The impetus for this resolution derived in part from the Truman Committee's having uncovered "mistakes of omission and commission in the domestic war effort." According to Ball, it was obvious that "lack of adequate planning" was at the root of those mistakes, planning that was objected to by the isolationists who were apparently "determined" that the nation should face "its vast post-war problems with as little planning and preparation as we had to meet the treacherous attack of December 7."[58] Other sentiments, equally prompted by opposition to isolationism, also lay behind this so-called $B_2 H_2$ resolution. Republican Senator Ralph O. Brewster of Maine in praising it expressed some of them: "Let us not again fumble the ball as we did after the last war in unfortunate divisions that arose between the two coordinate treaty making authorities—the President and the Senate. Let us sit down and talk it over in the great forum of public opinion and be ready for a continuance of the current collaboration of the nations in the post war world."[59]

Isolationist Republicans were taken aback by the $B_2 H_2$ resolution. It posed an obvious threat to their preferred strategy of caution and delay on the postwar issue. At first they tried to dismiss the resolution, as well as the threat, by laying ultimate responsibility for both upon internationalist leaders in the presidential wing of the party. They observed, correctly, that Ball, one of the sponsors, was a protégé of Harold Stassen, who had appointed him to a vacant Senate seat in 1940, and that having won election in his own right in 1942, Ball had interpreted the victory as proof of support for the commitment to international organization which he and Stassen both shared.[60] The isolationists also suspected that Wendell Willkie's hand might be behind the resolution since he had been making statements along the same lines. Vandenberg endorsed this suspicion of Willkie's influence and warned the internationalists that the $B_2 H_2$ resolution "could easily re-divide America at home," could divide the Allies abroad, "could precipitate a Senate debate which would be a total liability to unity," and "could threaten the war effort," thus jeopardizing victory itself.[61]

Eventually required to respond to the resolution directly, Republican isolationists opposed it on the grounds that it definitely would tend to promote disunity among the Allies and would give the president too much power to form the postwar organization. In a speech on May 7 before a Republican group in Ohio, moreover, Taft maintained that the Republican party was in favor of postwar planning in the international field. "We cannot escape the tremendous responsibility of rebuilding the world," he declared. "Whatever guaranties we assume or do not assume, we certainly should aid in establishing a world in which war is outlawed as far as humanly possible."[62] Taft, however, saw the point in the resolution regarding an international police force against aggression as a threat to American security and contended that the United States would never approve any permanent international police force, under the control of some international body, which might be greater than its own military force.[63] Senator Hiram Johnson, one of the Republican irreconcilables after World War I, thought the idea of an international police force simply "preposterous and absurd."[64]

Vandenberg also directed objections to the $B_2 H_2$ resolution. He argued that it sought "to *particularize* prematurely" about peace objectives on which there were as yet no specific agreements among the major Allies. Thus the resolution jeopardized "*war* unity (both at home and abroad)" and undermined "the indispensable Number One objective of all, namely, the quickest, cheapest possible conclusive military victory."[65] Vandenberg contended that the war objectives of the other Allies greatly complicated any planning for the future by the United States:

> In view of Russia's announced postwar territorial aspirations, a present statement of our own "war objectives" (which, under the Atlantic

Charter would certainly have to include the restoration of a free Poland, Latvia, Lithuania, Estonia, etc.) could easily split us apart *before*
we have won the war. In view of China's announced intention to produce a totally "free India" (while Churchill has announced that he
was not elected to "preside over the disintegration of the British Empire") our own "war objective" in respect to India *now* might split
the Far East wide open. Our "war objective" in respect to the Free
French may not be calculated to square things with Britain's contemplated pattern in North Africa. These exhibits could be multiplied.[66]

Such Allied objectives were already reducing the Atlantic Charter to
"mincemeat,"[67] according to Vandenberg, so much so that Americans
might discover too late that they "were not sufficiently specific when
the President laid out our primary partnership with our Allies" in that
document.[68] No postwar objectives are "worth the paper they are written on," he argued, until after victory was complete.[69]

Vandenberg's arguments resounded in Congress and in the administration. Leading Democrats also believed that the $B_2 H_2$ resolution might
be premature. Roosevelt was cool to the proposal while Hull was greatly
distressed by it. Hull feared that intensified isolationist attacks on Great
Britain and the Soviet Union might grow out of charges hurled in debate
on the resolution and harm relations with those Allies.[70] His fear was
well-founded. Suspicion of Allied war aims among congressmen did increase. Democratic Senator Albert B. Chandler of Kentucky argued in
May 1943 that with the campaign in North Africa winding down and
Britain and the Soviet Union no longer in danger of annihilation, the
United States should shift its emphasis to an all-out attack upon Japan
in the Pacific. Chandler thus revived a demand first put forth by many
isolationist Republicans in 1942. If victory in the European theater of
the war came first, he contended, the United States would lose what lev-
erage it might have there with the Soviet Union and Great Britain in
terms of the peace. Moreover, should the United States continue to center its main attention upon the European instead of the Asian front, the
British, according to Chandler, would gain ground in the Far East.[71]

True to Hull's sense of foreboding, Republican isolationists in the
Senate roundly applauded Chandler's speech. Henrik Shipstead of Minnesota echoed the anti-British element in Chandler's remarks and supported the call for a greater military effort in the Far East against Japan.
Shipstead also charged that the British were not putting forth a very active effort in the fighting there.[72] Vandenberg followed suit.[73] He even
wrote Chandler to say that the speech had admirably reflected his own
thinking on the matter. There was "a tremendous bulk of American pub-

lic opinion," Vandenberg remarked, "which while hating Hitler and enlisting for his total defeat, looks upon Japan as an equally prime enemy, particularly as respect our own American hazards."[74]

In addition to their concern over wartime relations among the Allies, both Hull and Roosevelt feared the beginning of an isolationist reaction comparable to the one of 1918-1920 which had ruined Woodrow Wilson and the hopes for his League of Nations. The election results of 1942 and subsequent political developments had done much to recall memories of Wilson's fate at the hands of a hostile wartime Congress. Concerned to avoid that fate as well as to achieve their own postwar objectives, the president and his secretary of state had adopted a strategy of caution and delay on the issue of international organization analagous to that of the Republicans. They had refrained from indicating specifically what their ideas regarding future world order might be and had attempted to restrain their associates, both at home and abroad, from doing so as well. In terms of anticipating and dealing with a congressional revolt against this strategy, however, Secretary Hull's and President Roosevelt's approaches differed.

Cooperation and extreme caution were the calling cards of Hull in his relations with Congress. Such an approach had helped to win considerable respect and esteem for him there, even among Republicans. As early as May 1942, Hull had included a Republican legislator, although admittedly one favorably inclined toward the administration's views on foreign policy (Senator Austin), on the State Department Advisory Committee which he had established to study problems of postwar foreign policy.[75] In part to defuse Republican demands for special executive-legislative committees to oversee the war and foreign policy and in part to remove these subjects if possible from the arena of partisan politics, Hull had moved in company with other administration leaders outside the White House to increase significantly the participation of congressional Republican leaders in the councils of the administration.

Following the elections of 1942, Hull, in addition to increasing his department's consultation with the standing committees of Congress, broadened congressional participation in his postwar Advisory Committee, adding Republican Senator White and Representative Eaton (both members of the G.O.P.'s internationalist faction) to the group.[76] After Republican resolutions calling for liaison committees had been introduced in the Senate, Tom Connally, chairman of the Foreign Relations Committee, had included Vandenberg in a special three-man subcommittee which he had established to consider such proposals. When the B_2H_2 resolution appeared, Connally expanded the membership of this select group to eight and included senators White and La Follette. The enlarged subcommittee was given charge of all postwar resolutions before the Senate; it was also instructed to recommend from among them a single resolution for the Senate's consideration.[77] In the War Department, General George C. Marshall had called a group of congressional leaders from both parties together to explain to them in advance the agreement between General Dwight D. Eisenhower, Allied commander of the campaign in North Africa, and Admiral Jean François Darlan, commander of the opposing Vichy French forces in that area, for a cease-fire following the landing of Allied troops.[78] Similarly, members of both parties in Congress had been consulted on the requirements for and development of the top-secret Manhattan Project, designed to produce an atomic bomb.[79]

Isolationist as well as internationalist Republicans derived political benefits from this cooperation. Given the administration's desire to confine the B_2H_2 resolution in committee, they were able to avoid the dangers of opposing the resolution's objectives too directly and of thus raising the image of post-World War I isolationism. They could even base their opposition to the proposal on the attitude of the State Department. Vandenberg, for example, replied to those anxious for the resolution's passage that the "most *responsible* opinions in our government (this does not exclude our own State Department) believe that we might easily *disunite* the *war* effort by prematurely seeking to *unite* the *peace* effort." Though "the demand for something like 'the Ball Resolution'" might be "perfectly logical upon its face," he wrote one of his constituents, the "State Department itself is advising extreme caution lest we create more problems than we solve."[80] Vandenberg was also able to turn his presence at the War Department briefing on North Africa to significant advantage. Crediting Allied collaboration with Darlan with saving American lives, he scored points both within the congressional wing of his party and elsewhere against Wendell Willkie, who had severely criticized the deal. As a result, Vandenberg strengthened his argument for increased consultation between the administration and Congress.[81]

The administration itself reaped sizable rewards from cooperation with the Republicans. It received the appropriations it wanted for the Manhattan Project without having to identify them publicly and violate the secrecy which the undertaking required. Lend-Lease was extended by an overwhelmingly favorable vote and the program's administrator, Edward Stettinius, Jr., himself a former Republican, drew special praise from congressional members of the G.O.P. for his obliging consideration of them in legislative hearings on the bill.[82] Secretary of War Stimson and General Marshall received similar praise as well as "the most complete respect" for their "judgment, thoroughness and soundness."[83] When the controversy over the deal with Darlan broke out in public, with Willkie emerging as critic and Vandenberg as supporter of the administration's

policy, Hull was able to turn reporters' questions aside by suggesting
that they await the outcome of the controversy between Willkie and
Vandenberg for their replies.[84] Finally, in what was a triumph for him
personally as well as for his cooperative approach, Hull saw his reciprocal trade program renewed in Congress by larger majorities than ever
before. As one commentator astutely observed, that action, accomplished
while a host of administration domestic policies were under attack, served
to point out a now "prevailing rule" among Republicans in Congress:
"Cordell Hull is one Administration official who is definitely tagged as
'no New Dealer' and beside the after-war foreign trade policies Vice-
President Henry A. Wallace and others are hatching, the old-fashioned
free trade Mr. Hull espouses has become arch-conservatism."[85]

In contrast to his secretary of state, President Roosevelt in 1943 took
a somewhat less cautious and cooperative tack with congressional Republicans on matters of foreign policy. Despite the view prevailing in
some Democratic circles that the administration ought to come out
strongly in favor of a postwar international organization, that its failure to do so had aided the Republicans in 1942, and that the first
task of Democrats looking to 1944 was to convince the country that the
Republicans were really repeating what they had done in 1919 and 1920,
Roosevelt was circumspect in his own views about what the future peace
might entail.[86] He was concerned to avoid the image of intransigent
idealism associated with Woodrow Wilson in 1919 and 1920 as well as
Wilson's fate at the hands of an equally intransigent Senate. The significance of Republican gains in the 1942 elections had not been lost on
him in this last regard.

On the one hand, therefore, Roosevelt had moved to counter Republican and other demands for exclusive concentration on the conduct of
the war (as well as to reassure the world and particularly the Russians
of Anglo-American dedication to total victory, despite the failure to
launch a second front in Europe in 1942) by issuing pronouncements
such as the one at Casablanca in January 1943 pledging a fight for the
"unconditional surrender" of the enemy. On the other, he had helped
prompt such congressional initiatives as the B_2H_2 resolution in the first
place by failing to indicate a preference for any specific postwar peace
plan. Certain questions, however, like those relating to the disposition
of war-torn Europe, were unavoidable. In dealing with them, the president displayed a predilection for making arrangements by executive
agreement rather than by treaty, a procedure guaranteed not to set very
well with a resurgent Congress (particularly the Senate) already conditioned by its Republican leaders to be apprehensive about the loss of
its traditional powers.

The first such question to which the president applied this penchant for doing things by executive agreement involved a conference of the wartime United Nations to be held in May 1943 at Hot Springs, Virginia, to work out the problem of supplying food to Europe following its liberation. The White House announced that no congressmen or reporters were to be permitted to attend the conference, despite warnings by Hull of likely public and partisan repercussions arising from this exclusion.[87] Indeed, Republicans as well as the press strongly criticized the Hot Springs gathering for its atmosphere of secrecy. Vandenberg and Representative Fred Bradley of Michigan introduced resolutions in Congress demanding that its members as well as the press be allowed to attend the food conference. In the House, Clifford R. Hope of Kansas sponsored another resolution to provide that members of its Agriculture Committee be made ex-officio delegates.[88] Some voiced the suspicion that Roosevelt and his New Dealers would be scheming behind closed doors at the conference to feed the world out of the collective pocket of the United States or to establish a currency standard which would leave Great Britain in a position of financial supremacy.[89] Others were upset that the administration, by moving in the direction of a general conference, was ignoring G.O.P. suggestions for providing food to countries invaded by the Germans (for example, by recalling Herbert Hoover to distribute it as he had in World War I).[90]

The State Department ultimately bailed the administration out of this controversy by submitting the plans for the conference to appropriate committees in Congress and by dispatching Assistant Secretary of State Dean Acheson to Hot Springs to handle difficulties on the scene with the press.[91] But the flurry over the food conference was just a warm-up for what was yet to come. It was, in fact, minor compared to the outburst occasioned in June when Roosevelt informed Republican and Democratic congressional leaders that he intended to seek United States participation in a proposed United Nations Relief and Rehabilitation Administration (UNRRA) by executive agreement rather than by treaty. "Without warning," according to Acheson, "a hurricane struck" when a draft of the UNRRA agreement appeared on June 11, 1943. The center of this hurricane "was filled with a large mass of cumulonimbus cloud, often called Arthur Vandenberg, producing heavy word fall."[92]

Writing to Secretary Hull and demanding to know whether the administration planned to submit the draft agreement to the Senate for ratification, Vandenberg declared the agreement of "tremendous significance" since it might "set the pattern for dealing with other problems of the peace to come."[93] The State Department scrupled over how to answer him. His capacity for "instant indignation," as Acheson put it, was becoming well known but, as the department's legal adviser, Green H. Hackworth, noted in an internal memorandum on June 26, "In view of Senator Vandenberg's attitude the matter of Senatorial approval may become important."[94] On July 7, Hull replied to Vandenberg that senatorial ratification had not been contemplated and referred him to the earlier meeting of the president with the leaders of both parties in Congress as the basis for that determination. "It has been decided," Hull wrote, "after consultation with the majority and minority leaders of both houses of Congress, that the United States' participation in the establishment of this United Nations administration should be through an executive agreement."[95]

Not at all satisfied with Hull's response, Vandenberg soon set out to create just the kind of uproar in the Senate that the State Department feared most. Perceiving a sinister significance in the president's failure to include members of the Senate or House committees on foreign affairs in his conference with congressional leaders on UNRRA, Vandenberg proclaimed the procedure "clearly a preview of the method by which the President and the State Department intend to by-pass Congress in general, and the Senate in particular, in settling every possible international war and post-war issue by the use of mere 'Executive Agreements.' " The move appeared to him to confirm earlier Republican forebodings in connection with Lend-Lease, mutual tariff reductions, the Panama treaty, and the United Nations food conference. These "far-reaching 'Agreements,' " for example, disclosed to Vandenberg yet "another reason why the Administration sought to keep the recent 'Food Conference' as secret as possible."[96] For him the question was "one of basic constitutional authority—to say nothing of the *policy* involved in thus making peace by executive fiat."[97]

Vandenberg immediately renewed his call for the establishment of a special war cabinet, claiming that the public had lost confidence in the president and his advisers.[98] In addition, he sent formal inquiries to both Republican congressional leaders, Senator McNary and Representative Martin, to find out "exactly *how far* 'the Minority House and Senate leaders' " had gone "in giving their approval (if they did) to this proposition because undoubtedly this will be urged by the State Department in support of their theory that these 'Agreements' are none of Congress' business." Apologizing for putting his question in the form of a letter, Vandenberg explained to McNary and Martin that he needed a reply from each of them which he could "quote by way of rebuttal to the Secretary of State's assertion that you gave this procedure the 'green light.' "[99]

Vandenberg also informed the Republican leaders that he had initiated a formal investigation of the matter by the Senate Foreign Relations Committee to determine whether the UNRRA agreement could be considered a treaty, thus requiring Senate ratification. "It seems to me," he opined, "that this 'Draft Agreement' involves the broadest possible commitments for the future—ultimately touching almost every phase of post-war reconstruction—and leaves us (as usual) to pay most of the bills *without* any adequate control over what the bills ought to be."[100] He added later to McNary that "as it was originally drawn, this 'draft agreement' pledged our total resources to whatever illimitable scheme for relief and rehabilitation all round the world which our New Deal crystal gazers might desire to pursue."[101] In response, both McNary and Martin telegraphed Vandenberg that neither of them in the conference with Roosevelt had agreed to any bypassing of Congress. "So sure as the sun shines over the mountains," claimed McNary, "our distinguished President never discussed with me the terms or conditions contained in any of the so called 'United Nations Relief and Rehabilitation Draft Agreements.'"[102]

Vandenberg was not the only member of the Foreign Relations Committee to be upset by the bypassing of the Senate being contemplated in the UNRRA agreement. Senator Connally, chairman of the committee, was also up in arms about the matter. After a five-man subcommittee which he had appointed to consider Vandenberg's complaint unanimously endorsed it, Connally summoned Hull and Acheson before the full committee to account for the administration's position. Although the State Department representatives appeared "very uncomfortable about the whole matter" and Hull seemed to give the impression that he was not in favor of attempting to bypass the Senate, a heated exchange between Connally and Hull quickly ensued over a proper formula for the UNRRA agreement.[103] After pressing the administration's legal and constitutional arguments for an executive agreement and observing that Congress would still have control over all appropriations for UNRRA, Hull agreed to discuss specific objections to the draft with senators from the committee. Connally suggested that the State Department could at least revise the agreement to provide for its passage through both houses of Congress by joint resolution.[104]

Sufficiently chastened by his encounter with the committee, eager to insure congressional approval of a postwar international organization, and anxious to avoid Woodrow Wilson's fate, Hull took Connally's suggestion to heart. Following a second conference of committee members with Acheson, Vandenberg himself acclaimed "a rather earnest desire on the part of the State Department not only to rewrite the draft agreement in some particulars, but also to concede the necessity for some sort of Congressional approval." He tempered his praise, however, by warning that it remained to be seen "whether this actually develops or whether they are just temporarily being 'good boys' under the pressure of the almost universal criticism which attaches to any plan to by-pass Congress in an obligation of this magnitude."[105] To insure that the department's resolve in the matter would not flag, Vandenberg and Democratic Senator Theodore Francis Green of Rhode Island continued to meet with Acheson in August, after Congress had recessed, to complete the details of a new procedure for UNRRA.[106]

In the end, an agreement was worked out among Acheson, Green, and Vandenberg that proved acceptable to the full Foreign Relations Committee. It provided for approval of the UNRRA draft agreement by a majority vote in both houses instead of a two-thirds vote in the Senate. Vandenberg publicly announced in favor of the revised proposal and urged a ban on political bickering about it.[107] Furthermore, he contended, the procedure of having executive agreements such as the one governing UNRRA come under the purview of Congress by joint resolution involved "a new and direct system of consultation" between the State Department and the Senate Foreign Relations Committee "which should be able to avoid many of the stalemates of which we are historically aware." The new procedure, if successful, would "clearly simplify the incidental and interim decisions which must be made in connection with the liquidation of the war," thus leaving longer-term commitments, like peace treaties, to the consideration of the Senate.[108]

Within the confines of the Republican party Vandenberg claimed a victory, remarking of the new UNRRA procedure that it was "the first direct and specific defeat of the president's original announced purpose to do this whole job by 'Executive Order.' "[109] The State Department had "surrendered at practically every turn in the road," he claimed, and although it remained to be seen whether President Roosevelt would "thus give up the totalitarian prerogatives which he clearly intended to exercise," Vandenberg was convinced that "a great and important and highly significant battle had been won."[110] To supporters who were critical of his role in giving up the argument for a treaty vote on UNRRA, he emphatically maintained that the agreement was "now practically nothing but an *authorization for appropriations*—with [a] specific statement in the text of the Agreement that we are bound to NOTHING unless and until Congress makes the subsequent SPECIFIC APPROPRIATIONS."

Vandenberg further asserted that the president was likely "to kick . . . over [the new agreement] at the last minute as being an insufferable invasion of HIS executive prerogatives." If Roosevelt did that, the politically astute Republican calculated, then his opponents could take issue with him on impregnable ground, for the president would appear to be rejecting a constitutional process and spurning an honest effort to solve some of the war's problems. On the other hand, if Roosevelt did finally sanction what Vandenberg labeled "the State Department's wholesale surrender in this whole episode," then he thought that Republicans would still be in a "far stronger position." They would simply claim a victory instead of dropping back "to a Treaty-argument" which he considered "very weak under the circumstances *now* surrounding the Draft Agreement for the Relief and Rehabilitation Agreement."[111]

Behind calculations of congressional and of party victory in the UNRRA affair lay another, more personal calculation for Vandenberg. "If I can force a highly reluctant Administration," he remarked during the controversy, "to submit the 'United Nations Relief and Rehabilitation Agreement' to Congress for the approval of an enabling Act— as I have already forced it to substantially re-write the text—I shall consider it a major one-man victory."[112] Vandenberg's was not a one-man victory, however. Senator Connally, for one, had forced the administration to concede as much as Vandenberg had. Moreover, it had not conceded that much. The State Department's revision of the UNRRA draft was more a matter of form than of substance, and even there it had carried the main argument against Vandenberg—that the agreement did not have to be submitted to the Senate as a treaty.

What was significant, and a kind of victory for Vandenberg in the UNRRA controversy, was the administration's decision to cooperate with him, an isolationist, as well as with internationalist Republicans in Congress like senators Austin and White. President Roosevelt had long distrusted Vandenberg, perhaps correctly suspecting that behind his demands for increased cooperation lurked latent presidential aspirations of the kind that had surfaced in 1940. In the State Department, however, Hull and Acheson became convinced during the UNRRA affair that they could and should work with Vandenberg, whatever his motives, for the benefit of the administration and its foreign policies in Congress. By flattering his considerable personal and political ego through such consultations as those involving UNRRA, they discovered, they could often get by with comparatively minor changes which Vandenberg would then defend to his colleagues as major ones wrung from the administration by his own hands. The State Department sought to co-opt Vandenberg, in other words, into championing its policies in Congress and in the Republican party and, perhaps with his help, to insulate sensitive issues of foreign policy from the heat of interparty competition. (In 1944, on a much larger scale, they attempted to do so again with the Republican presidential nominee.)

But it was a serious question in this case of who was co-opting whom. Vandenberg's admittedly large ego took pride in his newfound connection with the State Department, but his rather shrewd brain realized that he could use this connection to further his leadership among Republicans in Congress and in the party at large on foreign policy. Prolix, vain, and ingratiating though he was, Arthur Vandenberg was also a skillful and ambitious political operator, rivalling in a smaller arena the contemporary master of that art, Franklin Roosevelt himself. His close association with the State Department during the summer of 1943 signified an awareness in administration circles of Vandenberg's growing prominence among congressional Republicans in matters of foreign policy; moreover, the association itself accelerated that growth. On both sides, the connection was more a romance of political convenience, therefore, than a marriage of positions or views on foreign policy.[113]

The *appearance* of victory was all Vandenberg really wanted or needed in the UNRRA controversy, and he got it. The event marked a culminating point in his rise to prominence among Republicans in Congress as a spokesman on foreign policy in 1943. The reason for this rise, apart from his successful manipulation of the UNRRA controversy, was the political direction he provided for his colleagues, particularly the isolationists, on the question of postwar international organization. More so than Senator Taft (who was too principled to do so, according to some, too headstrong and inconsistent, according to others), Vandenberg offered fellow isolationist Republicans an appealing way out of their party's long-term problem in this area, a way that promised definite political advantages. Taft, on the other hand, was becoming more involved in leading the attack on New Deal domestic policies in 1943 and in his own campaign for reelection to the Senate in 1944.[114]

The principal object of isolationist concern in 1943, of course, was the B_2H_2 resolution before the Senate. Vandenberg's original objection to the resolution, it will be recalled, was that it sought to *"particularize* prematurely" on the question of international organization. Nevertheless, Vandenberg believed, one could "successfully generalize" on that question "to accomplish every good purpose and to avoid the pitfalls." With a keen sense of the direction in which public opinion was moving in 1943, he, like his internationalist colleagues, wanted to associate himself and the party with the issue of international organization in a favorable way, but a way less advanced than the one that the internationalists were advocating in the B_2H_2 resolution. The "average American," Vandenberg claimed, "even though he opposed the old League of Nations and even though he was a so-called 'isolationist' in pre-war days," was "willing to move in the direction of far greater international responsibilities than ever before." At the same time,

this 'average American'—(at least west of the Allegheny Mountains)—wants . . . to be very sure that American spokesmanship at the peace table is at least as loyal to America's own primary interests as Mr. Stalin is certain to be in respect to Russia and Mr. Churchill . . . to the British Empire. This average American is scared by the Vice President's "international milk route" and by kindred Pollyanna crystal gazing. He does not believe that America is big enough or rich enough to feed and clothe and finance and generally bless all the rest of the world forever. He is neither an isolationist nor an internationalist. He is a middle-of-the-roader who wants to win this war as swiftly and as cheaply as possible; who then wants a realistic peace which puts an end to military aggression; who wants justice rather than force to rule the postwar world; who is willing to take his full share of responsibility in all of these directions; but who is perfectly sure that no one is going to look out for us at the peace table or thereafter unless we look out for ourselves and who wants "enlightened selfishness" mixed with "generous idealism" when our course is chartered.[115]

At the very first meeting, therefore, of the subcommittee set up by Senator Connally to consider the B_2H_2 and other postwar resolutions in March, Vandenberg had objected to a suggestion by Senator White that the B_2H_2 proposal be tabled without further discussion. He feared that the administration would saddle congressional Republicans with responsibility for once again blocking plans for future world order, as they had in 1919 and 1920. Vandenberg had sought instead the cooperation of Democratic Senator Walter F. George of Georgia in sponsoring a bipartisan alternative to the B_2H_2 resolution.[116] Much milder than the latter, the proposed Vandenberg resolution called for prosecution of the war to total victory, endorsed the "aspirations" of the United Nations to create a world free from military aggression in which "justice rather than force" would prevail and self-governing peoples could work in close cooperation with one another, and finally, pledged "by due Constitutional process, to consider such co-operations to the full extent of American post-war responsibilities."[117] Aside from a copy being sent to Hull, from whom the suggested resolution received a "rather uncommittal reply," according to Vandenberg, nothing more came of the proposal at that time.[118]

In June 1943, at about the same time the UNRRA controversy was developing in the Senate, Democratic Representative J. William Fulbright of Arkansas introduced a resolution in the House which called upon Congress to express itself in favor of "appropriate international machinery" for the postwar period, "with adequate power to establish and to maintain a just and lasting peace among nations of the world."[119] This resolution, like Vandenberg's, was also milder than the B_2H_2 proposal. It did not include Fulbright's originally announced preference for a statement favoring an international police force. As a result, the resolution obtained considerable support in the House.[120]

Writing the president to request that he back the measure, Fulbright pointed out that most of the public support for it so far had come from Republicans. He complained that while many Democrats, including Roosevelt himself, had remained silent on the postwar issue out of belief in the political necessity of caution and delay, many Republicans were taking the lead in foreign policy by endorsing his resolution. Fulbright urged the president not to underestimate the importance of such Republican moves to nullify foreign policy as an issue in the next campaign and pleaded with him to regain the initiative by advocating some such postwar resolution himself.[121]

In response to Fulbright's earnest plea, Roosevelt wrote Hull to indicate a preference for the Fulbright resolution and to ask his congressionally minded secretary's opinion of the merits of supporting it in both the House and the Senate. Hull replied characteristically, advocating further caution and delay on the subject and warning of the Senate's jealousy of its prerogatives in foreign policy, a jealousy which a House resolution on postwar commitments might only inflame. Hull was just beginning to bear the brunt of that jealousy as a result of Roosevelt's decision to launch UNRRA by executive agreement. Furthermore, he informed Roosevelt that both Republican and Democratic leaders of the House had pleaded for more time to cut down initial opposition and rally potential support for the Fulbright resolution.[122]

There the matter rested, during the summer of 1943, with the Democratic leaders—but not with the Republicans. In the Senate, following introduction of the Fulbright resolution in the House and just prior to the summer recess, Vandenberg moved to seize the initiative as Fulbright had warned the Republicans would do. On July 2, he teamed up with Senator White to introduce "the first all-Republican 'foreign policy' Resolution" on the postwar issue. Similar to the draft resolution that Vandenberg had earlier proposed to sponsor with Senator George, the Vandenberg-White resolution pledged cooperation among "sovereign nations" to prevent future aggression, stipulated that all American peace-keeping activities in the future should follow "due Constitutional process," and promised "faithful recognition of American interests."[123]

In pursuit of "common ground" and perhaps to mend some fences broken earlier in the year during their feud over the assistant leadership, Vandenberg had first asked Senator Austin in the internationalist camp to cosponsor his resolution. Their efforts to agree on a text, however, proved unsuccessful. Austin, an advocate of the B_2H_2 resolution, considered that the United States ought to be counted on "without question" to participate in an international organization, "not merely . . . 'as a sovereign nation' but in a new way involving surrender of enough sovereignty to a world organization to establish the guarantee of peace and security."[124] He excused himself from participation in Vandenberg's resolution but recommended the old standby, Senator White, to him as an internationalist whose views and position on the Foreign Relations Committee might make him a more appropriate cosponsor.

In White, Vandenberg found a counterpart among Republican internationalists, much as Senator McNary had earlier, who proved most agreeable to Republican isolationists. White himself cautioned Hull, with whom both he and Austin had been consulting on postwar planning problems in 1943, "against the effort to do too much reconstructing too rapidly In July, following his collaboration with Vandenberg, White informed Hull that he was "now more fearful that we would attempt to do too much rather than that we would do too little." He added that he "thought we ought to be satisfied at the moment with laying a solid foundation for international cooperation" and building upon this foundation "only as later American sentiment might from time to time justify."[125]

To Austin, White later confessed to having a profound conviction "that as the war casualties pile up and as the war's immediate effects recede, there will be a cooling off on the part of the American people toward postwar commitments." As a cautious internationalist, he argued a line similar to Vandenberg's, that any "excesses" in postwar planning were "almost an invitation to the same sort of controversy within the Senate itself and between the Senate and the Executive as brought disaster at the end of the last war."[126] Austin respected this view but disagreed with it. He had an idea, he told White, "that by September eighteenth," when Congress reconvened following its summer recess, "Senators and Representatives in practically all of the states excepting five states in the constellation of the Chicago Tribune, will become convinced that the fears of controversy ought not to further postpone action." Conceding that their party would "probably lose some support in the middle west" if it took a stronger stand than the one contemplated in White's and Vandenberg's resolution, Austin contended that "everywhere else" it would gain much more than it lost.[127]

Austin had apologized to White in the end "for mixing up the partisan, political question with the rest of it," observing that he could not help doing so after the conferences he had been having with Vandenberg.[128] Indeed, in attempting to gain Austin's support for his resolution, Vandenberg had freely admitted to him that he was out to " 'kill two birds with one stone' in view of the probable passage of the Fulbright Resolution by the House." Comparing his own proposal to that of the

B_2H_2 group, he argued that his resolution, by "avoiding all invitation to a discussion of controversial details," would "point the way to *safe* action in the Senate" on the issue of international organization.[129] That was the first bird to be killed.

The second was the Republican party's troubles with its distinctive historical record in foreign policy. Acknowledging that the "Republican problem from a political point of view" was made more difficult "by the everlasting recurrence of the 'isolationist' theme," Vandenberg claimed to others (but not to Austin) that the Republican party had not had "*any*' isolationists' (in the original and literal sense of the word) since Pearl Harbor." He did not "blame the New Dealers for trying to keep this idea alive," he said, but he did "regret that some of our own [Republican] anti-isolationists continue to bestir the issue just as though nothing had happened since Pearl Harbor." It was "not the so-called isolationists" who kept the issue alive, Vandenberg complained, but "the anti-isolationists who sometimes act as though they were afraid that they might lose their shibboleth."[130] His resolution would demolish that shibboleth, he believed, as well as seize the initiative for the party in foreign policy for a change.

Some of Vandenberg's isolationist supporters in the party attacked him for his role in proposing the Vandenberg-White resolution, accusing him of having converted to internationalsim. To one such critic, Vandenberg remarked:

> If I have become an "internationalist" then black is white. It is perfectly clear—it seems to me—that when this war is over we cannot escape certain inevitable international cooperations to bring order out of chaos and to prevent another surge of military aggression. In my judgment there will be no escaping this necessity and it will be universally recognized in the United States.[131]

According to Vandenberg, the key questions were how far the United States should go and in what fashion. He was quick to emphasize to isolationist critics that his resolution differed fundamentally from resolutions proposed by the real "internationalists," like the B_2H_2 group, in that it provided for the permanent sovereignty of the United States, assured that there would be no international commitments without congressional approval, and insisted upon "a faithful recognition of American interests." He was "at total odds" on these points with Willkie, he claimed; his own views spoke up for "America first."[132]

Vandenberg further explained that he was "hunting for the middle ground between those extremists at one end of the line who would cheerfully give America away" and those at the other end "who would attempt a total isolation which has come to be an impossibility."[133] Amended to read that Vandenberg was playing both ends against the middle to achieve a certain kind of unity, the statement is valid. Vandenberg's concern was as much with the form of his resolution as with its substance and as much with the politics of the postwar issue as with the principles involved. As the strikingly nationalistic tone of the Vandenberg-White resolution suggested in such phrases as "constitutional process," "sovereign rights," and "faithful recognition of American interests," Vandenberg was out to appeal politically to that hypothetical middle-of-the-road American, suspiciously resembling his own constituents, whom he believed constituted the bulk of the body politic and whom politicians both before and since have invoked to justify their positions.

The unity toward which Vandenberg was working in his resolution was political rather than ideological. His objective was to obtain that unity as much between contending factions on foreign policy within the congressional wing of his party as within Congress or the nation at large. Hence, his initial appeal to an internationalist, Senator Austin, for co-sponsorship of the resolution as well as his willingness to settle for Senator White in the end. Vandenberg had already obtained approval of the resolution from a prominent fellow isolationist, Senator Nye.[134] By way of the Vandenberg-White resolution, therefore, Vandenberg sought to forge a united Republican front in Congress on the postwar issue and advance, at the same time, his own position as the leader of that front.

Why he chose to do so is another, more difficult question. A variety of motives could be advanced to explain Vandenberg's actions: histrionic thirst for the limelight stemming from personal vainglory; ultimate concern for his own reelection to the Senate in 1946; latent aspirations for presidential office, if not in 1944, then perhaps 1948; legitimate belief in the need for congressional power to balance that of the executive; and a kind of "natural loyalty" to his colleagues similar to that expressed by Austin. All seem plausible explanations of his behavior. One explanation, however, does not, namely, a "conversion" in foreign policy arising from a fundamental change in personal conviction as opposed to political necessity. Of the other possibilities, it is virtually impossible to say which one, more than the others, mattered most to him. Perhaps it is significant enough to observe that they all appeared to be operating in Vandenberg as a leader of congressional Republicans in 1943 and continued to operate for him and for others even after that. Shortly after the presentation of his resolution to the Senate, in fact, Vandenberg was hard at work on a draft statement closely resembling it for a general conference of the Republican party scheduled to convene on Mackinac Island in his home state of Michigan in early September. Austin and other internationalists, however, were also preparing for that conference. It remains to be seen whether Vandenberg's growing influence in the congressional wing of his party would extend to the presidential wing as well.

PRESIDENTIAL
5 REPUBLICANS SET THEIR SIGHTS ON MACKINAC

For the presidential wing of the Republican party, the 1942 elections had marked "the rolling of a great wave."[1] That wave promised to wash away forever the party's low-water point in the elections of 1936 and to carry Republicans forward to new heights of victory and the White House itself in 1944. The promise, so long in coming after the Republican political drought of the 1930s, also advanced inclinations within the presidential wing of the party to submerge controversies among members and to compromise issues which might produce them. The 1942 elections, however, had ended in a stalemate between the various competing factions on foreign policy. They had signified neither a victory for Wendell Willkie and his supporters who argued for increased Republican internationalism nor a full-scale retreat by their opponents to positions of prewar isolationism. Moreover, the elections had left behind within the party a sea of bitterness which threatened to drown its newfound political hopes. This bitterness soon precipitated a renewed struggle between isolationists and internationalists, as well as between presidential and congressional Republicans, for control of the party's presidential wing.

The immediate focal point of this struggle was Wendell Willkie himself. Because of his hostile attitude toward them in the elections, an old guard of prewar isolationist Republicans, primarily devotees of the party's congressional wing who had opposed Willkie on intervention before the war, redoubled their opposition to his assumptions of party leadership after November. As a result of the elections, there were now available to them a number of fresh political faces, especially among recently elected Republican governors, who stood a good chance of denying Willkie the Republican presidential nomination he so desired. The new governor of New York, in fact, Thomas Dewey, soon became the leading contender for that nomination. One survey of Republican opinion taken

shortly after the November elections showed Dewey ahead of all other
potential nominees, including Willkie. Asked to assess various candidates,
53 percent of the people polled favored Dewey; 49 percent, Willkie.[2]

Opponents of Willkie, however, could choose to back other contenders
for the Republican presidential nomination. Senator Taft, often named
as a potential candidate himself, had announced that he would not run
for the presidency in 1944. Instead, he supported Ohio's governor, John
Bricker.[3] Senator Vandenberg, like Taft a candidate for the nomination
in 1940, also withdrew his name from consideration in 1944 and predicted
that the next nominee would come from the new timber available to the
party, which would become all the more available as the war progressed.
Claiming that he wanted to be "entirely free of any suspicions of personal ambition in this direction" so that he could play a "full part in hunting for the *right nominee*," Vandenberg predicted that that nominee, who
was "going to be 'made' by events during the next eighteen months," would
be General Douglas MacArthur.[4]

One such event, which took place immediately after the elections, high-
lighted the conflict between Willkie and the old guard anew. The spark
for the incident was the deal with Admiral Darlan which General Eisenhower had concluded in North Africa. Designed to save lives in the Allied
landings there, the arrangement called for Darlan to issue a cease-fire order
to his defending French forces in exchange for his being left in control of
civil government in the area. The expediency of the arrangement—the notion that it was trading with the enemy for short term gains, while ultimate
war aims were being compromised—caused many Americans, including
Willkie, grave concern.

Learning of the deal, Willkie intended to criticize it in a speech he was
to deliver on November 16. A phone call from Secretary of War Stimson
on the eve of the talk, however, persuaded Willkie to withhold his criticism.
Stimson had warned him "flatly that, if he criticized the Darlan agreement
at this juncture, he would run the risk of jeopardizing the success of the
United States Army in North Africa and would be rendering its task very
much more difficult."[5] According to one account of their conversation,
Stimson also told Willkie that the cost of his criticism might be 60,000
American lives.[6]

The next day President Roosevelt himself publicly explained the Darlan deal and defended it against any adverse comment by outsiders. Willkie
believed that he had been duped. The administration had coaxed him into
withholding his criticism for political reasons, he suspected, so that Roosevelt could issue his own explanation of the event first. Loosing his censure
upon the Darlan deal in public, he took the administration to task and
spoke out against expedient international arrangements in general.[7] In re-

ply, Senator Vandenberg, speaking on behalf of wartime unity but also for the opposition to Willkie in the Republican party, accused domestic critics of the Eisenhower-Darlan arrangement of irresponsibility, of shooting at their own forces from behind the lines, "especially from the sanctuary of this safe home front."[8]

Another focal point in the struggle for party control also arose soon after the elections. On November 12, Representative Martin announced that he was resigning as Republican national chairman. Thus, the party's National Committee, scheduled to meet on December 12 in St. Louis, would have to elect a new head. Martin had originally been a compromise choice for the office. One reason he had remained chairman as long as he had in 1942 was to postpone until after the elections the conflict which had promised to break out between the pro- and anti-Willkie factions over the selection of Martin's successor. Up to the eve of the meeting in St. Louis, in fact, Martin was being urged to take the chairmanship again to stave off a possible bloodletting. The opportunity to resign, however, looked more propitious to him than ever following the Republican success in the elections and he took it, even though the St. Louis meeting still threatened to erupt into a power struggle of the kind that Martin and others had long hoped to avoid.[9]

Following Martin's resignation, a variety of possible replacements for him were suggested, including former presidential nominee Alfred M. Landon and Clarence Buddington Kelland, the party's outspoken publicity director. At the December meeting, however, the principal candidates came down to two. One was Werner W. Schroeder, a national committeeman from Illinois, the favorite of Colonel Robert R. McCormick and his *Chicago Tribune* as well as of Senator Taft. Schroeder had been campaign manager for Senator C. Wayland Brooks's successful drive for renomination and election in Illinois, which Willkie had openly opposed. Willkie now opposed Schroeder and favored Frederick E. Baker, a public relations man from Seattle and the second principal candidate for the chairmanship. Martin himself opposed Schroeder's candidacy, both "because of his distinctively German name," given the wartime situation, and because of "his association with McCormick."[10] The latter reportedly warned Martin on the eve of the voting "that if Schroeder isn't elected tomorrow, there is going to be a third party in America." Fearing such a possibility, Martin and other Republicans desirous of compromise took steps to head off the impending clash. While urging Schroeder to withdraw, they moved at the same time to promote the candidacy of Harrison E. Spangler, a Republican committeeman from Iowa and a figure "less objectionable to each of the contending forces than any other candidate."[11]

After the first round of balloting, Schroeder and Baker stood even at

40 votes each while Spangler had only 15. A second round saw Schroeder slip to 38 and Baker rise to 43. At that point, by his own account, Martin called for a recess and pressed his case on both sides for the necessity of Spangler's election to avoid splitting the party. The effort was successful. Walking arm-in-arm down the center aisle of the meeting place in a show of unity, Baker and Schroeder both withdrew and endorsed Spangler as the new Republican national chairman.[12] Both warring factions claimed victory afterwards. The Willkie forces contended that since their main objective had been to stop the election of Schroeder, they had triumphed. Willkie himself refused to comment to reporters on the election of Spangler on grounds that "a person should not boast after a victory."[13] McCormick's *Chicago Tribune*, on the other hand, bannered Spangler's election as a blow to the Willkie forces.[14]

In truth, both sides could claim what they wished. The new chairman was, after all, a compromise candidate elected for precisely that purpose. Although his selection was designed in part to appease the Middle West, and even though he had opposed Willkie's nomination for president in 1940 and had lobbied behind the scenes to promote his own candidacy for the chairmanship in 1942, Spangler's main claim to the office was simply that he did not offend anyone very much.[15] In that respect, he was comparable to another Republican who had received the party's nomination for president in 1920 for much the same reason, Warren G. Harding.[16] In fact, the outcome of the St. Louis meeting, as one Republican chieftain remarked of Spangler's election, "was not unlike that in the 1920 convention, in which strong men strove for either Lowden or Wood and, in the end, accepted a negative quantity."[17]

Spangler himself supported this assessment of his function in stating his views on the basic foreign policy conflict within the party. On the one hand, he observed for the benefit of the internationalists that the notion of the Atlantic and Pacific oceans as "moats around America" was no longer viable in the postwar world. On the other, he remarked for the isolationists that his main job was "to build up an army of voters in the United States to defeat the New Deal" and that he doubted there were "any votes in China, or Mongolia, or Russia" to be won for Republicans.[18]

Since the conflict between the party's pro- and anti-Willkie factions revolved to a significant extent around questions of foreign policy, Republican leaders who sought to prevent a split over the chairmanship in St. Louis also labored to avoid a falling-out there on the issue of postwar world order. They solved the second problem as easily as the first. The National Committee simply reaffirmed its resolution of the preceding April, already a compromise between the two camps. Significantly, Taft, who had originally opposed the resolution in April, moved its reaffirma-

tion in December. Heading into 1943, therefore, the presidential wing of
the Republican party was mapping out a strategy of caution and delay
on the question of postwar international organization similar to the one
that Republican leaders in Congress had embarked upon. The strategy
had proved so effective for the party in 1942, both internally in terms of
unity and externally in terms of the historical and political problems involved, that, for the time being at least, it seemed the best chance for
continued political success.

Republican hopes for a continued moratorium on the postwar issue,
however, were no more to be fulfilled in the presidential wing of the
party, than they were in the congressional. By the beginning of 1943, the
American public was beginning to favor the idea of a postwar international
organization more and more. One poll taken by George Gallup in December 1942 showed a sizable majority who wanted planning for the future
peace to begin immediately. Several independent groups, moreover, were
determined to push this trend of public opinion further and "avoid a
repetition of the postwar letdown which they believed had doomed the
League of Nations."[19] By the end of 1942, the League of Nations Association, the Commission to Study the Organization of Peace, and the
Free World Association had formed a Council of United Nations Committees to draw up a plan and to drum up support for a future world
organization.[20] Another such group, originating within the American religious community, was the Commission to Study the Bases of a Just and
Durable Peace of the Federal Council of the Churches of Christ in America. The commission's chairman was John Foster Dulles.

A New York lawyer and close associate of Thomas Dewey, Dulles
was related to two former American secretaries of state. His grandfather,
John W. Foster, had held the office under Republican President Benjamin
Harrison; his uncle, Robert Lansing, had served as secretary in the Democratic administration of Woodrow Wilson. Dulles himself had attended
the Second Hague Peace Conference in 1907 as his grandfather's secretary. In 1919, his uncle's influence had gained him a place in Wilson's delegation at the Versailles Peace Conference as a member of the reparations
commission. A disillusioned Wilsonian following that conference, Dulles
shared the view put forth by the English economist John Maynard Keynes
in his well-known account of the Versailles treaty, *Economic Consequences
of the Peace*, that the settlement was unfair and "Carthaginian" in its effect on Germany and Central Europe and that it needed to be rectified.[21]
As a result, Dulles was a non-interventionist before World War II; like
many an isolationist, although he opposed Hitler, he also opposed American entry into the conflict, blaming its origins primarily on selfish nationalism, especially as embodied in the peace treaty and in Great Britain
and France after World War I.[22]

In 1940, Dulles accepted the chairmanship of the Commission on a
Just and Durable Peace of the Federal Council of Churches in the general
hope, shared by members of both the British and American church com-
munities, that a future peace would not fail again as the one engineered at
Versailles had. To justify the carnage of World War II, they believed, a
truly lasting peace based on equity among nations and men would have to
be established. After the United States had entered the war, therefore, it
became "imperative" for Dulles and his group that the United States and
the United Nations "produce definite evidence" that they would "embark
on a program" to set up "concrete instrumentalities charged with the
task of replacing the anarchistic conditions which in the past have played
into the hands of ruthless men." His commission's objective, Dulles professed, was to "create public demand" which would in turn "force governmental action along such lines."[23] Toward that end, the group printed
and issued early in 1943 a widely circulated statement of political propositions. Popularly referred to as the "Six Pillars of Peace," these propositions maintained that any future peace must:

[1] . . . provide the political framework for a continuing collaboration of the United Nations and, in due course, of neutral and enemy
nations.
[2] . . . make provision for bringing within the scope of international agreement those economic and financial acts of national gov-
ernments which have widespread international repercussions.
[3] . . . make provision for an organization to adapt the treaty
structure of the world to changing underlying conditions.
[4] . . . proclaim the goal of autonomy for subject peoples, and
it must establish international organization to assure and to super-
vise the realization of that end.
[5] . . . establish procedures for controlling military establishments
everywhere.
[6] . . . establish in principle, and seek to achieve in practice, the
right of individuals everywhere to religious and intellectual liberty.[24]

In the presidential wing of the Republican party, where Dulles, through
his connections with Dewey, was soon to take roost, others were also determined to create public demand for action along these lines. Contrary
to the caution and delay on the issue evident at the National Committee
meeting in St. Louis, these Republicans aimed to spur the party onward
toward far-reaching American commitments in the postwar world. Chief
among them, of course, was Wendell Willkie. Lincoln's Birthday, 1943,
found him in the state of his birth, Indiana, addressing its General Assembly and summoning its members to realize the global nature of the

new world order which, he thought, the war's end would surely bring. The following day, before a group of conservative Indiana Republicans, Willkie advocated renewal of the Lend-Lease and mutual trade agreements acts then before Congress and recalled the party's internationalist inheritance from the days of Blaine, McKinley, and William Howard Taft.[25]

Shortly thereafter, in April 1943, Willkie's best-selling book, *One World*, appeared. In large part an account of his trip around the world the preceding autumn, it also contained a stirring plea that Americans recognize and plan to do something positive about the wealth of international opportunities for peace and prosperity that would be available to them after the war. The book's sales were astounding. Its first printing was gone in two days; after three weeks, over a half-million copies had been sold.[26] Like the B_2H_2 resolution in the Senate, *One World* became a symbol of, as well as a rallying point for, the increasing public sentiment in the United States for commitment to some form of postwar world organization.

In addition to Willkie among presidential Republicans, Harold Stassen of Minnesota also pushed in 1943 for a strong stand by the party on the issue of international organization. Stassen, who resigned his governorship in April to begin active service in the navy, advocated in March that a world government be formed out of the nucleus of the wartime United Nations. He argued that isolationism was dead and that in the wake of its demise the Republican party should tell the American people precisely where it stood in relation to postwar foreign policy.[27] Although Stassen took exception to Willkie for being highly critical of British colonialism in *One World* and insufficiently critical of Russian communism (an objection which reportedly hurt Willkie deeply), the two men's spirits were alike in attempting to steer the Republican party, and through it the United States, toward an unmistakably internationalist position.[28]

An ad hoc group of presidential Republicans had dedicated itself to the same end. Headed by two Midwesterners—Deneen Watson, a lawyer and former aide to Illinois Governor Dwight H. Green, and Dennison B. Hull, an architect and the opponent of Representative Stephen A. Day in the 1942 primaries—the Republican Postwar Policy Association originated among Illinois Republicans in Chicago on February 11. Shortly after the appearance of *One World*, 75 Republicans from 12 midwestern states met at the La Salle Hotel in the windy city on May 3 to hear Watson proclaim that in order for their party to defeat President Roosevelt, who seemed certain to run for a fourth term in 1944, it would first have to neutralize his obvious advantages in the field of foreign policy. Therefore, Watson argued, the G.O.P. ought to abandon its image of isolationism once and for all by way of a plank in the 1944 platform pledging the party's support for postwar international organization. The purpose of the Republican Postwar Policy Association, therefore, which Watson as its chairman hoped would mushroom into an organization with affiliates in the 48 states, was to put pressure on the party (and especially on the new national chairman, Harrison Spangler) "not to repeat the mistakes of 1919 and 1920," to be "positive about this battle for an enduring peace," and to neither "equivocate" nor "pussyfoot" about it.[29]

Addressed by, among others, Republican Senator Burton of Ohio and Representative Dirksen of Illinois, the Chicago meeting endorsed the B_2H_2 resolution, of which Burton was one of the sponsors, and adopted a four-point program deemed "essential to the establishment and preservation of peace." The four points read as follows:

1. A complete military victory of the Allies and the unconditional surrender of the aggressor nations is the first essential to world peace.

2. The United Nations must remain united if we are to secure international collaboration to prevent the recurrence of future wars.

3. For the preservation of peace, on the home front we must convert our war industries to peacetime production and establish a sound economic position with equal opportunity for all after the war is won.

4. We must establish a council of nations based on the United Nations to assume full responsibility in maintaining world order.[30]

These purposes of the association were reaffirmed at a gathering in New York during July of some 300 Republicans from 12 northeastern states, who were addressed by Senator Austin of Vermont and Representative Eaton of New Jersey.[31] In order to concentrate attention on the postwar issue, the organization and Watson gave assurances that "in attempting to anchor the party to an international program," they were "neutral as to candidates" for the 1944 presidential nomination.[32] They admitted, however, that eventually they would endorse internationalist candidates in preference to isolationist ones.[33]

One prominent candidate in New York, along with the regular Republican organization there, refused to participate in the Watson movement in his state. Governor Thomas Dewey, who was, according to a Gallup poll released in March, the party's leading contender for the 1944 presidential nomination, moved much more cautiously on the issue of postwar international organization than Willkie and Stassen.[34] An opponent of involvement in the war in 1940 but a supporter of Lend-Lease in 1941, Dewey warmed slowly to the growing internationalist trend in 1943.[35] At a Republican Governor's Conference in Columbus, Ohio, in June, he advised the party to take the lead in planning a cooperative program for the nations of the world after the war.[36] He lauded as an example of such a program the "Six Pillars of Peace" of John Foster Dulles and his Commission on a Just and Durable Peace.[37] But the New York governor refused to go more specifically beyond such general pronouncements.

In view of his presidential prospects, Dewey's caution seemed well advised, for at the same time that the drive was going on to rally public support for a permanent international organization, a reaction comparable in spirit and tone to the one produced in Congress by the B_2H_2 resolution was under way within the presidential wing of the Republican party. Herbert Hoover and Hugh Gibson helped spark that reaction. They published a series of articles in June 1943 which expanded upon ideas set forth earlier in their *Problems of Lasting Peace.* Hoover in particular opposed what he considered idealism or "damaging nonsense" in Willkie's approach to international affairs. He and Gibson argued instead for a self-styled realism in regard to postwar planning. They called, first, for the avoidance of an immediate postwar settlement and, second, for a long transition period during which the major victorious powers would run the peace, as well as provide essential relief and reconstruction. After stability and prosperity had been restored to the war-torn world, conditions might be settled enough for the establishment of a world organization.[38]

The publicity director of the Republican National Committee, Clarence Buddington Kelland, took this "realistic" approach to postwar planning a step further. In a speech delivered at the National Republican Club in August 1943, Kelland recommended setting up several "zones of safety" around the United States after the war to guarantee the nation's security. These zones would include military alliances with the major Allies for the occupation of defeated Axis countries and for the preservation of peace, a separate alliance with Great Britain in case the other alliances failed, and a final alliance with Latin-American nations for the protection of the Western Hemisphere. The last zone of safety for Kelland was the United States itself. Preservation and expansion of its military might, he argued, would in the end guarantee its security. Stressing the importance of maintaining American sovereignty and of refusing to sacrifice it to any world government, Kelland suggestively recalled in his speech the isolationist theme of American self-sufficiency with which he and his party had been closely identified prior to war.[39]

Isolationists in the presidential wing of the party launched into other familiar themes in reaction to the internationalist push for postwar commitments from the G.O.P. In conjunction with their counterparts in Congress, presidential Republican isolationists renewed their hostility toward Great Britain and the Soviet Union, long sources of suspicion in such circles, and their war and postwar objectives. Former Republican National Chairman Charles Hilles charged that Britain was not "excessively or affectedly religious in her post-war formula." The United States, therefore, should certainly not "undertake to underwrite the maintenance of an ideal global social state of well-being from the cradle to the grave" as some internationalists seemed to believe it should. Americans could not "safely drift into that condition and still serve the world," Hilles contended, without "mere pretense" and without lowering their own "standard of living to the average standard—indeed, below the average, be cause Great Britain will continue to seek a superior status."[40] Herbert Hoover, on the other hand, indulged in his perennial distrust of the Soviets. If Russian reports of victories in late 1942 and early 1943 were true, he observed, "it is a curious commentary upon their claims of insufficient forces to hold their lines when they were agitating a second front last summer."[41]

A principal object of concern among these Republicans was the Democratic administration and the postwar internationalist ideas of spokesmen like Vice-President Henry A. Wallace and Undersecretary of State Sumner Welles. To Hilles, it was "clear" that the definite purpose of the administration was:

(1) to at once chart the country's course for a period far beyond the war's end; (2) to commit the country to the abandonment of the policy of equalization of trade barriers; (3) to subordinate the courts and the Congress to the Executive; (4) to dissipate the savings of our people in global diffusions of luxuries to the impoverishment of our own standard of living; (5) to commit our country to a permanent international currency system; and (6) to commit it to an undertaking "to police the world for one hundred years," (as a Cabinet minister has announced).[42]

In order to defeat such purposes as well as to thwart an expected move by President Roosevelt to achieve them in a fourth term, Hilles and other like-minded Republicans sought to revive hopes from the late 1930s for a practical alliance, comparable to the one already existing in Congress, between presidential Republicans and anti-New Deal Democrats.[43]

In the Midwest, a mirror-image rival to Deneen Watson's Postwar Policy Association soon appeared. Billing itself as the Republican Nationalist Revival Committee, the group held a meeting in Chicago in May (shortly after Watson's gathering there), heard Senator Gerald Nye speak on

"Globalitis," and adopted a resolution denouncing attempts "to use the war to betray the American people into a Global Government" despite their "well-known opposition" to the League of Nations and "any other form of World Super Government which repudiates American principles." Although the Watson group had declared itself "neutral" as to presidential candidates, this one did not. It called upon "stalwart Americans to be candidates for delegates to the Republican National Convention and for other offices and to make straight-forward and understandable campaigns against Willkie or Willkie candidates for President and against any other candidate for public office who supports Willkieism."[44]

"WE DON'T WANT WILLKIE!" the Nationalist Revival Committee proclaimed. And it was not alone.[45] By and large, the bulk of Republican reaction to the issue of future world organization was directed against Willkie and his continuing attempts to maneuver the party toward advanced internationalist positions in foreign policy. Willkie was castigated in the congressional and presidential wings of the party alike for these attempts. Polls of party faithful in both wings showed support for him as the future Republican presidential nominee continuing to decline.[46] Willkie "is undoubtedly going to make a lot of trouble," observed Senator Taft, "and intends to rule or ruin the Republican Party."[47] Other critics recalled Willkie's former Democratic affiliations and charged that he was serving as a stalking horse for Roosevelt in the 1944 elections—that the president wanted him nominated by the Republicans more than any other candidate and would do all he could to bring that about.[48] Willkie was again censured for having failed to campaign for the election of Republican candidates in 1942 and for having taken his celebrated trip around the world instead.[49] Furthermore, he himself added to his difficulties by remarking in public that the party should be purged of the isolationist and ultranationalist elements making such charges against him.[50]

With battle lines forming on all fronts, therefore, the new Republican national chairman, Harrison Spangler, worked to maintain a cease-fire. In January 1943, shortly after his election, Spangler had written to G.O.P. leaders in both the House and the Senate requesting that the Republican conferences in each of those bodies select and designate members to act, in conjunction with floor leaders Martin and McNary, as an "advisory council" to the Republican National Committee.[51] In addition to strengthening the ties between the presidential and congressional wings of the party, one of the purposes behind Spangler's call for a council had been that the "brains of the party should get together to make a statement on foreign policy—to present a united front."[52] He had discussed this intention with Willkie but had gained the impression that he was not interested. Spangler was thus surpirsed to learn of the formation of Deneen Watson's Republican Postwar Policy Association, which he instinctively identified with Willkie and his followers. The Watson group, Spangler believed, had been hired and "financed by money from Wall Street and the New York *Herald Tribune*" and was at bottom a front to gain the 1944 Republican presidential nomination for Willkie.[53]

Fears that Willkie and the Watson group might take over the party and force it to take a stand in favor of international collaboration, winds of public sentiment blowing in favor of such stands, and a realization by even the old guard that the party needed some sort of compromise on the issue, all combined to reinforce and expand Spangler's original intention. On May 31, 1943, he announced creation of the Republican Post-War Advisory Council. As Spangler envisioned it, this council would "make exhaustive studies and research of all the postwar problems and be prepared to submit its findings and a suggested program to the Republican National Committee before the next National Convention." In order to do so, the council was eventually to consist of several subcommittees, but initially it would have two temporary ones dealing with domestic problems on the one hand and problems of foreign policy on the other. Foremost among those problems, according to Spangler's announcement, was that of "a lasting world peace," which must be approached "courageously and realistically" by the party "in a spirit of friendly cooperation with the other nations of the world, keeping in mind the welfare of our own country."[54]

In consultation with the Republican floor leaders in Congress, Representative Joseph Martin, Jr., and Senator Charles McNary, Spangler appointed 49 Republicans, consciously drawn from different geographical regions, to the Post-War Advisory Council. These included six senators, 13 representatives, the 24 Republican governors, and six members of the National Committee.[55] According to Spangler, the main criteria for selection were that members of the council "be truly representative of the rank and file" of the party and that they be "party leaders" who had "already been approved" by the party and "by the people."[56] In other words, all of Spangler's appointees to the council were party members currently holding elective office. Conspicuously absent from the list, therefore, were the last three Republican presidential candidates: Hoover, Landon, and, of course, Willkie.

Spangler tried to smooth over the absence of these three by claiming that the new group was to be the "official Advisory Council," that the National Committee would "confer with many other Republicans," and that it would also "seek the advice and counsel of former President Herbert Hoover" as well as the "last two Republican candidates, Alfred

M. Landon and Wendell Willkie."[57] Later, however, Spangler was to claim that he had specifically not asked Willkie to be a council member for fear that he would refuse and possibly discredit the group's work in advance. Moreover, the growing dislike of many rank-and-file Republicans for Willkie, according to Spangler, argued against his being put on the list.[58] The criterion of current elective office for council membership, therefore, provided a convenient excuse for excluding the party's most advanced and troublesome spokesman on postwar foreign policy from a group expected above all to produce a formula for party unity on the issue.

The membership of the council and Spangler's method of selection brought approval from the party's isolationists. The *Chicago Tribune* indicated that it was pleased and called upon the council to emphasize the leadership of Congress in the making of foreign policy.[59] Indeed, the congressional members of the council were the first to meet and discuss objectives. They determined that these would include the assumption of some sort of obligation by the party and the United States to prevent future war. In conjunction with Spangler, they also called for a meeting of the full Post-War Advisory Council in early September at Mackinac Island, Michigan, to draft a recommendation to this effect for the party as a whole.[60]

On the other hand, Republican internationalists were not especially pleased. Willkie objected that neither Senator Burton nor Senator Ball, two elected representatives of their party who were sponsoring the best known resolution on postwar foreign policy then before the Senate, had been included in the membership of the council. Regardless of what that body did, Willkie warned, he himself would continue to fight within the party for the international principles in which he believed.[61] The *New York Herald Tribune*, a staunch supporter of Willkie, also criticized the council's make-up, charging that "masterminds . . . have deliberately weighted down the committee with a group of men who may confidently be expected to do nothing at all."[62] In July, moreover, Deneen Watson of the Republican Postwar Policy Association spurned one of those "masterminds," Chairman Spangler, when he pleaded with Watson to dissolve his organization and support whatever stand on postwar foreign policy the council might take at Mackinac in September.[63]

Another prominent Republican internationalist turned back a similar request from the chairman. Senator Warren Austin, who had addressed the Watson group's meeting in New York on July 19 and applauded its objectives, had rebuffed Spangler's plea that he refrain from participating in that meeting.[64] Privately labeling the chairman's letter to him the "Palaver of an America Firster," Austin had replied that it would be "an act of perfidy" for him to cancel his talk. "My loyalty to the great cause for which the Republican Party ought to stand, officially as well as in the hearts of the people," he declared, "causes me to regard this meeting as an opportunity of considerable value to the party and to the cause."

Austin denied Spangler's suggestion that he would more effectively serve both cause and party as a member of the National Committee's Post-War Advisory Council, to which he had been appointed, than as a spokesman for the Watson organization. "As a member of your Advisory Council," Austin told the chairman, "my advice to you would be to make use of this organization instead of alienating it." He had no doubt that the Republican Nationalist Revival Committee would "bring its influence to bear on the Republican National Committee and the Republican National Convention."[65] Spangler's concern, therefore, that Watson's group and Austin's participation in it would promote disunity in the party and undercut the work of the Post-War Advisory Council was misplaced. The chairman's anxiousness to save the support of middle-western isolationists, Austin complained, was leading him to "trade out of the picture more people who are confirmed and zealous supportors [sic] of postwar collaboration than we can possibly save of the Chicago Tribune group."[66]

While one could look upon Spangler's Post-War Advisory Council as its early critics did and charge that it was stacked in the interest of prewar isolationists, it is noteworthy, in view of the council's later deliberations at Mackinac Island, that presidential Republicans outnumbered congressional ones among the appointees. Officially at least, particularly given the number of new Republican governors who were members, the Post-War Advisory Council did not appear to be dominated by an isolationist or congressional old guard. Nor did Spangler seem to be favoring this old guard unduly. He was primarily concerned with creating the impression of a council that was balanced in regard to office holding and to viewpoint, with effecting a compromise between the various factions on foreign policy, and with making it appear that neither widespread differences of opinion nor isolationism existed any longer among Republicans. To this end, for example, he would alternately recall the postwar resolutions adopted by the party in 1942 and promise a further statement by the advisory council in September.

The Watson group, Spangler believed, threatened his hopes for unity and effective compromise at that meeting by fostering the impression that vast differences still existed and that the party was hopelessly divided on postwar foreign policy.[67] Although he failed to convince Austin of the gravity of this threat, Spangler had more luck with Representative Eaton, who had likewise addressed the Watson group's gathering in July. Not long after that meeting Eaton issued a statement, circulated by

Spangler, which claimed that the Republican leadership and the rank
and file of the party were

> now in substantial agreement upon the forward-looking fundamental
> principles and policies upon which America must act in the Post-War
> period. We have in our elected office holders in Congress and over the
> country in our National Committee and in its official Post-War Ad-
> visory Council the leadership to successfully develop a program
> toward which America can look with confidence, and I am in
> hearty accord with the thoughtful and studious approach which the
> National Committee in full consultation with all interested parties
> is now making and will continue to make in the months ahead.[68]

Through his appointment of the Post-War Advisory Council, therefore,
Spangler was attempting to control the postwar issue in the presidential
wing of the party much as Senator Vandenberg was in the party's congressional wing. Spangler was also searching for "common ground" between
Republican isolationists and internationalists and he was later to receive
important help in this search from Vandenberg himself. A clue, in fact,
to the direction that the Post-War Advisory Council would be likely to
take in foreign policy at its meeting in September soon became apparent
in the appointment of Vandenberg to head its committee on foreign affairs.

Another indicator of the direction that the party would be taking in
this area lay in the separate attempts of Spangler and Watson to win over
John Foster Dulles to their respective causes in the summer of 1943. As
a leading advocate of postwar world order and a member of the party with
close ties to its leading presidential contender, Dulles was fast becoming
an important figure among Republicans. As such, his responses to these
overtures were significant and instructive. In general, Dulles believed,
as Spangler did, that it was both possible and desirable to find a formula
for Republican agreement on the postwar issue on which the great bulk
of party members could unite. On the basis of his conversations with
Willkie, Stassen, Taft, and Dewey, Dulles maintained that most differences between Republican leaders on foreign policy were imaginary rather
than real.[69] Dewey himself had suggested to Spangler that the Post-War
Advisory Council might want to pave over such differences by adopting
something similar to Dulles's "Six Pillars of Peace" as its statement on
postwar world order.[70]

Deneen Watson, however, was also interested in adopting the "Six
Pillars" for use by his Postwar Policy Association. In broaching this possibility to Dulles, Watson went to considerable lengths to assure him,

Dulles reported to Dewey, that the association was not a Willkie-for-president group in disguise and that it would not get involved in the matter of candidates, "certainly not until near the eve of the Republican Convention," and perhaps not even then.[71] Dulles, however, was wary of the Watson group's using the "Six Pillars." He did not want those principles becoming involved in partisan politics, he claimed. He was just "getting into a position to have some real influence throughout the country," and he did not want to relinquish that position or possibly jeopardize it and the work of his church group by involving them in partisan controversies.[72]

But Dulles was not as averse to political use of the "Six Pillars of Peace" as he claimed to be. In objecting to the Watson association's proposed adoption of his program, Dulles also objected to the association itself for "appearing to work from outside as a group attacking the regular organization" of the Republican party.[73] Thus, when Spangler commented favorably on Dulles's "Six Pillars" and indicated that the Post-War Advisory Council might consider adopting them at its forthcoming Mackinac Island conference, Dulles responded favorably.[74] If the Republican party could recognize that there ought to be a national and not a partisan policy for the entire country in foreign affairs, he rationalized, then party leaders might well look to his commission's "Six Pillars of Peace" as the best nonpartisan statement available on postwar foreign policy and adopt it, "expecting, or at least expressing the hope, that the Democratic Party might follow their example."[75] At bottom, Dulles had strong leanings toward the regular Republican party organization, as well as considerable desire to see it use his group's statement. He viewed that organization, not Watson's association, as the vehicle through which his own "real influence" in politics could be increased most effectively.

In connection with Spangler's overture to Dulles, H. Alexander Smith, a Republican national committeeman from New Jersey, member of the Post-War Advisory Council, and fellow alumnus of Princeton, sent Dulles the draft of a suggested resolution for the Mackinac conference. The resolution called, first of all, for prosecution of the war to total victory. Then it called for a stabilized, interdependent world of independent nations prepared to undertake new obligations and responsibilities in curbing rampant nationalism and its military and economic consequences at the war's end. Specifically, the draft advocated development of the United Nations Declaration of January 1, 1942, to include all self-governing nations and such postwar objectives as the peaceful settlement of international disputes; repression of future aggression; development of world trade and investment to maintain employment and raise living standards; and agreement on problems of aviation, shipping, colonial areas, equal access to raw materials, public health, and human interests.[76] In the broad reach of issues covered by the draft, especially in its calls for financial and economic stability as conditions for a future peace, it was remarkably similar to the Dulles Commission's "Six Pillars of Peace."

In his reply to Smith, Dulles praised the "highly spiritual note" of the pronouncement but urged that Republicans make clear in the finished product that the "interdependence" of nations called for in the draft did not necessitate a supranational agency. Dulles suggested opposition to world government as the issue on which the party should unite, for it seemed to him that "in some such way the Republican party might get away from the tentacles of a false issue" which had been imposed upon it by its political enemies and substitute instead an issue which was "thoroughly sound" and with which "the overwhelming majority of the American people would be in agreement." The "false issue" to which Dulles was referring was that of isolationism versus internationalism. He remarked to Smith that he had

> thought for some time that as a matter of political strategy the Republican party ought not to allow the issue to appear to be one between isolation and collaboration. So long as in the public mind that is the issue, the Republican Party, irrespective of anything that can be said, will be looked upon as tending more toward isolation than the Democratic Party. I think that the issue is a false issue. It is perpetuated by the Democrats for their own purposes.

By presenting the issue he had suggested—that of opposition to supranational authority—Republicans might be able to gain the upper hand in politics. Infused with the spirit of partisan calculation, he proclaimed that that way "the Democrats, or at least Mr. Roosevelt, might be put on the defensive."[77]

With a similarly shrewd sense of the political possibilities involved, Dulles also objected to the enumeration in Smith's draft of agreements on aviation, shipping, and colonial areas. Such a specific listing, he contended, might invite criticism for its omission of other items, such as monetary stability, relief and rehabilitation, and freedom of religion. And indeed, when a revision of the draft came back to Dulles from Smith for approval, the earlier enumeration had been replaced by a simpler statement calling for cooperation between the United States and other nations to achieve a wider exchange of goods, services, and investments, broader access to raw materials, and economic and monetary stability.[78] Party leaders like Smith and Spangler may have been working to impress Dulles, and through him Dewey, with their concern for his principles and views, but Dulles was working equally hard to impress them with his sympathy for their problems. Despite his original objections to any involvement of his church commission's proposals in partisan politics, Dulles as much as anyone sought to turn them in that direction.

Other views and interests besides Dulles's concerned party leaders prior to the Post-War Advisory Council's meeting at Mackinac. Chairman Spangler and Committeeman Smith, who was helping Spangler set up the meeting, worked hard in advance to accommodate different positions, obtain agreement beforehand, and guard against the possibility that the council might reach a politically damaging impasse on what the proposed statement on foreign policy should include. To this end, they solicited the support of Senator Austin. In writing to him in July to object to his addressing the Watson group's meeting in New York, Spangler had suggested to Austin that perhaps something along the lines of the Vandenberg-White resolution then before the Senate might serve as a basis for a statement by the Post-War Advisory Council on foreign policy. That resolution, according to Spangler, had prompted favorable reactions from internationalists and nationalists alike.[79]

Austin had failed to respond to that suggestion at the time, doubtless for some of the same reasons he had given in declining to cosponsor the resolution with Vandenberg in the first place.[80] To Spangler's delight, however, Austin, in his address to the Watson group in July, had warned Republicans to avoid details in postwar planning for the present and to concentrate instead on achieving agreement on general principles of international cooperation.[81] His note of caution appeared to be similar to that of John Foster Dulles and of the National Committee itself. In August, therefore, Committeeman Smith followed up Spangler's initiative with one of his own, forwarding to Austin a draft resolution comparable to the one he sent Dulles. Smith observed that this draft approved the adoption of the B_2H_2 resolution in the Senate and the Fulbright resolution in the House but included the language of the Vandenberg resolution, ostensibly to get the support of Vandenberg and Taft. He also noted that the proposed resolution included language, discussed above in connection with Smith's overture to Dulles, calculated to "insure the support of the New York crowd."[82]

Austin went over the document carefully, singling out the adjective "sovereign" before "nations" and the phrase "constitutional process" for attention and pencilling in a clause calling for "cooperative organization to maintain protection from military aggression"; he was preparing his mind, he remarked elsewhere, "for the keen contest which I feel impending at Mackinac Island." Soon, however, taking "Spangler at his word" that "the Republican National Committee does not want to be for un-

conditioned nationalism and does not want to appear to be so," Austin
proceeded to draft a resolution of his own for the forthcoming conference.[83] The question before the Post-War Advisory Council at that conference, Austin's draft proclaimed, would not be "WHETHER" the
United States would collaborate with other nations in the postwar period—that question had already been decided for the party by its National Committee resolution of April 1942—but "HOW." Having rejected isolationism, therefore, Austin called for total defeat and disarmament of the Axis powers and, in a reference to the B_2H_2 resolution, for the maintenance "of trained and well-equipped armed forces
of each of the United Nations, to maintain peace and order."

In regard to the important question of sovereignty, Austin's draft
recommended "such means of cooperation among the nations as require
the least amount of limitation or conditioning of nationalism as may be
consistent with maximum assurances of security." Nevertheless, it stated
that a "policy ought to be chosen by which sovereignty is conditioned if
it is found to be indispensable to the preservation of peace." With regard
to "constitutionalism," Austin provided that it "should be adhered to in
determining the substance of our policies and shall be followed in ways
and means of making international commitments." He also recommended
that "the Republican party promote the adherence of the United States
to the statute of the World Court." In its final form, the draft advocated
"tariff and exchange policies and an economic system designed to facili-
tate freer exchange of world goods and affording all nations reasonable
access to materials necessary to promote industry and to develop international commerce." Furthermore, it supported "the achievement of freedom by peoples who seek it and are qualified to maintain it and profit
by it," as well as "production and service" by the United States "great
enough to assist in the rehabilitation of distressed nations."[84]

This draft statement of Austin's soon became the principal alternative to the Vandenberg-White resolution in the Senate as the basis for
a forthcoming Republican declaration on foreign policy. The foremost
sponsor of that Senate resolution had himself been hard at work can-
vassing his colleagues' postwar views in advance of the "Republican 'policy pow-wow' " and redrafting his resolution in order to "get unity at
Mackinac on some such basis."[85] Vandenberg, in addition to Spangler and
Smith, was also searching the presidential wing of the party as he had the
congressional for that "common ground" of agreement on postwar foreign policy which he never tired of proclaiming his goal.

The essential elements of Vandenberg's Senate resolution were present
in the draft of a proposed Mackinac declaration which he sent several times
to Governor Dewey for approval. It called for prosecution of the war un-

til the enemy surrendered unconditionally and for the punishment and elimination of Axis leaders. In a key passage, the draft recommended "responsible participation by the United States in organized post-war co-operation between sovereign nations to prevent by any necessary means the recurrence of military aggression and to establish permanent peace with justice in a free world." It also advocated the achievement of these objectives "by due constitutional processes and with faithful recognition of American responsibilities and American interests." Of this passage, Vandenberg remarked once to Dewey that he had "taken out the word 'continuous,'" which Dewey had previously approved as a substitute for "permanent," having "found a great deal of resistance" to both words in his canvass of fellow Republican (presumably isolationist) colleagues. Vandenberg was quick to observe, though, in a show of further accommodation, that he had "left in the magic word 'organized'"—a significant but subtle addition to the original Vandenberg-White resolution—which Dewey (and probably Dulles as well) had recommended.[86]

Despite all such advance work to obtain a resolution on foreign policy which the Republican Post-War Advisory Council could adopt in harmony, however, the goal of party unity appeared to be in jeopardy when the conference on Mackinac Island convened. Governor Dewey arrived there on Sunday, September 5, the eve of the council meeting, and commented in response to reporters' questions that he would favor a postwar alliance of Great Britain and the United States—and possibly even the Soviet Union and China—to secure world peace. He remarked that he was not particularly worried that the United States would lose its sovereignty by participating in such an international arrangement, for it had had a de facto alliance with Great Britain since 1812 without compromising its independence. Furthermore, Dewey called upon the party and the country as a whole to discourage rampant nationalism in the future. In the spirit of Dulles's "Six Pillars of Peace," he urged them to assume, in cooperation with other nations of the world, new obligations and responsibilities for a wider international exchange of goods and services, broader access to raw materials, and greater monetary and economic stability.[87]

Dewey's suggestion of an Anglo-American alliance had an "electric effect" upon the Mackinac Conference, according to one observer who considered it an obvious blow to the party's old-time isolationists and a sign that Dewey had definitely moved into the "Willkie class of advanced Republican thinkers on international affairs."[88] Indeed, the old guard had expected more trouble from Willkie supporters than from Dewey. "Tom Dewey Goes Anti-American," a *Chicago Tribune* headline announced the next day, and the editorial beneath it condemned his alliance proposal.[89] Opposition to Dewey's suggestion also followed quickly from

Republicans attending the conference. Senator Taft, for example, immediately objected to it, recalling to reporters his own previously announced position against such alliances. Governor Bricker of Ohio said
that he was in favor of closer American-British cooperation after the war
but shied away from committing himself to anything like the military
alliance Dewey had suggested. Bricker contended that American sovereignty should be maintained along with complete freedom of action and
that the conference should emphasize the home front in its postwar
deliberations.[90]

On the other hand, governors Earl Warren of California and Raymond
Baldwin of Connecticut were receptive to Dewey's proposal. Warren, who
favored a pledge of military force in any pledge of cooperation for peace,
suggested adding assurances that the peace-keeping function would not
be restricted to the United States and Great Britain alone. Baldwin, observing that the United States would come out of the war the most powerful nation on earth, argued that Americans should maintain this commanding
position in order to prevent the growth of hostile, aggressive powers. The
United States should continue to play a role in world affairs consistent
with its military and economic strength, he believed, as well as with American ideas of liberty.

Dewey's alliance proposal, however, was more an off-hand, attention-
getting comment than a serious attempt to disrupt the conference.
Prompted initially by leading questions from reporters and perhaps by
his own increasing aspirations for the presidency, Dewey's statement was
blown out of proportion by the press in a search for good copy—and for
the controversy of which it is often made—from what otherwise promised to be a rather dull meeting. Given his pre-Mackinac cooperation with
party leaders like Vandenberg in drafting a postwar resolution, Dewey
hardly seems likely to have intended the results that followed his press
conference. Moreover, in response to further questioning by newsmen,
he refused to insist on any provision for an Anglo-American alliance in
the Mackinac resolution.[91]

The Dewey proposal, while delighting reporters, may have surprised
and upset party leaders at the council meeting initially, but not for
long. It soon seemed minor in comparison to the shock waves reported
on the day the conference began when governors Baldwin and Warren,
among others, demanded that the council adopt a stronger declaration on foreign policy than the one being offered, in a further semblance of harmony, by Representative Eaton on behalf of Senator
Vandenberg. Baldwin called for a statement advocating a council of
nations, a world court, and international military collaboration after
the war; in substance, he was calling for adoption of Senator Austin's

resolution. Austin himself was disturbed by what he considered an "attempt to keep [the] isolation position" at the conference. He threatened to file a minority report if his views and those of the dissatisfied governors were not accommodated.[92]

With reports of an internationalist and a governors' revolt brewing in the press, Senator Vandenberg, as chairman of the committee set up to write a foreign policy statement for the council, moved to avert the danger to his and Eaton's resolution and to the unity of the conference. He opened the sessions of the committee—which included, in addition to himself, Austin, and Eaton, Representative Frances P. Bolton of Ohio, and governors Dwight H. Green of Illinois and Edward Martin of Pennsylvania—not only to the dissident governors but to any other council members who might want to attend. Furthermore, Vandenberg saw to it that the record of these sessions reflected the committee's having received the recommendations of Republicans outside the council like former President Hoover and the prominent isolationist Reverend Gerald L.K. Smith.[93] The move seemed an impressive conciliatory gesture as well as a concession to Austin and the governors. In the end, however, it was also highly productive of Vandenberg's, and Spangler's, original objectives.

On Wednesday, September 8, the full Post-War Advisory Council approved a declaration on postwar foreign policy unanimously. While incorporating large as well as significant sections of Austin's draft into the one presented by Eaton and Vandenberg, it was by no means a surrender to the internationalists' views. The statement called for "responsible participation by the United States in postwar cooperative organization among sovereign nations to prevent military aggression and to attain permanent peace with organized justice in a free world." Through Austin's efforts, the phrase "cooperative organization" had been substituted for "postwar cooperation" in the original Vandenberg draft and the word "organized" had been inserted before "justice." Gone was the phrase "by any necessary means" after the word "prevent" in Vandenberg's version; instead, following its call for "prosecution of the war by a united nation to conclusive victory over all our enemies," Austin's more specific provision of means now appeared:

    (a) Disarmament and disorganization of the armed forces of the Axis;

    (b) Disqualification of the Axis to construct facilities for the manufacture of the implements of war;

    (c) Permanent maintenance of trained and well-equipped armed forces at home.[94]

Austin proclaimed these changes a triumph and considered that a major step had been taken in changing the "weasel-worded" phrases "postwar cooperation" and "peace with justice" to "postwar cooperative organization" and "organized justice." The last phrase provided for a world court, he contended, and the call for disarmament and permanent maintenance of armed forces, for the necessary deterrence against future aggression. A "switch-over from isolationism, or nationalism, to a constructive forward-moving world program" had been made with the declaration, Austin believed, but only after much debate, "hours of fighting and a threat by me to make a minority report."[95]

Considerable doubt, however, must be cast on Austin's conclusions. The permanent maintenance of armed forces "at home" was not a proposition to which many isolationists, or nationalists, would object; it was the permanent use of these forces abroad or in an international police force, as contemplated by the B_2H_2 resolution, which bothered them. Futhermore, as mentioned earlier, Vandenberg had already agreed with Dewey before the conference on inserting the word "organized" before "postwar cooperation." It was a comparatively short step from there to including it in the phrases "cooperative organization" and "organized justice." Vandenberg continued to use "postwar cooperation" in referring to the document later, and Austin himself admitted that the "gain made in getting an agreement upon 'organized Justice' did not represent a change in views of those who would not agree on the express provision for a World Court."[96] The essential magic of the word "organize," which Vandenberg had called to Dewey's attention before the conference, had been preserved. Furthermore, it continued to cast its spell over Austin and many of his internationalist colleagues.

When Governor Baldwin asked Vandenberg what the phrase "cooperative organization" might mean, noting that the members of the Post-War Advisory Council as well as Republicans in general would probably be asked that question, Vandenberg replied, "Governor Baldwin, I think it has to stand for itself." He did not believe, he added, that it was "possible to define the phrase" beyond the general objective of "supporting and sustaining any international effort to achieve the aims for which we are fighting, in the ultimate peace." Baldwin pressed Vandenberg further, asking him whether the phrase meant that Republicans as a party believed that the United States should join some form of world organization to establish peace and to advance commerce. Vandenberg's answer was again noncommittal:

> I think you are injecting something—some specifications which I might ultimat[e]ly agree to but which I am not yet prepared to fully

arpove [sic]. I think it means that—I know it means that we are prepared with open minds and with open hearts to proceed with any
ultimate discussion which contemplates the closest possible cooperation, cooperative action, thorugh [sic] organized means to make
permanent the objectives for which we fight. Now, I don't believe
I can go any further than that in detail at the present time and I
don't believe America can.

Baldwin replied that he was inclined to agree with Vandenberg.[97]

Despite Austin's rather lengthy consideration of the subject in his
draft, the Mackinac Declaration made no express reference to the issue of "sovereignty." Vandenberg assured one of the governors that, after "a very long and interesting and significant discussion over the question," the committee had concluded "that it is an act of sovereignty to
yield a portion of your sovereignty . . . if . . . you think you ought to
do it."[98] The document itself, however, employed Austin's language to
proclaim that, should there be a conflict between the "vital interests of
the nation" and "international developments," the United States should
then "adhere to the policy which will preserve its constitutionalism as
expressed in the Declaration of Independence, the Constitution itself,
and the Bill of Rights, as administered through our Republican form of
government. Constitutionalism should be adhered to in determining the
substance of our policies and shall be followed in ways and means of
making international commitments." Vandenberg's phrase "sovereign
nations" was left to stand unqualified.[99]

The committee overrode by vote any mention in the document of
tariff and exchange policies, access to raw materials, postwar economic
assistance to other nations, or the like in Austin's draft. He was satisfied
with that determination, however, contenting himself with the following
statement from the Vandenberg draft which appeared at the outset of
the declaration: "a specific program must be evolved in the months to
come, as events and relations unfold."[100] This followed an explanation
that since, at that time, no one knew what situation might obtain at the
war's end, "a detailed program . . . would be impractical, and specific
commitments by this Council, by the Republican Party, or by the nation, would be unwise." In the end, the statement finished as it had begun, with language from the Vandenberg-Eaton draft. It called upon
Americans to adhere to its principles and to abjure "domestic partisan
controversy and political bitterness."[101]

The Mackinac Declaration, as it came to be called, represented a compromise between isolationists and internationalists within the Republican party. It was that "common" or "middle ground" for which Spangler

and Vandenberg in their preconference efforts and the party as a whole in its National Committee resolutions of 1942 had been groping. In summarizing the work of his committee at Mackinac, Vandenberg explained that it had "put down in black and white, that basic truth that Americans can constructively contemplate their world duties without sacrificing their American allegiance."[102] The document itself carefully balanced the different versions of this "truth"; it captured and held them in suspended animation, with the balance tipping slightly in favor of the isolationists. The important point was, however, as Vandenberg later remarked, that neither side in the isolationist-internationalist controversy "got plowed under" at Mackinac.[103]

"The soundness of the Mackinac Charter," Austin wrote Spangler shortly after the meeting, "impresses me more as it matures."[104] Dewey, commending both Austin and Vandenberg for their work on the foreign policy committee, remarked that the results were so gratifying that the long trip to Mackinac and the long hours spent there had been worthwhile in every way.[105] Elsewhere within the party, Willkie and his associates commented favorably upon the declaration. While they were not necessarily enthusiastic about it, they nevertheless seemed to think, as Willkie put it, that it was "a step in the right direction."[106] Deneen Watson approved the foreign policy statement, considered it a repudiation of isolationism by the party, and claimed a victory because "that overworked word 'cooperation'" had been gotten rid of.[107] Shortly after the conference, in fact, Watson dissolved his Postwar Policy Association, declaring that the new resolution had fulfilled the group's initial purpose of persuading the Republican party to change its course in foreign affairs.

On the other side of the isolationist-internationalist divide, Senator Taft was equally impressed. Taking issue with a reporter's claim that an internationalist ultimatum on the foreign policy declaration had been issued to the "party group from Washington" by the governors attending the Mackinac Conference, Taft contended that "no such ultimatum was given or even intimated." Most of the language that had been added to Vandenberg's original draft made the declaration "less international rather than more so."[108] Other isolationist participants in the conference agreed. Congressmen Daniel A. Reed of New York and Roy O. Woodruff of Michigan, both members of the Post-War Advisory Council, as well as Representative Clare E. Hoffman of Michigan, who had attended the council's meeting in his home state and communicated his views to the committee on foreign policy, all proclaimed themselves satisfied as "America Firsters" with the statement.[109] Another such America Firster, Colonel Robert McCormick, also nodded in favor of the declaration; he much preferred it to Dewey's suggestion of an alliance between Great Britain and the United States, he indicated, or to anything smacking of Willkie's views on foreign policy. McCormick's *Chicago Tribune* hailed Mackinac's call for "responsible participation by the United States in postwar cooperative organization among sovereign nations" as visualizing "the America of the nationalist Americans."[110]

In other areas of public opinion, according to an analysis by the administration, the view that the Mackinac Declaration "was a straddle and was meant to mean all things to all men" oscillated with the opinion that "it showed substantial progress for a party in which isolationist sentiment had traditionally played such a powerful role."[111] Within the administration and among its supporters, reactions were similarly mixed. Vice-President Wallace "belittled" the meaning of the declaration, and the *New Republic* expressed deep-seated suspicion that the Republican leadership had not been converted at all to positive policies in behalf of effective international cooperation.[112] President Roosevelt was noncommittal about the declaration's passage, but Secretary of State Hull was delighted; in a speech delivered one week after the Mackinac Conference, he interpreted its results as evidence of Republican willingness to join with the administration in removing the issue of international organization from partisan controversy.[113] "The most general view," wrote one administration official of the reaction to the Mackinac Conference in Washington and in the country at large, "particularly among informed observers, was that Republican leaders at Mackinac, impressed by the weight of public opinion and spurred by determined elements particularly among the forward-looking governors, wished to register the party's break with isolationism and to advocate United States participation in some form of international organization for peace."[114]

On the whole, the Mackinac Conference, as one recent analyst has concluded, "was a major triumph for the Republican party."[115] This was not, however, as that analyst and others have believed, because Republicans had committed themselves to anything definite in regard to either postwar foreign policy or postwar international organization. One of the governors attending the conference, Arthur B. Langlie of Washington, described the foreign policy declaration rather well as "an elastic, and an elastic can stretch both ways."[116] The declaration was conditioned by future events, and there was still a substantial struggle going on within the party to determine which of its leaders—presidential or congressional, isolationist or internationalist—would gain the right to interpret those events for the party as a whole. In truth, the declaration differed little from the party's promise of "an international association . . . based upon international justice" in its 1920 platform.[117] Like that pledge, the declaration would become whatever the desire for political success might dictate.

The Mackinac Conference was a triumph for Republicans because it prevented an all-out war within the party over the issue of postwar international organization and promised, through its declaration on foreign policy, to continue in 1944 the electoral successes enjoyed in 1942. In addition to having forged an agreement for a cease-fire on foreign policy, the conference itself had resulted in some significant by-products. As Spangler noted afterwards, it had brought a "greater awareness" among party leaders from all sections of the country of their fellow leaders elsewhere, "literally dozens of new acquaintances" having sprung up "in place of hitherto 'correspondence acquaintances'"; it had helped "fuse" Republican leadership "into a more homogeneous, closely-knit group, working for common aims throughout the nation," and it had thus taken "a step toward party cohesion" that would make the party stronger "in the campaign ahead."[118] Nine months before the national party convention, moreover, the conference had begun laying the foundations of the 1944 Republican platform. Toward this end, it extended the life of Vandenberg's foreign policy committee and added to it seven others dealing with domestic problems, instructing all of them to draft detailed plans in the coming months for the Resolutions Committee of the convention.[119] Such features of the Mackinac Conference also help to explain the wholehearted endorsement of its work by so many different Republicans and, ultimately, by the G.O.P. members of Congress and the full National Committee.[120]

Equally important in explaining such endorsements, however, was the widespread conviction among party members that the Mackinac Declaration on foreign policy had laid to rest politically for the first time since Pearl Harbor the specter of Republican responsibility for the defeat of Woodrow Wilson's League of Nations and, by extension, for the outbreak of World War II. The party's leaders at Mackinac had helped foster this conviction despite, or perhaps because of, their resolution's ambiguity in regard to postwar commitments. In fact, Republicans had even gone a step further politically than their Democratic rivals by being the first of the two parties on record with at least some kind of official statement concerning postwar organization.

Spangler and Vandenberg were keenly aware of this last fruit of their labors over the conference. With the declaration on foreign policy, they hoped to maintain in the months of campaigning ahead if not the advantage, at least the absence of disadvantage for the party on the postwar issue. Vandenberg now proclaimed that "partisan politics, as such, should stop at the water's edge." He quickly associated the Mackinac Charter, as he dubbed the foreign policy declaration, "with precisely the same devoted hope . . . that partisan bitterness may be eliminated from foreign policy discussions" which, he noted, Secretary Hull had expressed in connection with the conference's results.[121] Senator Taft carried this hope a step further. As the chairman of a committee on domestic policy at Mackinac analogous to Vandenberg's committee on foreign policy, Taft had helped produce another unanimously accepted resolution which, not surprisingly, had assailed the New Deal for practicing unlimited government spending and for trying to "socialize" American business and agriculture. He now predicted that domestic problems would prove more important than international issues in the 1944 campaign.[122]

The significance of the Mackinac Declaration on foreign policy, therefore, was primarily political. Its obvious advantages in terms of party unity and electoral appeal go a long way toward explaining its adoption by the Post-War Advisory Council unanimously. The declaration was above all a political document designed by its authors, especially Vandenberg, to achieve the semblance of political unity on foreign policy and was accepted by its potential critics within the Republican party because they were, on the whole, party members first and world statesmen or stateswomen afterwards. Isolationists and internationalists, congressional as well as presidential Republicans saw in the ambiguous resolution a political position with which they could live, temporarily at least, without sacrificing too noticeably either principles or votes. Thus they were quick to proclaim the Mackinac Declaration a breakthrough in foreign policy for the party and the country as a whole. The evident political advantages of the declaration also account for its nearly unanimous, much relieved reception by party members outside the Post-War Advisory Council following the conference.

Vandenberg, of course, denied any such conclusions. Following the conference, he asserted "with total truth, that this Mackinac Charter, in respect to foreign policy, was framed with complete disregard for *partisan considerations*."[123] There was less than truth, however, in Vandenberg's assertion. By his own admission prior to the conference, he was going there in hopes of using "the occasion to differentiate between Republican and New Deal foreign policy. . . . We *must* beat the 4th Term," he had asserted. "It is the 'last roundup' for the American way of life. I do not believe we can beat it if we split the Party (and its Jeffersonian Democratic Allies) by going either to an isolationist extreme or to an internationalist extreme."[124]

Following the conference, moreover, Vandenberg himself provided an object lesson in how the Mackinac Declaration could and would be used in future political battles by Republicans. To a critic who worried about possible qualifications on sovereignty in the resolution, he replied that the United States could participate in the postwar "cooperations" envisioned by the declaration "*without* yielding its basic self-determina-

tion and its basic independence and its essential sovereignty and a vigilant protection of American institutions and American interests. If . . .
this proves to be satisfactory to . . . 'the Willkieites' then we have a
united Party and we can win the next election." But more than this on
the subject of sovereignty Vandenberg did not want or have to say. There
were definite limits to his own acceptance of any specific commitment in
the Mackinac Declaration, just as there were limits built into the declaration
itself. Given these limits, Vandenberg had only to explain after the conference that he did not "care to engage in any public discussion of the matter"
because he was "completely satisfied with the well-nigh universal editorial
approval of the Mackinac Charter by practically all of the American press
regardless of its pre-Pearl Harbor attitude."[125]

On the other hand, with critics urging a greater degree of Republican
commitment to postwar world order, Vandenberg could still argue that
"the American people generally" would "accept the responsibilities of
reasonable post-war cooperation" but would "reject the Henry Wallace
viewpoint which in its latest edition seems to say that we cannot have
high living standards and abundant resources in America unless the rest
of the world enjoy similar standards and resources; that if we attempt
to maintain our superior economic position, the rest of the world will
band together and wage war against us." The Mackinac resolution had
been designed for and had appealed to these Americans, he maintained;
therefore, it deserved the support of all Republicans.[126]

Before the Mackinac Conference had adjourned, the members of the
Post-War Advisory Council had adopted yet another resolution unanimously, by a standing vote. The resolution expressed to Spangler the
council's "appreciation of his vision, initiative and courage in the formation of the Council, his care and labor in the making of plans and
preparations required for the holding of this conference, and his skill
in connection with the conduct of its business."[127] Certainly the party
chairman as well as Senator Austin, who had claimed a victory himself
at the conference, deserved credit for the political success achieved there.
Both Governor Dewey and Senator Taft attested to the importance of
Austin's role in drafting the declaration on foreign policy. They, however, reserved the lion's share of their praise for Senator Vandenberg
and his efforts at conciliation and compromise both on the foreign policy committee and before the council.[128]

Of his role in the Mackinac Conference, Vandenberg was as self-
congratulatory as he was proud. "I know that *you* want a unified
American 'foreign policy,' " he wrote a newfound associate in that endeavor, Henry Luce, the Republican internationalist publisher of *Time-
Life*, "and I continue to believe that when I succeeded in putting forty-

nine prima donnas together at Mackinac I discovered the necessary formula. Furthermore, I think it is an utterly *sound* formula."[129] Vandenberg had in fact succeeded at Mackinac in extending his growing influence on matters of foreign policy from the congressional wing of the party to the presidential. His own willingness to compromise helped him do so, to be sure. More important, however, was the willingness of others to compromise with him and to begin looking to him as one Republican leader who could be trusted from now on to blunt the edges of politically damaging controversies. He could be relied upon in the future to devise formulae for agreement on foreign policy that would be politically desirable as well as safe.

Vandenberg, moreover, succeeded in increasing his influence among presidential Republicans at Mackinac by putting his already increasing influence in Congress to maximum advantage. He did not hesitate, for example, in one of his interchanges with Governor Baldwin during the conference, to argue that during the past eight months, "in intimate consultation not only with the leaders of our own country[,] and I am speaking of the administration, speaking of the State Department, but in conversations with the leaders of our responsible allies, we have been constantly warned that it would be inadvisable, it would be dangerous, it might even threaten to disunite the war effort, if we sought to set down any details respecting our post war commitments."[130]

After Mackinac, for a time, neither Vandenberg nor his fellow Republicans, whether in the congressional or the presidential wings of the party, had to remain entirely on the defensive in regard to those commitments. They could point to the Mackinac Declaration as evidence of the party's desire to undertake them, provided they were sufficiently defined in terms of basic American interests and procedures. Republicans were able in fact to bask in the glow of a considerable political triumph, for the declaration on foreign policy had been painstakingly designed for them to be able to do so. No one was more responsible for that design nor more deserving of credit for its success than the irrepressible senator from Michigan.

CONGRESSIONAL
6 REPUBLICANS
REDEVELOP MACKINAC

Following the summer recess, congressional Republicans reassembled on Capitol Hill in September and listened there to a report by senators Vandenberg and Austin on the foreign policy declaration successfully decided upon at Mackinac. What they heard seemed to promise even further success, for with the Mackinac Declaration's appearance in advance of an election year, the Republicans had stolen a march on their Democratic opponents in the ongoing battle of American politics. The declaration had launched a brief period of Republican initiative in foreign policy. And the party's members in Congress were among the first to demonstrate the political uses to which that initiative, as well as the new document itself, could be put.[1]

A prime reason for the Mackinac Declaration's immediate success lay in the strong public sentiment for some sort of national declaration of intent on postwar foreign policy. Such sentiment had been building throughout the summer of 1943, having developed in response to a campaign conducted on behalf of the B_2H_2 and Fulbright resolutions by internationalist congressmen during the congressional recess. According to the administration's own analysis, the public, while indicating a desire for "some kind of international organization for peace," did not favor a commitment by Americans to any specific form of organization or to the use of military power to maintain international security.[2] Such sentiments, of course, had not been obscured from Republican leaders as they drafted the resolution on postwar foreign policy for their party at Mackinac; the declaration adopted there fitted in nicely with prevailing public attitudes.

Coming as it did, in advance of any congressional resolutions on postwar foreign policy or any specific indication by the administration of its objectives in that area, the Mackinac Declaration put the Democrats on the defensive. Secretary of State Hull himself attempted to remedy this

situation in his nationwide radio address shortly after the Republican conference. In the talk, Hull strove to outline the administration's approach
to the problem of postwar world order, but his remarks served more to
confirm than to dispel the impression of an administration defensiveness
in the matter. His lack of specificity in enunciating six moral principles
to govern the future peace disappointed leading internationalists. By comparison with Hull's presentation, the Mackinac Declaration seemed certainly no more, and possibly even less, evasive. Hull may in fact have encouraged a belief in the similarity of Republican and administration views
by calling in his talk for a nonpartisan approach to the problem of a future peace—a call, it will be remembered, which Vandenberg had quickly
seconded.[3]

If Hull or Vandenberg did not encourage this belief, then perhaps the
diversity of Republican responses to Hull's speech did. Another measure
of the Mackinac Declaration's political success was that Republicans with
widely varying positions on foreign policy could now attack such pronouncements by the administration on different fronts, yet retreat in
common to the Mackinac resolution to justify their party's position on
international organization. The isolationist *Chicago Tribune*, for example,
charged that Hull went too far in his reference to the role of force in the
postwar period and interpreted his address as a declaration of the administration's desire for an international army and a world government after
the war. The *Tribune* preferred the Mackinac resolution, which, it declared,
would preserve American sovereignty and permit Congress alone to determine when Americans were to be sent into battle.[4] The internationalist *New York Herald-Tribune*, on the other hand, rejected the "whole
system of ideas" contained in Hull's talk as being too antiquated for the
mid-twentieth century and demanded a broader commitment to the
concept of international organization; at the same time, however, it was
highly enthusiastic about the Mackinac Declaration.[5]

Further estimates of public opinion in September 1943 had indicated
widespread support for nonpartisan approaches to foreign policy, interest in the bipartisan sponsorship of the B_2H_2 resolution in the Senate, and
approval of the campaign conducted in its behalf by members of both
parties throughout the summer.[6] What had developed most specifically
during the summer of 1943 was a desire on the part of the public at large
for some sort of bipartisan statement by Congress pledging that the United
States would participate in a postwar international organization. A considerable amount of sentiment appeared to favor the Fulbright resolution in the House for this purpose over the B_2H_2 resolution in the Senate.
The former, in calling for "the creation of appropriate international
machinery with power adequate to establish and to maintain a just and

lasting peace among nations of the world," had omitted any reference to a postwar international police force; it appeared, therefore, to stand the best chance for immediate passage.

Republican opposition to the measure, however, readily in evidence before the summer recess, still remained in the fall, even after the Mackinac Conference. When the majority leader of the House, John W. McCormack of Massachusetts, called for suspension of that body's rules to expedite passage of the Fulbright resolution, representatives Fish and Reed of New York and a number of other isolationist Republicans objected. Fish worried that "secret commitments" would be entered into by way of the resolution and that Congress would be bypassed, while Reed demanded an opportunity to amend it in order to safeguard American sovereignty in the postwar period.[7] Congressman Maas of Minnesota insisted that "the world cooperate from now on with the United States" and that this country be considered the "senior partner" in that cooperation.[8] Congresswoman Jessie Sumner from *Chicago Tribune* country in Illinois charged that the Fulbright resolution was "the most dangerous bill ever presented to an American Congress" and contended that its language furnished internationalists with all the power they required to "rob Americans of their independence."[9] Even Representative James W. Wadsworth, Jr., of New York, one of the original supporters of the measure in the spring, felt obliged to justify his support for it in the fall in distinctively nationalist terms. "Let us be strong and patient and decent," Wadsworth enjoined his colleagues, "and, again, let us be strong."[10]

In view of the gathering Republican storm of protest, Democratic Representative Sol Bloom, chairman of the House Foreign Affairs Committee, moved to amend the Fulbright resolution to read that the United States favored participation in "appropriate international machinery" for peace "through its constitutional processes."[11] Bloom had been under pressure to do so not only from Republican members of his committee but also from House Minority Leader Martin. Martin, in turn, had been urged by Senator Vandenberg to hold out for inclusion of "sovereignty" and of "constitutional processes" in the measure before passage. In the end, however, both Martin and Vandenberg had settled for the last term, and Bloom, by wording his amendment so obviously to resemble the recently approved Mackinac Declaration, insured substantial Republican support for passage of the resolution.[12]

Hamilton Fish, the ranking minority member of the Foreign Affairs Committee, supported the amended version and another leading Republican on the committee, John Vorys, joined him in defending it on the floor of the House. Speaking to the nationalistic sentiments lying behind Republican opposition to the Fulbright resolution, Vorys noted an advantage in approving it as amended; "by wise participation in appropriate international machinery for peace," he contended, "we will regain more . . . sovereignty than we will lose."[13] Earlier, he had argued that the resolution was "not just a pious generality" or the "blueprint of a supergovernment," that it was neither "a commitment" nor "a pledge," but "merely a statement of congressional preference in postwar foreign policies."[14] Another prominent Republican on the committee and a veteran of Mackinac, Representative Eaton, also urged fellow Republicans to approve the measure. Eaton added to the thrust of Vorys's argument by declaring the resolution "in full accord, so far as it goes, with the policy we devised at Mackinac Island."[15]

When the Fulbright resolution passed the House by a vote of 360 to 29 on September 21, scarcely two weeks after the adoption of the Mackinac Declaration, 26 Republicans remained in opposition to it.[16] The resemblance of the resolution in the end to the document produced at Mackinac undoubtedly helped account for the great majority of Republicans, including arch-isolationists like Fish, who voted for it. However, the preoccupation with potential threats to American nationalism in debate on the resolution, the attention drawn to the limited nature of its commitments, and the number of those who still opposed it, all tended to indicate that any changes in congressional Republican attitudes toward postwar organization following the Mackinac Conference were probably more apparent than real.

Following passage of the Fulbright resolution in the House and intimations that the Senate might simply concur, Tom Connally, Chairman of the Foreign Relations Committee, decided to take the matter of a Senate resolution on international organization into his own hands. Connally was determined that passage of the House Resolution would not preempt the Senate's prerogatives in foreign affairs.[17] As an alternative to either the Fulbright measure in the House or to the B_2H_2 resolution in the Senate (which had originated outside of his committee, gone "too far" for him, and been bottled up since spring in the special subcommittee that he had appointed to deal with such measures), Connally proposed a new resolution, similar to the Vandenberg-White proposal and the Mackinac Declaration. For Republicans, following promptings by Vandenberg again, Connally's resolution incorporated the key terms "sovereign nations" and "constitutional processes" in its call for the establishment and maintenance of international authority with power to prevent aggression and preserve world peace. Vandenberg had reportedly served notice on Connally that he would fight any resolution which did not include a reference to sovereignty and that 30 of 38 senators whom he had polled would go down the line with him.[18]

The Connally resolution was attacked from both sides of the isolationist-internationalist spectrum. The sponsors of the B_2H_2 resolution and internationalist Senators Austin and Claude Pepper, a Florida Democrat, opposed Connally's resolution for being too weak. They wanted to amend the text to stipulate that the United States would join "an international organization" (instead of Connally's less definite "international authority") which would have "authority to settle international disputes peacefully, and . . . power, including military force, to suppress military aggression and to preserve the peace of the world."[19] Despite the advance work by Vandenberg, Republican isolationists led by Senator Danaher of Connecticut also opposed the resolution as it stood. Envisioning a possibility that the administration might construe it to justify joining an international organization by executive agreement (the means it had sought to employ in the case of UNRRA the preceding spring), the isolationists supported an amendment to the resolution offered by Senator Raymond E. Willis of Indiana which specified that any adherence to an international organization must be approved by a two-thirds (treaty) vote of the Senate. The amendment also aimed a blow at suggestions, based on the Senate's performance in 1919 and 1920, that the two-thirds rule for treaty ratifications might be abolished.[20]

One of the early hopes behind Connally's resolution in the Senate had been to have it passed before Secretary of State Hull departed for a conference of foreign ministers from the United States, Great Britain, and the Soviet Union in Moscow in the fall of 1943. The hope had been to provide Hull, in advance of his negotiations with the Allies and in contrast to 1919, with an obvious symbol of the Senate's support for an international organization. Debate on the resolution continued, however, throughout Hull's stay in Moscow. In the end, the secretary of state succeeded in persuading the British and the Russians to agree on the matter before Connally or Vandenberg, who supported Connally in return for his acceptance of Vandenberg's language, could convince the Senate.

With Hull's success in Moscow adding to the pressure at home for passage of some sort of Senate resolution, the section on postwar world organization from the Moscow Declaration—point number four to be exact—was incorporated into Connally's text. It called for recognition of "the necessity of establishing at the earliest practical date a general international organization, based on the principle of the sovereign equality of all peace-loving states, and open to membership by all such states, large and small, for the maintenance of international peace and security." This call satisfied internationalists like senators Austin, Pepper, and the B_2H_2 group, who, in a change of tactics soon after its announcement, had begun lobbying for its inclusion in the resolution in preference to their own amendments. Further amended to include the isolationists' call for an eventual treaty vote on the issue (the Willis amendment), Connally's resolution passed the Senate on November 5 by a vote of 85 to 5. Only three die-hard Republican isolationists—William Langer of North Dakota, Hiram Johnson of California, and Henrik Shipstead of Minnesota—opposed it. Others, including Nye, Brooks, Taft, and, of course, Vandenberg, voted for it.[21]

As in the case of the Fulbright resolution, however, one has to question the degree of commitment to postwar world order represented by Republican support for the Connally resolution. Many G.O.P. senators adhered to extremely limited interpretations of the resolution, undoubtedly voting for it because it omitted any mention of an international police force and contained reassuring references to "sovereignty" and "constitutional processes" taken from the Republican declaration at Mackinac. Senator Lodge, for example, who was soon to resign his seat for active duty in the army, stated: "If I thought this resolution were in any way tying the hands of the United States Government, the United States Senate, or the people of the United States, I would not vote for it." He favored "international cooperation to maintain peace between nations," Lodge added, but did not favor "having such cooperation perverted into a device to siphon off the power, prestige, and resources of the United States."[22] In voicing his approval of the Connally Resolution, Taft singled out its provision for a two-thirds vote of the Senate on a final peace treaty for praise and reiterated his belief in "the policy of America first." A policy insuring "freedom and peace for the United States," as opposed to "the purposes set forth in the Atlantic Charter," was still "the only proper basis for foreign policy" for Taft.[23] Indeed, there was more truth than humor in the question that President Roosevelt put to Connally while congratulating him on the resolution's passage, "why, oh why did you let Nye vote for it?"[24]

When Hull returned from the Moscow conference of foreign ministers, approval for the fruits of his labors there seemed well nigh complete. The public's confidence in the administration's postwar policies and hopes for an effective international organization to prevent future aggression reached a peak. Moreover, Republicans, in view of their party's performance at Mackinac and in connection with final approval of the Fulbright and Connally resolutions, were accorded a measure of credit for this development. Hull himself, in a speech to a joint session of Congress on his return from the Moscow conference, indirectly paid tribute to the G.O.P. by praising the "nonpartisan" approaches to foreign policy that he discerned in the large majorities by which both the House and the Senate had passed their respective postwar resolutions.[25]

With the Moscow Declaration and the passage of the Fulbright and

Connally resolutions, the administration and the Democrats evened the political score with the Republicans on foreign policy, ending the latter's brief period of initiative following Mackinac. Both parties had now responded in significant ways to a discernible sentiment in the country at large for some sort of international organization to keep peace which would not limit America's freedom of action unnecessarily. For both parties, the Moscow Declaration, followed by the Connally resolution, brought the issue of postwar organization temporarily under control and, for the first time in months, removed it from the spotlight of public attention.

Among Republicans in Congress, these developments fostered signs of harmony between isolationists and internationalists where controversy had reigned before. In the absence of Senator McNary, who was suffering from an illness that was soon to prove fatal, Senator White continued to act during the latter part of 1943 as minority leader of the Senate. Despite recurrent rumors following Mackinac that the isolationists were seeking to oust him, install Vandenberg in his place, and make Senator Taft Vandenberg's assistant, White was confirmed in his position when the Republican conference met in January 1944, with Taft making the motion to approve him. White in turn appointed Taft chairman of a committee "to review the need of the party with respect to further organization."[26] That committee ultimately recommended a form of organization for Republicans in the Senate when their numbers exceeded 30 which restored importance to the position of conference chairman (as opposed to that of floor leader), established a steering committee to formulate party policy on legislative issues, and prescribed the duties and procedures for selection of various party officials in order to dispel former controversies.[27]

The center of one such controversy the preceding year, Senator Austin, applied in February 1944 for a seat on the Senate Foreign Relations Committee that became available to Republicans upon the death of Democratic Senator Frederick Van Nuys of Indiana. Although Austin had collaborated with fellow internationalists to broaden the Connally resolution, he had also announced his intention to vote for the measure whether or not it incorporated the internationalists' amendments.[28] When he applied, therefore, to the Republican Committee on Committees headed by Senator Nye for the vacant Foreign Relations Committee seat, Austin received it, as Senator McNary had indicated he would the year before. Doubtless, his willingness to cooperate with the leadership on the Connally resolution (as well as to close ranks with Vandenberg at Mackinac)—his "natural loyalty"—had as much to do with his ease in obtaining the position as seniority or the absent floor leader's promises.[29]

The signs of ease and harmony, however, were deceptive. As evidenced by all the maneuvering required for approval of the Fulbright and Connally resolutions, neither the Mackinac nor Moscow declarations had removed the issue of postwar international organization very far from the arena of political controversy. In other areas of foreign policy, moreover, congressional Republicans in late 1943 and early 1944 continued to flex their partisan political muscle.

One issue which evoked this partisanship grew out of the secrecy surrounding certain decisions being made by President Roosevelt and Prime Minister Churchill at the Quebec Conference in August. Speculation among congressional Republicans had it that General Marshall had been chosen there to lead the forthcoming European invasion. With the possible exception of Secretary of State Hull, Marshall in the War Department was viewed by Republicans on Capitol Hill as the most completely trustworthy official serving in the Democratic administration. One motive hypothesized for his supposed removal from Washington sheds light upon the high degree of trust placed in him by Republicans as well as upon their continued criticism of the administration in foreign policy. It was widely rumored among congressional Republicans that in Allied strategy sessions for planning the future conduct of the war, Marshall was generally the one—in contrast to his malleable commander-in-chief—who resisted arguments favoring British positions and interests in the war and held consistently to a pro-American point of view. Marshall's presumed transfer to Europe ("because he stood up for our American rights"), Republicans now charged, was but another success for British over American interests.[30] Although Roosevelt in his report to Congress on the Quebec Conference defended the policy of secrecy on the basis of wartime necessity and General Marshall remained at his post in Washington, Republican apprehension over what was actually taking place during the president's conferences with Churchill and, later, Stalin, hardly diminished.[31]

Suspicion of America's two major allies, of course, had long been a key element in Republican congressional dissent on foreign policy. So great did it become toward the end of 1943, however, that the Speaker of the House himself, Sam Rayburn, thought it necessary to issue warnings against recurrent outbursts of anti-British and anti-Soviet criticism.[32] Fears concerning British gains at the expense of American interests vastly multiplied when, in the fall of 1943, five members of the Senate Military Affairs Committee, including Republicans Lodge of Massachusetts and Ralph O. Brewster of Maine, just back from a tour of the war's battlefronts, reported to Congress on the information and impressions which they had gathered. They confirmed charges that widespread waste and mismanagement of Lend-Lease funds were taking place among the Allies, especially the British. The senators accused Great

Britain of using Lend-Lease supplies to win friends for itself and of promoting its own policies at the expense of the United States in areas of the world which interested both, particularly distant oil-producing centers in the Middle and Far East. Brewster called for Senate investigations of Lend-Lease operations abroad as well as the ratio by which the war was depleting American versus British oil reserves.[33]

When Lend-Lease came up for renewal again in 1944, many Republicans were as vociferous in their criticisms of it as they had been before. Deprecating its results in the case of the British, some charged that Lend-Lease was saddling the economy of the United States with more debt than it was worth. In the end, however, both houses overwhelmingly approved renewal of the measure for one more year. As in 1943, Republicans who supported the bill did so for the most part because they understood Lend-Lease to be limited to items of wartime necessity and confined to the period of actual fighting. This understanding helps in part to explain why, for example, in the case of the Soviet Union, Senator Taft was to demand, ten days after the German surrender in 1945, immediate cessation of Lend-Lease to the Russians.[34]

The Soviet ally received its share of congressional Republican criticism also. In addition to a continuing anxiety over the Russians' form of government, Republican fears extended in late 1943 and early 1944 to their repeated demands for a second battlefront in Europe and to their general reliability as a partner of the West. The major Republican criticism of the U.S.S.R., however, related to its intentions regarding the smaller nations along its prewar borders. Sympathy for Finland (then at war with Soviets), the Baltic States, and Poland combined with fears of Russian postwar designs upon their territories to fill Republican ranks with mounting distrust of the Soviet Union.

In their concern for the fate of the Russians' neighbors, Republicans in the Senate had supported an amendment to the Connally resolution, sponsored by Southern Democratic Senator Robert R. Reynolds of North Carolina, calling for specific recognition of the independence and territorial integrity of subjugated nations after the war.[35] Vandenberg, whose constituency in Detroit alone was outranked in its number of ethnic Poles only by Chicago and Warsaw, proclaimed to the editor of an influential Polish-language daily in his state that

> It would be a travesty upon good faith if the victorious conclusion of the war should fail to be as faithful to the Free Polish Republic as were the crusaders who started this war on Poland's behalf. It would be a travesty if Poland did not emerge from this war in strength and integ-

rity and in greater security than ever. Furthermore, if the Atlantic Charter means *anything*, it *must* mean a new Poland when it says that there are to be "no territorial changes that do not accord with the freely expressed wishes of the peoples concerned"; and when it promises to "respect the right of all peoples to choose the form of Government under which they live"; and when it asserts that "sovereign rights and self-Government are to be restored to those who have been forcibly deprived of them."

Despite a prior agreement among the members of the Foreign Relations Committee that none of them would support amendments to the Connally resolution on the Senate floor, Vandenberg "broke away from the Committee in this one instance" and by his own account supported the unsuccessful Reynolds Amendment.[36]

Another member of the Foreign Relations Committee, Senator Robert LaFollette, refused to support the Connally resolution at all. LaFollette had informed Vandenberg, "with all due respect" for his and other committee members' work on the resolution, that "a great mistake" was being made in trying "to commit the United States to a future course in world relationship[s] when the Committee and the people of the United States are still in the dark as to the peace table demands and the post war policies of the other United Nations, including Great Britain, China and Russia."[37] Vandenberg acknowledged that the State Department was worried about Russia and fearful that a poor showing by the Senate on postwar collaboration might give the Russians an excuse to conclude a separate peace. In contrast to the Progressive isolationist LaFollette, however, the regular Republican Vandenberg went along with the resolution and urged others to do so as well, arguing that otherwise Roosevelt would blame his opponents on foreign policy for any Russian failure to cooperate.[38]

Following Hull's announcement of the Moscow Declaration, with its anticipation of increased Allied cooperation on postwar matters, public confidence in the U.S.S.R. had appeared to increase. Among Republicans, however, there was disappointment over the failure of the Moscow Conference to deal with the question of the Soviet Union's western boundaries.[39] Vandenberg remarked to his friend, the Polish editor, that he did "not like the implication when the Conference *did* deal with postwar Austria but left all of these other questions (including Poland) alone. The future is imponderable at the moment. All I can say is that the friends of Poland (among whom I want always to be vigorously enrolled) need to be constantly vigilant."[40] Troubled as always by the likelihood that wartime conferences were producing secret postwar deals, Republicans began to raise a cry, which became more and more familiar as the 1940s wore on, that the administration was handing over Central and Western Europe to the Allies, particularly the Russians, in order to satisfy its own dreams of postwar world order.

This dark impression appeared to be confirmed following the first meeting of the big three at Teheran in December 1943. In his report to the United States on that conference, President Roosevelt hinted that the major Allies themselves were going to be responsible for keeping the peace after the war. Roosevelt implied that he was taking a traditional balance-of-power approach to world peace—one which would have the world divided up into spheres of influence and regional alliances—rather than pursuing the ideal of universal equality among nations which many advocates of a postwar international organization had in mind. Internationalists as well as isolationists, therefore, quickly deplored the suggestion of great-power predominance in the postwar picture glimpsed from the president.[41]

Leading the attack among Republicans in Congress was Senator Taft. As indicated by his chairmanship of the committee on Republican postwar domestic policy at Mackinac—the counterpart to Vandenberg's committee on foreign policy—and by his frequent assertion that domestic issues ought to dominate the 1944 campaign, Taft was now increasingly identified among his congressional colleagues with leadership of the party on domestic affairs.[42] In late 1943 and early 1944, however, he came to the fore again, as he had in 1942, as a critic of the nation's foreign policy, particularly of the president's secret dealings at his wartime conferences with Churchill and Stalin. Taft categorically rejected any alliances that might be involved in Roosevelt's agreements at Teheran, just as he had rejected Dewey's suggestion of an Anglo-American alliance at Mackinac. He also opposed plans for a world government after the war, for American control of the globe through economic generosity, or for establishment of the four freedoms in the Atlantic Charter. Steadfastly refusing to recognize any irrevocable national commitment by the United States to such Roosevelt-inspired pronouncements as the Charter, Taft looked forward to a future Republican administration which would structure its own plans and priorities in foreign affairs.[43]

Personally, Taft favored international collaboration for peace along the lines of the League of Nations and even suggested rejuvenating that organization for the task. Like his father (the former president and chief justice, William Howard Taft) before him during World War I, he urged establishment of an international law that would govern all nations, be adjudicated by a world court, and find enforcement in a climate of opinion backed by military power only when necessary. He wanted to delay revival of the League, however, and defer the entry of the United States into it until the war's end, when the conditions of a future peace treaty might be better known.[44] In this desire, Taft also resembled his Republican predecessors in the Senate of some 20 years before. Finally, he supported the proposals of former President Hoover and Hugh Gibson in their *Problems of Lasting Peace* but failed to see "much use in the Republican Party taking any position very different from that of the Mackinac Resolution."[45]

With Senator Taft in the vanguard, criticism of the administration and its Allies soared to new heights after the Teheran conference, seriously threatening hopes for further cooperation between Democrats and Republicans on foreign policy. In the House, G.O.P. Representative Jessie Sumner of Illinois, whom Assistant Secretary of State Dean Acheson later referred to as "the worst of the rabble rousing isolationists of *Chicago Tribune* fame," urged that the anticipated invasion of the European mainland be postponed. Distressed by the failure of the Moscow Conference to define postwar national boundaries, particularly those of the U.S.S.R., she proposed, as Senator Albert B. Chandler had the year before, that the United States begin concentrating on the war in the Pacific against Japan and introduced two resolutions in the House to this effect.[46] In a similarly nationalistic vein, Republican Alexander Wiley followed up these proposals in the Senate by advocating that the United States resolve before the war's end to keep certain Pacific territories for itself.[47]

Congressman Fish weighed in on the side of these sentiments by raising once again the charge that the administration was trying to stifle General MacArthur. He proclaimed to the House in March that "the wolf pack of communistic smearers and radical New Deal and fellow traveler stooges" were out "gunning" for MacArthur. He was the country's "greatest fighting general," Fish declared, "the best-known and the best-loved officer in our armed forces." "With little to fight with," MacArthur had been winning "victory after victory over the Japs while our invasion troops have been bogged down in Italy for 6 months."[48] Such changes, of course, also reflected continuing Republican concern over the fate of China and the Far East, a concern based in part on a fear that the British (as well as the communists) would use American preoccupation with the European invasion to advance their own interests in the Orient.

Congressional Republicans moved, furthermore, to keep charges of administration responsibility for Pearl Harbor alive and bring them to trial before the 1944 elections. Representative Dewey Short introduced resolutions in the House calling for extension of any statute of limitations on the prosecution of civilian and military officials responsible for the "catastrophe of December 7, 1941." Hoping to force the issue before the elections, he demanded that Secretary of War Stimson and Secretary of the Navy Knox promptly instigate court martial proceedings against the military officials involved.[49] The resolution embodying this demand passed the House by a vote of 305-35, with Republicans virtually unanimous in their support of it. In the end, however, a Senate amendment to the resolution prevailed, providing that an investigation of the mishap take place before any prosecutions. Thus the issue was effectively postponed until after the 1944 elections.[50]

With regard to those elections themselves, it was widely conceded among Republicans that Roosevelt would run for a fourth term and that he would do so largely on the basis of his knowledge and experience as wartime commander-in-chief, the presumed danger of changing captains in midstream, and the as yet unannounced plans of his administration for seeing the nation through to victory and lasting world peace.[51] The advantages inherent in the president's position were obvious. Even Taft acknowledged them and appreciated the dangers implicit in Republican attacks on administration foreign policy. "The difficulty is," he wrote in April 1944,

> that we still have seven months before the elections. Anything may happen. Roosevelt knows the facts and can guide and change his policy to a considerable extent. If we make an attack upon any particular feature of the policy, he can make some announcement that will cut the ground out from under our feet. Churchill and Stalin will probably cooperate with him to help him there.

In explaining his own attacks on Roosevelt's foreign policy, Taft contended that individual representatives of the party could voice criticism, and he intended to do so, but that the party as a whole could "well afford to wait until after the Convention." By that time there would probably be a second front, he argued, and Republicans could judge its effect. Then they could decide "just how strong" they could afford to be in their criticism and, "without stirring up popular disapproval," could "pick out the weak points in the foreign policy and go to town."[52]

Not all congressional Republicans, however, proposed to deal with the administration along the lines of Senator Taft, by simply hanging back and attacking whenever the coast seemed clear. Vandenberg, in particular, held a different view. Both before and after the Mackinac Conference, he had been suggesting to his G.O.P. colleagues that a cautious bipartisan approach to foreign policy, one aimed at neutralizing the administration's presumed advantages in this area, would be the most effective policy the party could pursue. This suggestion had been part of Vandenberg's unsuccessful attempt to obtain Democratic cosponsorship of his alternative to the $B_2 H_2$ resolution, as well as of his persistent demands for increased consultation with the administration. The favorable public reaction to bipartisanship aroused by the B_2H_2 proposal, moreover, had led him to portray the Mackinac Declaration, and Secretary Hull's recognition of it following the conference, in the same light.

Like Senator Taft, Vandenberg was apprehensive about the element of secrecy involved in the wartime conferences, remarking on one occasion: "None of us knows what President Roosevelt's commitments on our behalf have been at Quebec and Moscow and Teheran. We can guess—but we do not know."[53] In the case of Pearl Harbor, he "felt that the postponement of the court martial trials . . . was not unrelated to a reluctance on the part of the Administration to have the basic record laid bare," and he speculated that the reason for this was "that the Administration dare not face these trials prior to Armistice (and—shall we say—prior to next November)." Like Taft also, Vandenberg argued, as he often had in the past, that there were "natural limits" to partisan Republican attacks on the administration during wartime. He cautioned those who wished to make more of an issue of the Pearl Harbor trials, for example, that the subject was "necessarily a delicate one so far as *public* discussion" was concerned, for no one wanted "to contribute to national disunity or to national anxiety in respect to the management of the war." Nor, he might have added, to such an obvious preelection reminder of the Republicans' old image problem. He did add that "the Navy has magnificently retrieved itself since Pearl Harbor."[54]

Unlike Taft, however, Vandenberg went a step further. In embracing the more positive-sounding strategy of bipartisanship in foreign policy, he pursued an unfamiliar alternative to traditional opposition and staked his hopes for continuing leadership of congressional Republicans upon it. The rising criticism of administration foreign policy following the Teheran conference threatened that alternative and jeopardized Vandenberg's hopes. A prime example of his bipartisan approach, the UNRRA agreement, came before Congress as a joint resolution in early 1944 during the height of the Republican outcry over Teheran. The previous September, shortly after their collaboration on the agreement, Vandenberg had warned Assistant Secretary of State Acheson that they were "not yet 'out of the woods' in respect to the Congressional argument over 'Treaties vs. Enabling Acts'" in connection with UNRRA.[55] His warning proved to be correct.

Republicans fresh from attacking the Roosevelt administration for secret diplomacy quickly channeled their criticisms toward the UNRRA proposal when it came before Congress. Despite Vandenberg's consultation with the State Department, Representative Sumner of Illinois continued to view the agreement as an attempt by the Executive to bypass the Senate. She proclaimed it unconstitutional and joined with Represent-

ative Bertrand W. Gearhart of California in predicting that the administration would also move to have the postwar peace treaty approved the
same way, by simple majorities in both houses instead of a two-thirds
vote in the Senate. Representative Edith Nourse Rogers of Massachusetts
opposed the kind of relief contemplated by the measure; she wanted relief taken out of the hands of civilian authorities completely and handled
by the military. Sumner, on the other hand, argued that it should be taken
care of voluntarily by private organizations like the Red Cross.

Hamilton Fish objected that the United States was being asked to pay
more than its share for the relief program envisioned by the UNRRA proposal and charged that the organization itself would turn into an international W.P.A. Other congressional Republicans maintained that the
funds for rehabilitation would ultimately work to the disadvantage of
Americans by reviving European industries to compete with those of the
United States. Senator Willis of Indiana offered an amendment to the
proposed appropriation designed to prevent the spread of communist propaganda; the amendment prohibited any expenditure of funds for promo-
tion of educational, religious, or political programs in the countries to be
rehabilitated. Finally, opponents of the measure argued that UNRRA
would further involve the United States in European power politics with
no one yet knowing exactly how far the country had been involved already as a result of President Roosevelt's wartime conferences.[56]

Vandenberg staunchly defended the UNRRA proposal, paying particular attention to his own and the Senate Foreign Relations Committee's consultation with the State Department in framing it. He contended
that such consultation was itself a way to implement the constitutional
requirement that the Senate give consent "in respect to treaty obligations" and the Congress give consent "in respect to appropriation responsibility."[57] Maintaining emphatically that "UNRRA dealt only with
a limited part of the *war* machinery" as opposed to "the *peace* machinery," Vandenberg argued that it was inseparably "part of the war itself."
He distinguished between UNRRA and the Food and Agricultural Organization of the United Nations, both of which the administration had
proposed to handle as executive agreements. FAOUN he proclaimed "a
long-term part of the *peace* machinery." In contrast to UNRRA, it was
"implementing the Atlantic Charter—in respect to 'the end of want and
fear from want,'" he reasoned, and he argued "that obligations of *this*
nature" could not be handled "other than by Treaty." Vandenberg
doubted that "Congress would approve any precedent which might imply
some other method for writing the formula for our relationships in the
postwar world."[58] He did not believe that the appropriation for UNRRA,
however, was such a precedent.

For those who believed that UNRRA did not go far enough in providing a program of reconstruction for Europe, Vandenberg balanced his approach with the argument that it was "necessary to draw a sharp distinction between 'relief' and 'rehabilitation'" in order to secure congressional approval.[59] There was a "total" lack of information, he noted in reference to recent Republican criticisms, about "the commitments which are being made on our account in all of these various international 'conferences' where the President always acts exclusively upon his own initiative and then maintains totally effective silence upon his return." If there was to be any "rehabilitation" in the future, therefore, "it must be preceded by a new candor between the White House and the Capitol" and by comprehensive planning. Approval of the UNRRA agreement, Vandenberg contended, on which Congress had been consulted to some degree in advance, was a necessary but not a sufficient step in this direction.[60]

In the end, Vandenberg's approach and leadership prevailed. An amendment designed to reduce the appropriation was defeated in the Senate, with Republicans voting two to one in favor of its defeat, while Senator Willis's amendment prohibiting the use of UNRRA funds to promote educational, religious, or political programs passed, Republicans voting for it 23 to 1. The resolution itself cleared the Senate by a vote of 47 to 14 and the House by a vote of 338 to 54, a minority of Republicans opposing it in each case. Although a Senate-House conference committee eliminated the Willis amendment, the Senate as well as the House, including a majority of Republican members in both, proceeded to approve the final bill.[61] Even Taft announced that, despite continuing doubts and a fear that the procedure employed for approval of UNRRA would "be used as a precedent," he would vote in favor of the joint resolution because he deemed it "all-important in the war effort."[62]

In recognition of his cooperation, support, and leadership, Vandenberg was warmly thanked after passage of the UNRRA resolution by Assistant Secretary Acheson on behalf of the State Department. Acheson shared Vandenberg's sentiments, he declared, regarding the effectiveness of the cooperation which they had achieved and expressed a hope that they would soon have occasion to work together again.[63] Vandenberg in reply complimented Acheson's own "fine cooperation across the months." He warned, however, that they would both be "less than realists" if they did not recognize that "there is a tremendous latent 'suspicion' of this entire enterprise in the Senate; and that it was far from being reflected by the wide margin in favor of UNRRA on the final roll call. It is highly important, therefore, that UNRRA should be kept strictly and rigidly within the 'specifications' which have been laid down."[64]

This interchange between Vandenberg and Acheson signified more than simply routine injunction or polite form. It further cemented the political liaison they had contracted the previous year and it added a boost to their various hopes for bipartisanship. Within the administration, increased co-operation with Congress and selected members of the opposition party was fast becoming standard policy. Although some Democrats had warned that the bipartisan approach to foreign policy would simply play into the hands of Republicans like Taft, who would jump at the chance to conduct the 1944 campaign on domestic issues alone, the administration itself was worried about the consequences of failing to move in this direction.[65] The potential assertiveness of Congress, evidenced in debates over the different postwar resolutions, had been troublesome, regardless of the subsequent passage of the ones most favored by the administration. Some comfort could be taken in the approval of the UNRRA agreement, but even that had been accompanied by clamorous demands for more details concerning the administration's postwar plans.

Following the Moscow Declaration, Democratic leaders had lapsed into circumspection once again in regard to such plans, just as Republican leaders had after Mackinac. Pressure was building on the incumbents, however, to divulge the specifics of what they had in mind. Internationalists of all political persuasions implored the administration to reveal its intentions. Twenty-four Republican congressmen seized the opportunity and addressed an open letter to Hull. They demanded to know what his department was planning for the future order of the world and argued that such knowledge was all the more necessary given the administration's record of secrecy in the wartime conferences. President Roosevelt himself warned his slower-moving secretary of state that the Republicans would make the question of postwar organization a campaign issue and would do so to advantage if the Democrats did not announce their own plans soon.[66]

Hull heeded such warnings as well as his own recollections of congressional and Republican reaction to international organization in 1919 and 1920. Appearing before the Senate Foreign Relations Committee in March, he requested the formation of a special bipartisan committee to consult with the State Department on the plan for postwar world order which it had been developing for more than a year. Hull wanted to secure both Senate and Republican approval of the plan before proceeding to negotiate its acceptance with Great Britain and the Soviet Union. Senator Connally responded to Hull's overture by appointing a committee of eight senators—four Democrats (Connally, George, Guy M. Gillette of Iowa, and Alben W. Barkley of Kentucky, the majority leader) and four Republicans (Vandenberg, White, Austin, and LaFollette, the Progressive)

—after consulting with Vandenberg on the make-up of the group's minority representation. For Vandenberg, who had been advocating such bipartisan consultation between the administration and members of Congress, the opportunity was a windfall. It promised to give congressional Republicans a greater share as well as more say in foreign policy, at least in the publicly prominent area of postwar planning. Participation in policy making in that area might, in turn, enable them to neutralize it as an issue in the forthcoming elections.[67]

The principal obstacles to this strategy, of course, were Republicans like Taft who almost instinctively shied away from such bipartisan collaboration. Within the confines of the party, therefore, Vandenberg proceeded to deal with Taft's potential opposition. Before accepting the offer of seats on the committee for himself and the other Republicans, Vandenberg asked Taft whether he would approve such a move. The latter replied that if the proposed collaboration were merely to write a blueprint for a League of Nations, Vandenberg's question was not important. If, however, the committee was to confer on all matters of foreign policy, Taft would agree to Vandenberg's cooperating only under certain conditions. The conditions were, first, that the invitation come from Roosevelt himself, not from Hull, since the president had primary responsibility for foreign affairs; second, that the conferences cover every phase of current and postwar activities; and, third, that Republicans be fully informed and given a chance to render advice before, not after, decisions were made.

Taft further recommended that Republicans on the committee reserve the right to consult other minority members of the Senate and to resign if their views were consistently ignored. Suspecting that the president was not going to be truly cooperative, Taft urged that steps be taken to guard against this possibility. He warned Vandenberg that the proadministration press might play up the committee in such a way as to make Republicans appear responsible for everything that went wrong. For his part, Vandenberg acknowledged Taft's concerns and agreed to his conditions.[68] He communicated them to Connally who in turn forwarded them to Hull. The president in the end did not have to issue an invitation, for Hull confined the committee's initial meetings to the State Department's plan for a United Nations organization, kept them informal, and agreed that congressional Republican participants would not be under any obligations.[69]

Having obtained clearance in advance from the principal Republican opponent to cooperation with the Democrats, Vandenberg joined the special Senate committee and was pleasantly surprised when he learned the details of the administration's plan for a world security organization.

"The striking thing about it is that it is so *conservative* from a national-ist standpoint," he declared. "It is based virtually on a four-power al-liance."[70] Vandenberg satisfied himself that there was nothing remotely approaching a "world state" or a standing "international police force" in Hull's proposal; moreover, he was "deeply impressed" and surprised "to find Hull so carefully guarding" an American veto power "in his scheme of things." Hull, he noted, was "manifestly eager to avoid Wilson's mistake of attempting commitments designed for ultimate congressional rejection." On the whole, Vandenberg concluded, the State Department's plan for a post-war international organization, with the possible exception of some of its details, was "excellent."[71]

Despite his favorable reaction to the plan, Vandenberg soon had oc-casion to remind the secretary of state and his colleagues on the committee that above all else he was participating "as a *Republican* in these confer-ences."[72] When Hull requested from the committee a letter, according to Vandenberg, "virtually endorsing" his plan before proceeding to negoti-ate it with the British and the Russians, both Vandenberg and LaFollette flatly refused. "It seems to me," Vandenberg warned Hull, "that one of the lessons we should have learned from Versailles is that a *League*, no matter how nobly meditated, cannot cure the defects of an unsound peace."[73] Elsewhere he remarked, as LaFollette had earlier in connection with his refusal to approve the Connally resolution, that he was "dis-turbed by Russia's unilateral announcements from time to time as to what she intends to do, for example, with Poland and the other Baltic States; and by Churchill's constant reiteration of restoring the British Empire intact." The peace would create "a new *status quo* in the world," and the new "League" would have to defend that status quo.[74]

Over all the members of the Committee of Eight, Vandenberg ob-served, hung the shadow of a doubt as to whether they or even Hull himself were "in possession of *full* information as to what peace terms may have *already* been agreed upon between Roosevelt, Stalin and Churchill." None of the committee, the Senator noted in his diary, "is *sure* that Hull *knows* the whole story."[75] The appearance in the press in May of a report on Roosevelt's peace plans served to confirm such impressions. Based on an interview with the president conducted by Forrest Davis shortly after Teheran, the account made public for the first time some specific thoughts of Roosevelt on solutions to postwar problems. According to Davis, the president envisioned the world being policed in the future by four major powers—the United States, Great Britain, the Soviet Union, and China—each keeping order in its own distinctive section of the globe.[76]

This disclosure convinced Republican isolationists and international-

ists alike that Roosevelt had in fact made the kind of secret deals with
Churchill and Stalin that had been feared. Vandenberg and LaFollette,
therefore, became even more insistent on the Committee of Eight that
any congressional acceptance of a postwar organization await the peace
settlement and more reluctant than ever to commit themselves to any of
the administration's plans. Vandenberg demanded that Hull negotiate his
proposal with the Allies first before trying to obtain any kind of Senate
approval. Hull, unwilling to risk a public outburst against the plan of the
kind that had occurred in the committee, finally agreed.[77]

Once again, as in the case of his consultations with the State Department on UNRRA the year before, Vandenberg had apparently forced the
administration to back down from an intended course of action. In the
process he confirmed his own leadership of Republicans in Congress on
foreign policy as well as the bipartisan approach upon which it was based.
Facing an implicit threat to both in the partisan political resurgence led
by Taft in 1944, Vandenberg's responses, as in the case of the UNRRA
resolution and the Committee of Eight, were persuasive ones, particularly
among congressional Republicans like Taft who were up for reelection
that year and in something of a quandary about how to handle questions
of foreign policy. Vandenberg's approach not only maintained a distinction between issues related to the war and those related to peace, as Taft's
did, but also demonstrated that bipartisan collaboration did not necessarily mean commitment. Such distinctions were important for Republicans who wished to refrain from either approving or opposing a postwar organization until political conditions, both foreign and domestic,
were better understood.

In contrast to what one biographer has described as Taft's "almost
off-hand approach to foreign relations" which failed to provide sustained
leadership for congressional Republicans in 1944, Vandenberg's policy of
collaboration with the administration promised to guide them in an at-
tractive political direction.[78] It offered isolationists and internationalists alike a certain voice in the administration's policies without forcing
them into potentially dangerous positions (given their different constituencies and their party's historical image problems) on the question of
international organization. Vandenberg's approach further promised, just
as the Mackinac Declaration had, to avert the danger of intraparty war-
fare over the question prior to the 1944 elections. If the postwar policies
of the Democrats proved successful, congressional Republicans, by associating themselves with their development, could claim part of the
credit; if anything went wrong, they could still hold the administration
accountable because of its primary responsibility in foreign affairs. Furthermore, if the Democrats refused to cooperate with Republicans, the

latter could continue to charge, as they had in the past, that the administration was conducting a sinister "secret diplomacy."

Two senators from New Hampshire—an internationalist, Styles Bridges, and an isolationist, Charles Tobey—provide illustrations of how congressional Republicans of either persuasion could find a home away from home in the bipartisan strategy being developed by Vandenberg. Bridges had supported aid to both Britain and Russia before the war, had won renomination and election from New Hampshire in 1942, and had allied himself afterwards with Republican   internationalists like Austin and Ball. In the spirit of Vandenberg and LaFollette, however, Bridges charged Roosevelt, after the appearance of the Forrest Davis articles, with "risking the whole future and the future of the postwar world on the good will of Mr. Stalin." Stalin and Churchill, Bridges noted, were "speaking in such a manner that with every passing day the prospects of an enduring peace become more and more remote." He demanded to know whether the president was acquiescing in their "rampaging demands, which will surely scuttle any peace if left unchallenged?" If he was, then, despite its emphasis on bipartisanship, Hull's approach to American foreign policy, Bridges warned, would "never secure the kind of peace we seek if it rests upon unity at any price with any nation, or clique of nations."[79]

Tobey, on the other hand, had given the best that was in him, he proclaimed before Pearl Harbor, to fighting the "deceptive methods used by the President and his leaders in the Congress to take us into war step by step" and vowed to continue doing so "regardless of the consequences." After Pearl Harbor, it will be recalled, he had created a congressional uproar over his demands for an immediate investigation of the disaster.[80] As a result, Tobey later observed, he had been "crucified" in New Hampshire and throughout the nation.[81] Republican internationalists launched a concerted drive, following Senator Bridges's reelection and the defeat of an isolationist congressman from New Hampshire, Arthur B. Jencks, in 1942, to oust Tobey from the Senate; they opposed him for renomination in 1944 with another congressman, Foster Stearns, whose "only talking point," Tobey noted, "is on the foreign situation."[82] Reading the political omens well in advance of the primaries, Tobey underwent something of a conversion in foreign policy in 1943. By June, he was "glad to advise" one of his constituents that it was "not too early now to lay a foundation of basic principles for peace in cooperation with the other United Nations and to make that position as permanent as possible."[83] To this end, he encouraged Vandenberg's efforts at Mackinac, declared himself in favor of the Fulbright resolution in the House, and vigorously supported the Connally resolution in the Senate, declaring that he would vote for it "with satisfaction and hope that it may make a contribution to an effective and permanent peace."[84]

Casting about in 1944 for more such associations with the postwar issue, Tobey found one in connection with his position as ranking Republican on the Senate's Banking and Currency Committee. Secretary of the Treasury Henry Morgenthau had proposed inviting Vandenberg instead of Tobey, whose reputation as an isolationist still rankled memories, to participate in the Bretton Woods Conference, which was scheduled to meet in the White Mountains of New Hampshire in July to draft plans for an international bank and monetary fund. Vandenberg ultimately declined in favor of Tobey, but, in the meantime, Assistant Secretary of State Acheson had intervened to avert the insult to "the sacred rights of seniority" that Tobey's exclusion from this important conference in his home state would have implied. He convinced Morgenthau of the "folly" of his proposal and got Tobey invited to the conference. Acheson even extended the State Department's efforts in behalf of bipartisanship futher. He arranged for Tobey to speak at the opening of the Bretton Woods Conference on the Fourth of July and to enjoy the "gratifying publicity he would receive for it throughout the state" in advance of the Republican primary.[85] Tobey survived that primary with his political skin, if not his former principles, intact. "I have never been an isolationist," he proclaimed prior to the elections. While acknowledging that he had not been "in favor of precipitating our nation into war before we were prepared," he nevertheless contended in 1944 that "no man in Washington has more fully cooperated with the Administration in the prosecution of the war effort."[86]

As developed by Vandenberg in 1944, therefore, the policy of bipartisanship was aimed at maximizing the advantages of this cooperation for every congressional Republican. Being confined primarily to issues of postwar international organization, the policy allowed them to criticize other aspects of wartime foreign policy from the comparative political safety of an apparently united front. Furthermore, bipartisan cooperation on postwar organization did not necessarily imply a Republican commitment to such organization, as Vandenberg himself continued to indicate. One of the reasons he refused to attend the Bretton Woods Conference, he observed to Republican senators (apart from the "affront" to Tobey that would have been implied), was that he would have been "expected to support" the American plan "and to promote it among the other United Nations. I cannot possibly put myself in a position where my advance assent is thus presumed."[87] In regard to postwar collective security, moreover, he wrote late in May 1944 that

When this war is successfully concluded, we Americans must never for an instant relax our totally adequate international defense—with particular emphasis on sea and air. We shall strive for the security which flows from international cooperation for peace and justice. We shall confidently hope for a better and a safer world from which military aggressors have been banished. We can then strive for relative limitations upon armaments. But there must never again be a moment when we are not equal to the total defense of the United States against any potential enemy.[88]

For Vandenberg as for others, the old isolationist ideal of a fortress America, armed to the teeth in the postwar period, was still the best option, regardless of their political participation in bipartisan efforts to secure an alternative.

Secretary Hull called the Committee of Eight back into session late in August to apprise its members of the progress in negotiations for an international organization then taking place among the United States, Great Britain, and the Soviet Union at Dumbarton Oaks in Washington. Vandenberg together with LaFollette immediately objected to the American position on the question of national contributions to the proposed organization's peace-keeping force. Specifically, they opposed the idea that a United States representative to the new world body might be able to commit American troops to future military operations without prior approval from Congress. The two prewar noninterventionists lobbied among fellow members of the committee for retention of a congressional veto over the employment of American forces, especially since it might take "another world-wide war" to deal with a future aggressor.[89] In the process, they alarmed Democrats like Hull who feared that at any moment the Republican objection might break out of the confines of the committee's executive sessions into a full-scale partisan attack on the results of the Dumbarton Oaks conference.[90]

Indeed, such an attack appeared imminent. Republican Senator Harlan J. Bushfield of South Dakota arose in the Senate on September 5 to charge that, according to unofficial accounts of the conference appearing in the press, the United States was surrendering its sovereignty and liberty at Dumbarton Oaks by giving the president the power to commit American troops to future combat roles without specific congressional consent. Senator Connally, on behalf of the Democrats, simply dismissed Bushfield's attack as partisan rhetoric forged in the midst of the political campaign then in progress. For the Republicans, however, Vandenberg responded to Bushfield's charges much more sympathetically and effectively. In line with the policy of bipartisanship, Vandenberg prevailed upon his irate colleague to forego criticism of the Dumbarton Oaks deliberations for the present, but he reminded him and others that they would ultimately

have their say when the final proposal for an international organization
came before the Senate for approval—after the campaign.[91]

In 1944, therefore, Vandenberg firmly established his primacy among
congressional Republicans on foreign policy. That primacy was formally
recognized by his colleagues in 1944 when they elected him chairman
of the Republican Conference in the Senate, under the plan of party
reorganization developed there by Taft. Taft himself became the chairman
of the new steering committee created by that plan. Between the two of
them, Vandenberg and Taft were symbolically dividing the leadership
of Republicans in Congress, just as they had divided it at Mackinac, along
foreign versus domestic policy lines. Once again, as at Mackinac, Vandenberg's success in Congress had largely derived from his ability to sustain
and articulate positions on foreign policy which promised maximum political advantages for a minimum of commitment.

Vandenberg, in fact, was virtually repeating in 1944 the pattern of
leadership that he had established the previous year. While serving on the
Committee of Eight in May, he also was hard at work with his committee
on foreign policy from Mackinac, negotiating acceptance of a statement
on that subject for the 1944 Republican platform. More will be said of
these negotiations in the next chapter. It is interesting to note, however,
that with the Republican convention scheduled to begin in June, Vandenberg was again moving, as he had with the Mackinac Declaration the preceding summer, to extend his congressional leadership on foreign policy to
the party's presidential wing. In this connection, Vandenberg wrote in
May to the likely Republican nominee by then, Governor Dewey. Indicating his presence on the Committee of Eight, informing Dewey of the
stand he was taking there on postwar organization, and recommending
its adoption by the Republican party as a whole, Vandenberg declared:

> I am more than ever convinced that a new "League of Nations" will
> only succeed if it has a just peace to administer. Wilson gave away
> his "14 Points" at Versailles on the fallacious theory that he could
> cure these infirmities through his subsequent "League" which couldn't
> be done. It can't be done now. In other words, it seems to me that
> our first emphasis must be on a "just peace." It seems to me that
> the extent of our own ultimate commitments to a "league" must in-
> evitably be somewhat contingent upon the *kind* of a "peace" (the
> *kind* of the status quo) which the "league" shall sustain.

Vandenberg, the Republican congressional leader on foreign policy, was
advising Dewey, the future presidential leader, that, whatever bipartisan
appearances might suggest, Republican acceptance of a plan for collective
security would and should ultimately depend on the establishment of a
"just" (and politically acceptable) peace.[92]

PRESIDENTIAL
7 REPUBLICANS WEATHER THE 1944 ELECTIONS

In the presidential wing of the Republican party, the outstanding champion of a cooperative approach to foreign policy, comparable in form at least to the bipartisan strategy being advocated by Vandenberg in Congress, was, of course, Wendell Willkie. The substance of Willkie's approach, however, was different, for he had his own distinctive ideas about what such bipartisanship should entail. Essentially, his strategy was to get out in front of opponents on the issues and urge them to catch up. Thus, he had reacted to the Mackinac Declaration by calling it a step in the right direction but had soon begun insisting that the party advance even further. Willkie, more than anyone else in 1944, including the Democrats, loomed in that election year as the greatest potential threat to efforts by Vandenberg and others to down the party's long-term historical problem: its record of having thwarted America's original attempt to join an international peace-keeping organization following World War I.

By September 1943 Willkie's attempts to move the party in the direction of greater, more specific commitments to postwar world order had taken the form of his own announced candidacy for the Republican presidential nomination. In an article in *Look* magazine, he had declared his intention to run for the office provided he could obtain a liberal Republican platform which would promise among other things a new, internationalist foreign policy.[1] Soon afterwards Willkie began a tour of several western and midwestern states to rally support for his campaign. Along the way, he continued to remind Republicans and other potential voters of the partisan tactics in 1920 that had resulted in the nomination of Harding and the death of American entry into the League.[2] He cautioned them to avoid such an outcome in the future and to insure against it by backing his candidacy.

A torrent of opposition from presidential and congressional Repub-

licans alike greeted Willkie's campaign for the nomination. Substantial
segments of the party viewed him as a stalking horse for Roosevelt. The
president wanted the Republicans to nominate a liberal, internationalist
Republican, they believed, and was doing everything in his power to foster Willkie's candidacy. If Willkie should be elected president, Senator Taft
remarked, "he would be just as New-Dealish as Roosevelt, only it would
be worse because he would be in control of the Republican Party"; moreover, "in the post-war reorganization there would be very little left of the
American system."[3] In the Midwest, the Republican Nationalist Revival
Committee, which had condemned the Moscow Declaration as the "unconditional surrender of the United States to Europe," urged Colonel
McCormick of the *Chicago Tribune* to enter the Illinois presidential primary to blunt Willkie's drive.[4] Willkie added to the conflict by announcing that he would gladly challenge the isolationist publisher in his home
state should the latter decide to run.[5]

Elsewhere within the party, Willkie was charged with having "antago-
nized almost every member of Congress and a very large number of men and
women who work patiently and painstakingly for the Republican party."[6]
Party regulars launched a concerted drive to stop his renomination. Former
Republican National Chairman John D. M. Hamilton followed Willkie's
tour throughout the heartland and the West. In the wake of Willkie's passage, Hamilton urged support for favorite-son candidates and encouraged
consideration of Thomas E. Dewey as an alternative. At the same time,
Willkie's candidacy and views came under extensive attack from G.O.P.
members in Congress, such as Senator Taft, who were up for reelection in
1944.[7]

Willkie refused to abate his course. He continued to fuel Republican
resentment against him, portraying such resentment as further evidence
of a desire within the party to move the country back into isolationism.[8]
Despite his bravado in the face of challenges, however, Willkie's candidacy and views on foreign policy were fast being eliminated from serious
consideration by the party's faithful. A variety of indicators showed him
continuing to decline in popularity among Republicans. In a survey of
206 G.O.P. members of the House, 89 considered Dewey best qualified
to lead the party in 1944; only six believed Willkie so qualified. Mac-
Arthur, Bricker, and Taft all outranked him.[9] The Republican National
Committee met in January and without incident reaffirmed the Mackinac Declaration as the party's basic position on foreign policy, at least
until its forthcoming convention in June. Moreover, a poll of the members at that meeting showed Dewey and not Willkie the favored candidate among members of the National Committee.[10]

A simultaneous poll of 3,581 Republican party officials at state and

local levels throughout the United States confirmed a belief that Senator
Vandenberg, for one, had long held. This poll revealed that the "grass
roots" Republican leaders, though willing to have the United States
join an international organization to keep the peace and promote economic cooperation, were against extensive disarmament after the war, the
surrender of island outposts, and "the idea of Uncle Sam masquerading
as an international Santa Claus."[11] Indicating their familiarity with and
approval of the views on foreign policy of prominent national party figures, the state and local leaders on the whole ranked Willkie's positions
third, behind those of Dewey and Herbert Hoover.[12] According to Republican National Chairman Spangler, the mail to Republican National
Headquarters in late 1943 and early 1944 ran nearly nine to one against
Willkie, who was alienating more Republicans practically every time he
spoke.[13] Although top-ranking Democrats, reportedly, continued to regard him as Roosevelt's toughest potential opponent in 1944, a Gallup
poll early that year found Willkie commanding only 27 percent of Republican support, down 8 percent from the preceding November.[14] The
same survey showed that Dewey's support among Republicans had risen
9 percent by early 1944, to a total of 64 percent. As Willkie's star continued its descent, therefore, Dewey's continued to rise.

Together with Dewey, another important figure rose to prominence
in the Republican party in 1944, John Foster Dulles. As Dewey's adviser
on foreign policy, Dulles in his person and views provided many Republicans with a welcome alternative to Willkie in foreign policy. Something of
an isolationist himself prior to the war, Dulles, like Senator Taft in the
congressional wing of the party. appealed to Republicans who believed
in late 1943 and early 1944 that the administration's foreign policy
ought to be criticized openly. "Actually Mr. Roosevelt's foreign policy
is highly vulnerable if it were properly attacked," Dulles observed.

> Indeed, it is difficult to perceive if he has any foreign policy other
> than drifting into war and out of war. However, because of the Re-
> publican ineptitude he stands before the country as a great master
> of foreign policy and most Republicans have come to feel that while
> they disagree with him on domestic issues, they accept his leadership
> in foreign affairs. At a time when foreign affairs are outstanding in
> everyone's mind, this is a suicidal policy for Republicans to adopt.[15]

Dulles remarked once that Taft and he were not far apart on foreign
policy.[16] As chairman of the Commission on a Just and Durable Peace
of the Federal Council of Churches, Dulles had criticized the Atlantic
Charter, as had Taft. His commission had also stood with Taft in opposing the kind of big-power domination of the postwar world suggested in

President Roosevelt's report on the results of the conference at Teheran.[17] Moreover, Dulles was of the opinion, as was Taft, that any proposed military alliance which would tie the destiny of the United States to that of another power, without giving Americans a voice in that power's policies, was fundamentally unsound.[18]

When Dewey reportedly advocated such an alliance between the United States and Great Britain at Mackinac, Dulles was naturally put on the spot. He quickly resolved any conflict, however, by contending that Dewey did not mean to suggest a long-range military commitment. He was merely demonstrating his good will toward the British and his approval of continued Allied collaboration.[19] Nevertheless, Dulles shared with Taft and the Republican isolationists a fundamental distrust of the British. In his case, as mentioned earlier, such distrust stemmed largely from the view that selfish British nationalism had been responsible for a second world war.[20]

On the other hand, Dulles, in contrast to Taft and other midwestern isolationists in the party, was a confirmed believer in international organization, especially after the outbreak of the war. As such he also appealed to Republican internationalists on foreign policy, particularly those on the eastern seaboard—Wendell Willkie's natural constituency. Warning against overemphasis on security, reliance on force, and desires to preserve the status quo, Dulles and his church commission stood opposed to narrow nationalism. They favored a world organization for peaceful change as an alternative to violence and aggression.

On behalf of his commission, Dulles had written to Senator Connally in October 1943 requesting that the word "sovereignty" be omitted from Connally's resolution on postwar policy which was then before the Senate.[21] Sovereignty, Dulles had explained elsewhere, "is made up of a bundle of rights and certain of these rights need to be vested in authority having a broader responsibility than purely national responsibility."[22] Following Roosevelt's post-Teheran indications, therefore, that a postwar peace settlement based on limiting responsibility to a select few nations might be in the offing, Dulles and other members of his commission had called upon the president at the White House and urged him to work for an international organization for peace that would seek to cure the world's problems, not simply perpetuate the status quo.[23] To this end, Dulles had approved the Moscow Conference and its subsequent declaration, proclaiming the latter a great improvement over the Atlantic Charter and a notable step toward realizing the international order envisaged by his commission's "Six Pillars of Peace." He noted, however, that some significant omissions remained in the document; it had not, for example, dealt with colonial or economic matters.[24]

It is interesting to note in this connection that Dulles, like many of the eastern Republican (and Democratic) internationalists to whom he would appeal—Senator Austin and Representative Eaton in Congress, Governor Baldwin of Connecticut, National Committeeman Smith of New Jersey (all of whom had expressed views similar to his at Mackinac) —was as much an economic as a political internationalist. In fact, the need for political internationalism, according to Dulles (who was a senior law partner in the Wall Street firm of Sullivan and Cromwell, which had important clients and interests abroad), arose in large measure from prior considerations of what was economically desirable.[25] His opposition to national sovereignty as well as his views on the origins of the war in Europe derived largely from this base. For him, world peace and order depended upon economic unity and the enlightened businessmen who, he believed, tended to bring that unity about. Such unity in Europe, Dulles argued along the lines laid down by John Maynard Keynes, had "primarily been held back by a small group of self-seeking politicians in every nation."[26] Their self-seeking had contributed directly to the outbreak of World War II. Furthermore, according to Dulles, politicians were still "highly insular and nationalistic."[27] They persisted in trying to "hold on to the trappings of sovereignty."[28] As a consequence, the political organizations of the world under their influence had become "backward."

In the absence of rational international political organization, therefore, Dulles defended such devices as international cartels. Businessmen, he argued, "have had to cope realistically with international problems" and "have had to find ways for getting through and around stupid political barriers."[29] Nor was the problem centered in Europe alone, he wrote to an executive of the Pennsylvania Railroad:

> There is a powerful group in Washington who want foreign investments here and American business connections abroad to be conducted on the theory that we are perpetually in a state of war—actual economic war and potential military war. Of course that is the surest way to make that war a reality. Seemingly the policy is in contradiction to what the President and others around him publicly profess. However, there is no one in government who seems to have the will or capacity to curb activities which, it seems to me, are most menacing from the standpoint of future world order.[30]

Dulles was not alone in these beliefs. In varying degrees, he shared them with the Republican internationalists mentioned above and with Willkie and his supporters. He shared them most, however, and succeeded in identifying them for internationalists, with Dewey, whom

Dulles had recruited for his law firm in the late 1930s, just before circumstances intervened to catapult Dewey into a political career. When that career reached its summits in 1944 and 1948, Dewey, Dulles, and the other Republican internationalists gave expression to their economic views in part by moving the G.O.P. platform away, to some degree, from its traditional reliance on high protective tariffs.[31]

Above all else, however, John Foster Dulles, as an alternative to Willkie on foreign policy for many Republicans, was a realistic internationalist. He acknowledged that the "so-called 'democratic countries' alone" could not "organize to enforce peace." If the Allies won the war, Dulles maintained, it would be "largely with the help of the Russian and Chinese manpower which at the end of this war will be a formidable force." As neither of these countries was "democratic" (nor for that matter were the South American countries "truly democratic"), "some form of world organization" was needed which would be "representative of, and feel a sense of responsibility toward, all of these peoples as well as the vanquished nations."[32] To the idea that at least the new world authority itself might be set up by democratic procedures, Dulles responded in a similarly pragmatic vein that the United States and the internationalists "would probably have to get along with something less ambitious for the time being."[33]

It is to this political realism of Dulles that one must turn in the end to understand the basis of his and Dewey's appeal to both extremes on foreign policy in the Republican party during 1944. Much like Senator Vandenberg in the congressional wing, in fact, Dulles and Dewey together in the presidential wing of the party defined a certain politically advantageous "middle ground" for Republicans in foreign policy. Dulles in particular, by virtue of his work with the churches on international organization, provided a kind of moral sanction and appeal for positions which, however politically motivated, Republicans might want to adopt on that especially touchy subject. Despite his aversion to "nationalistic politicians," Dulles demonstrated a ready willingness to cooperate with them in the party and a basic solicitude for their needs. In opinions similar to Vandenberg's, he questioned "whether it would be wise to precipitate" problems and differences among the allies over postwar policies while the war was still on "and victory far from sight." He also acknowledged and warned in relation to pronouncements on the postwar period that "the concrete constantly threatened a breakdown of allied unity."[34]

Given his function as middleman and priest in the presidential wing of the party, therefore, Dulles's approval and advice on foreign policy was soon being solicited from all sides. Alf Landon asked Dulles for comments on a speech he was to deliver calling for cautious appraisals of the wartime conferences and, by inference, criticizing Willkie, who had already approved them.[35] On the other hand, Willkie himself asked Dulles for help in the 1944 campaign should Dewey turn out not to be a candidate. Dulles declined the potential commitment, however, for his sense of political realism was acute.[36] Willkie was not at all likely to win the presidential nomination; besides, Dewey, with whom Dulles had long since invested his own political fortunes was clearly out in front.

The arrival of Dewey and Dulles at the front and center of the Republican party's presidential wing took place during the presidential primaries of 1944. There too, the opposition to Willkie in the party culminated. Willkie attacked Dewey in the primaries for espousing a traditional, balance-of-power approach to postwar problems by his proposal of an Anglo-American military alliance. He charged that this was a sure way to divide the world and bring on another war.[37] The Willkie campaign held up through the New Hampshire primary, in which the former nominee won six delegates to Dewey's two. In Wisconsin, however, where the campaign was to encounter its first big test, Willkie was in trouble from the start. Indeed, because of the poor reception generally accorded his views there, he even considered stepping out of the race before the voting began. He remained in, though, and when the balloting was over, Dewey emerged with fifteen of the twenty-four delegates, followed by Stassen with four and MacArthur with three. Willkie ran last and failed to win a single delegate. Afterwards, he quit the race, charging that his defeat in Wisconsin had been a victory for isolationism and pledging himself to continue the fight for acceptance of his internationalist views.[38]

Willkie's exit from the presidential primaries was soon followed by that of General MacArthur, who issued a statement from his headquarters in the Pacific reminiscent of Civil War General William T. Sherman. He did not "covet" the Republican presidential nomination, MacArthur declared, nor would he accept it.[39] Reports that the general was considering running for the presidency had begun appearing in 1942, but they were denied by MacArthur, who disclaimed any such political ambitions.[40] The reports nevertheless continued and became politically linked with Republican congressional demands that MacArthur and his men, as Vandenberg put it, "be promptly sustained with more 'tools' for an earlier and less costly Pacific victory than may otherwise be possible."[41] It was sometimes difficult to tell, in fact, whether congressional Republican fixation on the war in the Pacific led to support of MacArthur for president or whether a desire for MacArthur's candidacy led to concentration on the Pacific phase of the war. The two became intimately intertwined.[42]

Vandenberg had been one of the prime instigators of the MacArthur-for-president reports in 1942 and had sponsored a movement in the general's behalf afterwards in company with Republican Congresswoman Clare Boothe Luce of Connecticut, Robert Wood of Sears, Roebuck and Company, and Frank Gannett, the publisher of a chain of eastern newspapers who had himself been mentioned as a possible Republican candidate for president in 1940.[43] In MacArthur, Vandenberg hoped to provide his Republican colleagues in the presidential wing of the party as well as on Capitol Hill with an ideal candidate, one who would neutralize any advantages Roosevelt might claim on the basis of his wartime leadership.

While highly active in promoting MacArthur's candidacy, Vandenberg was also highly cautious about the operation. To his cohort and the principal financial backer in the endeavor, Robert Wood, he admitted that he was "still in something of a quandary" over what ought to be done to gain MacArthur the nomination. Not wishing to be "responsible for any defaults" in promoting the general's candidacy, Vandenberg maintained that "any 'campaign' for him must be kept divorced from any ordinary political routines which might embarrass him or even ultimately force his irrevocable retirement from consideration."

In view of the then-prevailing War Department policy which prohibited military men from running for office, Vandenberg advised Wood that their "primary obligation to the General" was "to protect him against *any* untoward political activities which would in any way embarrass his present status." Furthermore, he declared:

I continue to believe that this nomination must essentially be a spontaneous draft—certainly without the appearance of *any* connivance on his part (of which he would never allow himself to be consciously guilty). The fact remains that much can be judiciously done—strictly within the letter of these limitations—to see on the one hand that no mistakes are made by unwise friends and, on the other hand, to encourage the ultimate favorable attitude in the Republican National Convention.[44]

By the beginning of 1944, therefore, MacArthur-for-President Clubs were springing up throughout the country in anticipation of forthcoming presidential primaries, and in Congress there was a good deal of talk in favor of the General's candidacy as well. Too much so for Senator Taft, in fact, who protested against Vandenberg's "extreme position" that the Republican party could win the election only by nominating MacArthur.[45] Taft suggested to John Foster Dulles that one reason behind the close association of Vandenberg with MacArthur was that the latter, if elected president, "would be good for only one term so that those presently ambitious [presumably, Vandenberg himself] would soon get another chance" at the office in 1948, when the political difficulties of the wartime situation might be behind them.[46]

In the end, however, what happened to the MacArthur campaign realized the worst of Vandenberg's original fears. A Republican congressman from Nebraska, A. L. Miller, released some of his personal correspondence with MacArthur to the press. Miller's disclosures implicated MacArthur (not for the last time in American history) in some directly hostile criticism of the Democratic administration under which he served. Thereupon, MacArthur completely dissociated himself from the campaign in his behalf, giving as his reason the "widespread public opinion that it is detrimental to our war effort to have an officer in high position on active service at the front considered for President."[47]

Vandenberg and his associates in the movement for MacArthur's nomination were naturally upset, Vandenberg himself suggesting sardonically that the errant congressman from Nebraska perhaps "ought to join the submarine service."[48] His proven sense of political strategy had indicated to him all along that any campaign for MacArthur had to be conducted entirely by others in his behalf and that nothing ought to be done to mar MacArthur's greatest political asset—his image as the complete military commander, totally dedicated to winning victories over the nation's enemies and unconcerned with the squabbles of political partisanship during wartime. With that image now compromised, Vandenberg, his political sense still intact and his hopes for neutralization of the commander-in-chief's wartime advantages still high, soon began moving in the right direction. While reaffirming to associates in the MacArthur affair that the general "would have been our most eligible nominee and our greatest President," Vandenberg now maintained that there was "no denying the tremendous momentum of the Dewey Campaign."[49]

Indeed, there was no denying that momentum, particularly after the withdrawal of Willkie and MacArthur from the field. Taft, a supporter of Ohio Governor Bricker's candidacy, conceded after Wisconsin that Dewey was "practically nominated," despite the anti-Willkie nature of the vote there, and that "the bandwagon feeling" was "very strong."[50] The only real question remaining in Republican circles about Dewey pertained to his views on postwar foreign policy: what exactly were they? Since his alliance proposal at Mackinac, which had sparked considerable criticism from both Taft and Willkie as well as from their various supporters, he had not specifically addressed himself to the postwar issue.

In a Lincoln Day speech in early 1944, Dewey had followed Taft's initiative and accused Roosevelt and the Democrats of commiting the same

mistakes (secrecy, lack of cooperation with the Republican opposition) in
their approaches to the peace that their predecessors had in 1919.[51] His
charges may have mollified isolationist Republicans somewhat, especially
after Mackinac, but the Democrats effectively countered that Dewey was
assaying the role of Warren G. Harding for the forthcoming campaign.[52]
Following Willkie's withdrawal from Wisconsin, therefore, in an address
to the American Newspaper Publishers Association that Dulles helped
him write, Dewey responded more to the internationalist concerns of
former Willkie supporters. He declared himself in favor of organizing "in
cooperation with other nations a structure of peace backed by adequate
force to prevent future wars . . . and [to foster] conditions calculated
to promote world-wide economic stability." Hoping to down the Harding
image, he also urged that the United States not "repeat the tragic error
of twenty-five years ago." "We have learned much since 1919," Dewey
proclaimed. At the same time, however, he was embracing only the most obvious part of the lesson and simply trying to associate himself with what
had, by that time, become a popular position in American politics.[53]

On the internationalist side of the Republican divide, Dewey won some
plaudits from Willkie's supporters for his belated advocacy of an international organization. *Time* magazine now labeled the New York governor a "realistic," practical internationalist who had removed the issue of
postwar organization from the 1944 campaign.[54] Among the isolationists, however, Dewey's views were less well received. There was considerable resentment in the Republican Midwest over his apparent failure to adhere strictly to the Mackinac Declaration, just as there had been
earlier to his proposal for an Anglo-American alliance.[55] A brief flurry
of campaign activity followed on behalf of Governor Bricker of Ohio,
whom the Republican internationalist, William Allen White, labeled
"an honest Harding" and whose positions on postwar issues were minimal.[56] Bricker gave a set speech, approved by Taft, in which he affirmed
support for the key sentence from the Mackinac Declaration on postwar organization and indicated that he might favor revival of the old
League of Nations. But even Taft, whose views these replicated, had already conceded the obvious—the bandwagon for Dewey was too strong.[57]

Among former supporters of MacArthur, Robert Wood communicated
to Vandenberg his doubts about the wisdom of nominating Dewey and
the opinion that he personally could not get enthusiastic about the New
York governor's candidacy.[58] Vandenberg replied to such doubts with
characteristic political pragmatism. If Dewey "*is* to be nominated—regardless of our doubts and preferences—I want him nominated under the
best possible auspices and with the greatest possible sendoff so that he
can have a maximum chance to win."[59] To another MacArthur supporter,

Vandenberg now remarked that Dewey had always been his second choice.

> As a matter of fact he probably would have been my first choice if I
> had not felt that General MacArthur would be an easier candidate
> to elect. But I feel that Dewey has continued to grow immensely
> during these last few months and if he is nominated I shall whole-
> heartedly give him my *total* support to the last possible resource.[60]

Vandenberg had good reason for switching to Dewey so enthusiastically.
His attempts to lead the presidential as well as the congressional wings of
the party in 1944 had suffered a serious setback in the demise of the
MacArthur campaign. It had been expected that Vandenberg would be
elected temporary chairman of the Republican National Convention,
scheduled to meet in June. The Miller incident and Vandenberg's close
connection with the MacArthur cause, however, had quashed these hopes.
Furthermore, a fight for control of the Michigan delegation to the convention was going on between the pro- and anti-Dewey forces back in
Vandenberg's home state. The pro-Dewey group reportedly would not
even give assurances that Vandenberg would be a delegate to the convention.[61] Given this state of affairs, Vandenberg was hard at work again,
broadening his lines of communication with the future Republican nominee and shoring up his weakened leadership position in the best way he
knew how.

In March, almost a month before the results in Wisconsin were known,
Vandenberg had begun writing fellow members of his Mackinac committee
to remind them that it had been agreed at the conference that they would
make "a final recommendation" of a statement on foreign policy to the
Platform Committee of the Republican National Convention. "We could
'stand' on our previous declaration," Vandenberg explained, "which seems
to have met the acid test, and which certainly has not yet been rivaled by
our Democratic opponents." But, he added, "it would be preferable, perhaps, to bring our statement down to date and to condense it for platform
purposes."[62]

Members of the Mackinac committee, however, were not the only Republicans with whom Vandenberg consulted. On March 30, writing just
before the Wisconsin primary and anticipating its result, Vandenberg con-
tacted Dewey about the matter. Noting that he was "very anxious—for
obvious reasons" that any recommendation of the Mackinac committee
should "at least not be repugnant" to Dewey, Vandenberg sent the future Republican nominee the following draft of a suggested platform
plank, which, he indicated, had already been approved by the Senate's
Republican steering committee:

The Republican party favors the prosecution of the war against Japan and Germany to total victory. We shall support our military forces with every civilian resource. We shall cooperate with the United Nations to the limits of our national strength. Our relentless aim will be to win the war against all our enemies for the sake (1) of our American security, welfare, and interests; (2) in order that the Axis forces never again shall be capable of renewed tyranny and attack; (3) to the end that peace and freedom shall be the hope of an emancipated civilization.

We favor responsible participation by the United States in postwar cooperative organization among sovereign nations to prevent military aggression and to attain permanent peace with organized justice in a free world. We favor the re-establishment of the authority of international law on firm foundations.

We believe that peace and security should not rest upon sanctions of force alone; but they should prevail by virtue of inherent, reciprocal interests and spiritual values in the voluntary agreements by which nations live. We are opposed to any form of intervention on the part of one State, however powerful, in the domestic concerns of any other sovereign State, however weak. We respect the rights of all peoples to choose the form of Government under which they will live; and we wish to see sovereign rights and self-government restored to those who have forcibly been deprived of them. We shall seek practical programs by which these objectives can be supported and sustained by effective international cooperation. We shall faithfully follow the dictates of the Constitution of the United States in the attainment of all such international commitments; and whenever there is any conflict in objectives we shall adhere to the policy which is essential to the independent welfare of the United States and which will preserve our republican form of government under the Declaration of Independence, the Constitution and the Bill of Rights.[63]

Vandenberg observed to Dewey that the sentence beginning "We favor responsible participation by the United States" in the draft was taken verbatim from the "key sentence at Mackinac." The " 'Mackinac Charter,' " he explained, "has stood up so well that I hesitate to touch it again. On the other hand, its discussion of foreign policy is much too long and involved to become a plank in our Chicago Platform—if we are to have the short, succinct platform for which I hope." Furthermore, "for frank campaign purposes," according to Vandenberg, there were one or two points which seemed to invite new emphasis. The language in the sentence starting with "We are opposed to any form of intervention," he noted, was from an official State Department statement in 1941, while the sentence begin-

ning "We respect the rights of all peoples" was taken directly from the Atlantic Charter. Vandenberg thought that these two sentences were "vitally
important" because they related to the point at which the Roosevelt administration was "deserting the hopes and prayers of all our American na-
tionals from Poland, Finland, Latvia, Lithuania, Estonia, etc." The plank as
a whole, he concluded, was "intended to make a forthright pledge to international cooperation (with emphasis upon the priority which we would
give to *justice* over *force*)." On the other hand, it was "equally intended
to give our great Middle Country (where the issue will be a *controlling*
one) the dependable assurance that America is *not* going to be 'sold down
the river.' " Vandenberg earnestly solicited Dewey's comments on the
draft, emphasizing again that he was "aiming at *condensation*—for the sake
of an effective impact" on the electorate.[64]

Dewey replied that he wished to study the document with great care before venturing any comment upon it.[65] Senator Austin, however, Vandenberg's former adversary on the Mackinac committee, responded immediately
to his colleague's overture in March.[66] Throughout the next month, while
Dewey (and Dulles) pondered the draft, Austin struggled with Vandenberg
over the section devoted to international organization. Austin wanted to
change the document "to bring out in bold relief the precise point" at which
Republicans were advancing "toward a more specific program." He was in-
strumental in substituting for the sentence on international law the following explanation:

> Such organization requires facilities to deal with regulatory ques-
> tions in international relations; the maintenance of an impartial tri-
> bunal to deal with justiciable disputes and to establish international
> law on firm foundations; and means of effective consultation to pro-
> vide peace forces to prevent or repel military aggression.[67]

Vandenberg assented to this addition, claiming that he himself wanted to
go far enough in the document to establish clearly the Republicans' good
faith with regard to postwar international cooperation. He begged Austin
to remember, however, that the resolution was "primarily a *political* document" which must win the approval of the great Mid-West.[68]

Forwarding the revised draft resolution to Dewey, Vandenberg explained that he and Austin had been "struggling for an agreement on
basic ideas." Austin, he claimed, could be considered a representative of
"what we may loosely call the 'Eastern internationalist' school of thought."
In the same loose way, Vandenberg believed, he himself represented "the
'Middle Western nationalist' school of thought." It was "obviously essential" that the two schools find "common ground," as they had at Mackinac.
He was convinced that they could find that common ground at the con-

vention in Chicago, but only if the platform adopted there should plainly
state that the party did not favor "a world State," that it intended
"to keep the flag on the Capitol," and that it would "protect and conserve
the *legitimate* self-interest of the United States precisely as Mr. Churchill
constantly asserts his primary devotion to the British Empire."

These points "must be asserted," Vandenberg maintained, "in order to
save our situation in the Middle West where I believe there is great danger
of a resurgence of what could *really* be called 'isolationism' unless we Republicans provide effective spokesmanship (as we did at Mackinac)." He
had "no fear of the response of the Middle West to 'international cooperation,'" he professed, "if the basic elements of the principle of 'sovereignty'"
were maintained. Moreover, he denied "using the word 'sovereignty' in a pro-
vincial sense," but, rather, "with frank acknowledgment that 'sovereignty'
is not impaired when the 'sovereign' *voluntarily* parts with some of it for
value received."[69] Accordingly, Vandenberg also added a sentence to the
revised draft that he sent Dewey; immediately following Austin's addition,
his proclaimed: "We shall achieve these aims by organized international
cooperation and not by joining a world state."[70]

Following his victory in Wisconsin, Dewey responded to the revised
resolution with some recommendations of his own. He suggested several
relatively minor changes (the substitution of the phrase "all our enemies"
for "Japan and Germany" in the opening sentence; a rewording of the
second point regarding war aims to read more smoothly; and a specifica-
tion that the pledge to include sovereign rights did not include Germany
and Japan), all of which Vandenberg immediately accepted and sent back,
incorporated in the resolution, to Dewey. With regard to the pledge to
restore sovereign rights, Vandenberg noted that he had "confined it to
'the victims of Axis aggression,'" and explained that Republicans ought
to "express the general '*wish*' to see 'sovereign rights restored to those
who have been deprived of them.'" Surely "we *do* have this 'wish,'"
Vandenberg reasoned; while a statement of it in the platform would not
oe "a commitment to 'restore the pre-war status of Poland and the Baltic states,'" it would nevertheless be "a gesture in this *general* direction
so far as practicable." The Republican party, he contended, was "entitled to take advantage of this tremendous political potential."[71]

In his recommendations concerning the draft plank, Dewey had himself questioned the political wisdom of Senator Austin's elaboration of
the proposed international organization, with its reference to "peace
forces to prevent or repel military aggression." Vandenberg heartily
supported the sentiment behind Dewey's question but could do little
else than proclaim the passage "Senator Austin's fetish." He had to
leave it in, Vandenberg explained, "in order to satisfy Austin" and "to

have a *unanimous* report from my Committee." Elsewhere, Vandenberg
added to the proposed resolution at Dewey's suggestion a point completely
ignored in the original draft—a statement about the importance of economic
considerations in building the foundations of an effective peace. All in all,
Vandenberg concluded in response to Dewey's recommendations, he was
"delighted to discover" that there was no *"fundamental* disagreement" between them "as to what the Republican platform should say" on the subject of foreign policy.[72]

Vandenberg then sent the draft, complete with Dewey's recommendations,
to other members of the Mackinac committee for their approval, advising
them in advance, however, that it had already benefited from "the views
of some of our more prominent Presidential candidates" and been agreed
upon by Senator Austin and himself.[73] Following a further consultation
by Vandenberg with John Foster Dulles (who again suggested eliminating Austin's reference to "peace forces," but not adamantly), Dulles remarked that the draft was so adequate that he believed the Resolutions
Committee at the convention could adopt it outright.[74] Vandenberg was
thus able to write members of his Mackinac committee (*"very confiden-
tially"*) that the draft had now met "with the approval of those who speak
for our "leading candidates.'" Personally, he added, "I think it is an even
better job than we did at Mackinac."[75]

Vandenberg had good reason for putting these triumphant conclusions
in confidence. Although he and other regular Republicans were much relieved when Willkie withdrew from the presidential race, they were nevertheless apprehensive that he would either throw his support to President
Roosevelt or move to discredit Dewey and the Republican platform.[76] In
first writing to Dewey for approval of his committee's draft, Vandenberg
had assured him that his interests would be protected and that the draft
would not be made public until Vandenberg himself presented it to the
Resolutions Committee in Chicago. He hoped to avoid, Vandenberg said,
"needless pre-Convention controversy in the public press and elsewhere,"
as well as to "greatly simplify the Party problem (which might otherwise
blossom into a battle in the Resolutions Committee at Chicago).[77]

Vandenberg's and Dewey's objectives were threatened not only by the
"Party problem"—factions ready, as before Mackinac, to tear each other
and the party apart if their platform requirements were not met—but by
serious distractions from sources outside the party as well. In early June,
the administration announced the long-awaited invasion of the European
heartland at Normandy and made public soon afterwards an outline of
the State Department's draft plan for an international organization. These
developments heavily overshadowed the Republican National Convention
scheduled to begin later in June. In terms of foreign policy as well as na-

tional politics, the Democrats had seized the initiative once again and put the G.O.P. back on the defensive.

The time available to Republicans for continued compromise, postponement, and generalization on the postwar issue along the lines of the Mackinac Declaration had been considerably shortened. Assistant Secretary of State Breckinridge Long thought the hour propitious enough to suggest to Senator Austin and Governor Dewey that a statement approving the administration's draft plan be included in the Republican platform. Not surprisingly, given the divergence of opinion on the matter within the party, Long's preconvention gambit failed. As a consequence of this failure, however, and the other Democratic successes, the troublesome specter of the G.O.P.'s former reaction to the League of Nations began to bulk larger in the consciousness of both Democrats and Republicans.[78]

An added distraction from attempts to compromise differences among Republicans and to minimize the threat of the prewar image in foreign policy was provided, as expected, by Wendell Willkie. In May 1944, true to his pledge following the Wisconsin primary, Willkie set out to influence both the Republican platform and the future nominee on the question of postwar world order.[79] He began writing a series of articles on positions that he believed the party should espouse in the forthcoming national platform. One such position was a strong stand in opposition to narrow views of national sovereignty and a commitment to the immediate creation of an international organization out of the wartime United Nations.[80]

With an assault on party unity gathering on different fronts, Republican leaders redoubled their efforts to obtain agreement on a foreign policy plank in advance and keep it under wraps until the Resolutions Committee could approve it in Chicago. To insure such approval and to avoid any last-minute tampering with their agreed-upon text, Dulles for Dewey and Vandenberg for the Mackinac committee hastened to enlist support for it from Senator Taft, who was going to be chairman of the Resolutions Committee in Chicago. On June 14, two weeks before the convention, Vandenberg was able to report to Dulles that he had just shown the draft to Taft personally and believed that it had met with the Ohio Republican's "complete approval." At the same time, Vandenberg reaffirmed the widespread conviction "that the wisest and the safest course would be for the Resolutions Committee to take this draft as a 'closed text.' There would be inevitable danger in any changes—no matter how nobly meditated—on the spur of a Convention moment."[81]

Other steps were taken to keep the convention "closed" to further questions regarding the stand that the party should take on postwar foreign policy. National Chairman Harrison Spangler, considering that "Willkie had practically seceded from the party" by refusing to assure him after

Wisconsin that he would support the party's candidate for president, who-
ever that might be, pointedly refused to invite the 1940 nominee to address
the 1944 convention.[82] Moreover, efforts were redoubled to keep the draft
resolution on foreign policy a secret—to avoid drawing Willkie's fire—until
the Resolutions Committee had approved and presented it to the convention.

Despite the concerted attempt to exclude him from deliberations on the
foreign policy plank at Chicago, Willkie obtained knowledge of it in advance and in confidence from Senator Austin, the chairman of the platform subcommittee on foreign affairs. Much to Austin's regret, however,
Willkie proceeded to attack what he considered the plank's undue emphasis
on national sovereignty and enigmatic reference to "peace forces" (Austin's own term). He compared the document to its predecessor in 1920
for ambiguity on the issue of international organization, inviting the conclusion that the 1944 platform plank was designed to produce the same
results.[83]

Willkie was not alone in his objection to the platform. Most of the nation's Republican governors had also been excluded from the preconvention deliberations on the foreign policy plank, as well as from access to
the final draft. The only ones who had been consulted, in fact, were governors Martin and Green, of Vandenberg's Mackinac committee, and, of
course, Bricker (through Taft), and Dewey. At the convention, in a vir-
tual replay of the early scene at Mackinac, other governors, led by New
Jersey's Walter E. Edge and in league with Senator Joseph Ball, demanded
and received from Senator Taft, as chairman of the Resolutions Committee,
an opportunity to inspect the plank on foreign policy and suggest changes
before the committee finally recommended it to the convention. Before
the committee, the governors argued, along the lines advanced by Willkie,
that any ambiguities in the platform should be supplanted by positive
statements in favor of a strong and forceful international organization
for peace. They even threatened a floor fight if this demand were not
met. However, they quickly abandoned their position after being informed that extreme nationalists like Gerald L. K. Smith, Colonel McCormick, and Robert Wood were equally well-prepared to recast the platform in an isolationist mold, if the matter were thrown open to debate,
and that Dewey, the sure nominee, had already approved the foreign
policy plank as it stood.[84]

As at the Mackinac Conference, therefore, a flurry of opposition
among presidential Republicans to a prearranged resolution on postwar
foreign policy—one promoted by Vandenberg again and compromised
with Senator Austin—was laid to rest. Stressing the political advantages
to be gained by the resolution, Vandenberg triumphantly retraced the

history of its development in presenting it to the Resolutions Committee
at the convention as the *"UNANIMOUS"* report of his Mackinac committee:

> In its Mackinac Conference last September—and in its resultant Mackinac
> Charter—the Republican Party presented a "foreign policy creed" which
> united the Party on solid ground where divergent minds found a common
> meeting place. That creed was almost totally immune to *any* attack from
> *any* source. It was so sound that it became the basis of almost literal
> bi-partisan paraphrase by the United States Senate when, by a vote of
> 85 to 5, it passed the so-called "Connally Resolution" as an expression
> of *American* purpose. It is warp and woof of the subsequent "Moscow
> Declaration." From this record, I submit that we have given the country
> pre-view proof that the Republican Party and its fast approaching Re-
> publican administration are wholly competent to be trusted with our
> foreign affairs. I also submit that no *other* Party, as a Party, has even
> remotely approached our record.[85]

Without further to-do, the resolutions was approved by the Resolutions Committee and adopted by the 1944 Republican National Convention.

In its final form, the foreign policy plank followed in the footsteps of the
Mackinac Conference again by expressing the party's support for "responsible
participation by the United States in postwar cooperative organization
among sovereign nations to prevent military aggression and to attain permanent peace with organized justice in a free world." The pronouncement
added Austin's provision that this organization "should develop effective cooperative means to direct peace forces to prevent or repel military aggression." It qualified that provision, however, by declaring in Vandenberg's (and
Dulles's) words that all such aims should be achieved "through organized international cooperation and not by joining a World State." Furthermore, the
plank promised that the party would "sustain the Constitution of the United
States" and the two-thirds vote in the Senate in relation to "any treaty or
agreement to attain" America's international aims.[86]

Reaction in the party to the platform resolution also followed a pattern
derived from the Mackinac Conference. Although Willkie maintained his
opposition to the foreign policy plank, other prominent internationalist
Republicans, including senators Ball and Burton (of $B_2 H_2$ fame), supported
it. Among the isolationists, Senator Taft and the *Chicago Tribune* approved
the plank, the latter noting its presumed concessions to the internationalists
but nevertheless proclaiming it "satisfactory."[87] In another show of near
unanimity, Dewey was nominated by the convention on the first ballot
with only one dissenting vote. That came from a lone MacArthur delegate whom Convention Chairman Joseph Martin and Vandenberg (in
another little service to his old favorite candidate as well as to his new)

maneuvered out of nominating the general for the embarassingly lost cause, but not out of voting for him.

In his acceptance speech to the convention, Dewey defined the meaning of the platform further.

> There are only a few, a very few, who really believe that America should try to remain aloof from the world. There are only a relatively few who believe it would be practicable for America or her allies to renounce all sovereignty and join a super-state. I certainly would not deny these two extremes the right to their options; but I stand firmly with the overwhelming majority of my fellow-citizens in that great wide area of agreement.

Once again, as at Mackinac, the party had sought to appeal to the "middle ground" (as Vandenberg put it then), or "the overwhelming majesty of that broad area of agreement" (as Dewey put it in his acceptance speech), in a major pronouncement on foreign policy.[88] Once again, within the party at least, the appeal had largely succeeded.

The official Republican position on international organization, however, still remained qualified. In a subsequent press conference, Dewey clarified his acceptance speech to mean that he did not favor an international police force under international as opposed to national control; nor did he favor, he said, surrendering the right of the United States to make war alone.[89] Mapping out with his advisers a campaign based largely on domestic issues, the importance of American society's reconversion to peacetime endeavors, and the advancing age and obviously deteriorating health of the wartime president, the youthful, energetic Dewey planned to address himself formally to issues of foreign policy only a handful of times during the campaign. Moreover, he rejected a suggestion that he tour the world's battlefronts (*à la* Willkie) in preparation for the campaign.[90]

His was to be a "peace" administration, Dewey reasoned with his advisers, following in this line Taft's prediction that the next elected president would have only one year of war to deal with but three years of peace.[91] To solidify his position among middle-western isolationists, who still distrusted Dewey for his alliance proposal at Mackinac, Bricker of Ohio was selected as his running mate. (Bricker was also nominated for the vice-presidency by the America First party of presidential candidate Gerald L. K. Smith, but he declined that nomination.) Even though Republican internationalists, like Senator Ball, who seconded Dewey's nomination at the convention, seemed to be rallying to his side, Senator Taft himself could now write constituents that he was "quite certain" Dewey "would stop far short of the New Deal plans to establish an international WPA over all the world."[92]

Unlike Willkie, Dewey in 1944 was not one to overestimate the sources of his political support or the regular Republican organization upon which it was based. He replaced Harrison Spangler as national chairman with his own lieutenant, Herbert Brownell, another New York lawyer, but he appointed an old-guard favorite and Willkie foe, Werner Schroeder of Illinois, vice-chairman.[93] Stressing his ability to work with Republicans and their Southern Democratic allies in Congress, Dewey dedicated himself from the start of the campaign to preserving the volatile mixture of his supporters and to keeping the party united. His strategy of minimizing foreign policy issues was consciously calculated to do so. It aimed at bypassing not only the problem of the G.O.P.'s isolationist image but also the danger to unified party organization that conflicts over foreign policy might evoke.

Despite what Taft remarked as a tendency in Dewey "to boss everything and everybody" and "to be entirely surrounded by New Yorkers and to look at the issues from the New York standpoint," cooperation, not conflict, had been the meter of his success in gaining the nomination. To that would now be added centralized organization and planning to "get rid of" what Taft and every other regular Republican could no longer endure—"Roosevelt and the countless bureaus and radical bureaucrats whom he supports." In many ways the mirror image of the hypothetical New Deal bureaucrat which he proposed to eliminate, Dewey (and his advisers, including Dulles) typified the "organization man" whom the regimentation of war as well as of economic and political development in the twentieth century was rapidly bringing to the fore. Dewey and his "team" of associates lacked the personal flair of a Willkie, a Roosevelt, or even a Vandenberg, but they rivaled the last two (and set a pattern for future Republican nominees) in their concern for old party ties, patient labor, public opinion polls, and skillful political manipulation. Even Taft conceded that while Dewey and his advisers had "too much of the New York viewpoint," he admired "their spirit in trying to understand the whole country."[94]

Dewey's objective in the 1944 campaign was to stick to his predetermined strategy and timetables as precisely as possible and make no mistakes. When in late August he spoke out on foreign policy for the first time in the campaign, he expressed alarm over reports that the proposal for international organization which the United States had just presented to the major Allies at Dumbarton Oaks aimed at subjecting the smaller nations of the world to the coercive power of the Big Four. Clearly abandoning any notion of an Anglo-American alliance left over from Mackinac, he now condemned the possibility of such a big-power alliance (in the administration's plan) as the rankest form of imperialism. Dewey called for a more democratic form of world order.

He urged Americans, in view of their traditional concern for the rights of minorities and small nations, to abjure power politics and champion full rights for all nations in any future international organization.[95]

Dewey's speech drew favorable comment from the press and a quick response from the State Department. In a news conference called the day after the talk, Secretary Hull denied Dewey's charges and invited him to Washington where Hull promised to satisfy him on the nature of the administration's draft plan.[96] The secretary's invitation was viewed in the Dewey camp as "purely a political ploy," but after thinking it over for a day, Dewey decided to take advantage of Hull's offer. He issued a public reply to Hull announcing that he was sending Dulles to Washington to confer with him.[97]

The first meeting between the two took place on August 23. Hull presented Dulles with a copy of the draft plan in question, as well as a memorandum on the role of small nations in the proposed organization, and the two men talked for over two hours. They could agree on removing the issue of international organization from partisan controversy in the campaign but not on much else. Hull wanted to withdraw all issues of foreign policy from partisan debate, but Dulles, interested in preserving as many options for Dewey as possible, refused. Hull also wanted to employ the adjective "non-partisan" in a joint communiqué to be issued by both men announcing the results of their discussions. He contended that that was the most appropriate description of an agreement which purported to remove an issue from the realm of political controversy. Again Dulles balked. He held out for the word "bi-partisan," maintaining that it more accurately connoted his sense of the agreement, namely, that the two parties were cooperating in a commonly approved foreign policy. The two men argued for hours over the choice of words. In the end, following a three-way telephone conversation with Dewey in Albany, Brownell in New York, and Dulles in Washington on August 25, the latter bowed to Hull and the word "non-partisan" was used. Both sides agreed that "the American people considered the subject of future peace as a non-partisan subject which must be kept entirely out of politics." Dulles, on behalf of Dewey, however, stipulated that the agreement "did not preclude full public non-partisan discussion of the means of attaining a lasting peace."[98]

Much to Hull's dismay, Dewey continued the general Republican attack on the element of secrecy surrounding the wartime conferences, singling out the Dumbarton Oaks gathering itself as a particular case in point.[99] In a campaign address on foreign policy written by Dulles and delivered in Louisville, Kentucky, in September, the Republican candidate also placed considerable emphasis on the fate of small nations again, stressing that they should play a significant role in any future international organization.[100] Furthermore, Dewey discussed the Hull-Dulles agreement in that speech in such a way as to suggest that the Republicans were taking the initiatives in the direction of international organization and bipartisan foreign policy. Extolling the virtues of a "non-partisan approach to the shaping of a peace structure," he proclaimed:

> I have made a practical beginning with Secretary Hull in a bipartisan cooperation to establish an internal organization for peace and security. Both parties are working together today in this great labor so it can go forward year after year, decade after decade, regardless of the party in power. . . .
>
> That is why I have taken [the] unprecedented action of promoting the non-partisan character of the conferences now in progress. Experts of both parties and members of the Senate of both parties are now conferring and will continue to confer as the work progresses. So long as I have anything to say about it, I shall insist on two things. First, that the American people shall be fully informed of our efforts to achieve the peace of the world. Secondly, these matters shall never be subjects for partisan political advantage by any individual or party either in or out of power.[101]

Dulles, the author of Dewey's speech, had similarly tried to claim credit for the Republicans by arguing, as he had with Hull, that their original agreement ought to be described as "bipartisan."

Dewey's participation in the Hull-Dulles agreement as well as his subsequent handling of the postwar issue in the campaign sparked criticism not only from Hull but also from members of his own party. Republican nationalist conceded that Dewey had gained a strategic political advantage, temporarily at least, by responding to Hull's original offer and concluding an agreement with him. Gerald L. K. Smith, the presidential candidate of the America First party, had even sought to have his own representative, Colonel Robert McCormick, included in the Hull-Dulles discussions. The isolationists objected, however, that the G.O.P. nominee was accepting by default, instead of attacking, an international organization designed to commit the United States to fight in future wars.[102]

Dewey and Dulles had accepted more than these isolationists knew. Following conclusion of his agreement with Hull, Dulles had indicated in private that the two had tacitly agreed to remove the proposed international organization not only from partisan but also from "destructive" political discussion.[103] On the day of his final consultation with Dulles, Hull had called the special Senate Committee of Eight back into session to advise them of the Dumbarton Oaks negotiations. The major Repub-

lican criticism of those talks, it will be recalled, as voiced by senators
Vandenberg and LaFollette on the committee and, later, by Senator
Bushfield's attack in Congress, centered around questions regarding an
international police force and how American troops were to be committed to it. Such questions were effectively the ones to be excluded
from "destructive" discussion under the terms of Dulles's agreement
with Hull.[104]

When Bushfield's attack occurred, therefore, Hull asked Hugh
Wilson, a Republican and a former ambassador to Berlin who had been
posted to the State Department by the Dewey organization to maintain continuing contact with Hull, to inform Dulles and Dewey of "the
movement under way to call for Congressional approval of all specific
applications of force under the security organization." Declaring that
"this movement might endanger the whole peace program if it were not
nipped in the bud," Hull maintained that "it was up to the Republican
leaders to do something about it," presumably because of their agreement, "before it was too late."[105] Taking Hull's warning to heart, Dulles
began exploring the possibilities of a compromise on the issue with Republican congressional leaders. Before he could work one out, however, Hull
came up with one of his own. Drawing upon an agreement just concluded
with the major Allies at Dumbarton Oaks, Hull suggested to the Committee
of Eight that the question of who should commit American troops be considered by the Senate separately from the question of international organization per se. With that offer, Hull won tentative approval of the agreements
negotiated at Dumbarton Oaks from Vandenberg and LaFollette, as well as
from Dewey and, ultimately, Dulles (despite the latter's reservations, deriving from the work of his church commission, about an international organization relying too heavily on force).[106]

Questions of the Hull-Dulles agreement and international organization
aside, presidential Republican leaders refrained from exploiting other issues
in criticism of the administration's foreign policy during the 1944 campaign.
The Dewey forces had received information from a representative of the
Ford Motor Company which purported to show that the administration
had learned beforehand that the Japanese were going to bomb Pearl Harbor. Furthermore, they believed this information to be authentic. Despite
an outburst of charges by congressional Republicans in September and
October to a similar effect, however, Dewey and Dulles decided not to use
the material or make responsibility for Pearl Harbor a campaign issue.[107]

On another matter of concern, the question of Allied and especially
Soviet postwar intentions, the Republican leaders likewise remained sur-
prisingly silent. Neither Dulles nor Dewey, as the latter put it, "ever shared
Roosevelt's delusions that the Russians were going to lie down and be nice

boys."[108] Nevertheless, they ignored suggestions that Dewey denounce in advance any secret international agreements that Roosevelt might have made at the wartime conferences. Except for Dewey's comment about secrecy at Dumbarton Oaks and occasional forays against the concept of presidential secrecy in general, particularly in the case of Poland, Republicans for the most part refrained from directly criticizing the administration in these and in other areas of foreign policy during the campaign.[109]

Various explanations of these omissions were offered after the campaign was over. Addressing himself to the failure to make an issue of Pearl Harbor, Herbert Brownell, Dewey's choice for Republican national chairman, observed that General Marshall had informed Dewey "that if he discussed this, he would be damaging the public welfare, because the Japanese were using the same code at that time as they had at the time of Pearl Harbor." Such discussion would constitute notice to Japan that the United States had broken its code and was daily receiving messages of great intelligence value.[110] Patriotism, not politics, in other words, had determined the course of action. Dewey himself later contended that no greater issue was made of Roosevelt and the Russians in 1944 precisely because the administration's secrecy at the time concealed the extent to which mistakes had been made.[111]

Others have argued that Republican leaders like Dewey and Dulles generally refrained from criticizing the administration on foreign policy during the 1944 campaign because they essentially agreed with the Democrats in that area. The Republican leaders followed the White House line on the need for accommodation with the Russians, that is, in the hope that the Soviets would change after the war and peace would be achieved.[112] Thus Dewey and Dulles collaborated with the administration in the agreement with Hull because as eastern internationalists they wanted above all else to see world order established through an international organization. Finally, the absence of more significant congressional criticism in the campaign is explained by a belief that Dulles, while in Washington conferring with Hull, held simultaneous talks with Vandenberg which helped convert the congressional Republican leader from isolationism to internationalism, thus insuring a uniform foreign policy in the party as a whole.[113]

What is lacking in all the foregoing explanations of Republican reluctance to attack the administration on foreign policy is an indication of the political consequences such an undertaking might have involved. Republican leaders like Dewey and Dulles were acutely aware of these consequences and, as mentioned earlier, had consciously formulated campaign strategy with political considerations foremost in mind. First among these considerations was that of the party's adverse historical image in foreign policy prior to the war. Second, but closely allied, was the problem of maintaining unity on foreign policy among the party's divergent factions, both isolationist-internationalist and presidential-congressional.

Faced with the difficult and delicate task of running against an incumbent president who by the fall of 1944 was leading an obviously successful war effort, Republicans stood more to lose than to gain, the presidential leaders believed, by attacking Roosevelt's wartime policies directly.[114] If they were to make an issue of responsibility for Pearl Harbor, for example, or of Roosevelt's dealings with the Russians, they might be charged with sabotaging the war effort or at least the wartime unity. Furthermore, they stood a good chance of reviving the party's prewar image of isolationism, particularly in relation to the League of Nations, if they took too much exception in public to the plan for international organization being developed at Dumbarton Oaks. Whatever they might think of the old isolationist position, Republicans in 1944 did not want to be associated with it. Instead, they did all they could to identify with their Democratic opponents, especially on the question of international organization; hence, the genesis of the Hull-Dulles agreement as far as the presidential Republicans were concerned.

At the same time, however, Dewey and Dulles were also hard at work trying to maintain party unity among the various factions on foreign policy and to tailor their positions on issues accordingly. During the course of his meetings with Hull, therefore, Dulles conferred daily with Republican congressional leaders like Vandenberg, Taft, Austin, and White; afterwards, he continued to maintain contact with them. Furthermore, Dulles endeavored to ingratiate himself with isolationist Republicans like Nye and Shipstead. Writing to Shipstead following his trip to Washington, for example, Dulles emphasized that he had "had quite a time in arriving at a joint statement with Mr. Hull which would make it clear that foreign policy was left open as a subject for discussion during the campaign."[115] According to Vandenberg, he and Dulles in reviewing the course of the latter's meetings with Hull were agreed "that the great advantage (to us) of these conferences is that they may rob the Administration of its campaign argument that it would 'break the continuity' of the peace negotiations if Roosevelt is defeated; also that the great danger is that Dewey may be handicapped in his campaign discussions of foreign policy if he becomes the recipient of too much 'confidential information.' "[116] (The information regarding Pearl Harbor was apparently a case in point.)

Dulles and Dewey also agreed with Vandenberg that, in addition to the party's image of former isolationism, they had other political reasons for being "careful not to 'play politics' with 'foreign policy.' " They stood to lose more than they would gain, the congressional Republican had argued, if they gave "any of these foreign born groups (like the

Poles) any right to feel" that the Republicans were making "political promises" to them. Vandenberg maintained that it was "impossible" to make a specific pledge to the Poles "which would actually be worth the paper it is written on" because the administration's "current defaults to Mr. Stalin" were "rapidly putting him in the 'drivers seat.' " Therefore, Vandenberg advised, "we must not *promise* anything which we cannot *perform.*"[117] The presidential leaders generally followed this advice in the campaign and failed to make an issue of Poland's ongoing boundary dispute with the U.S.S.R. They often hedged their bets, however, in bidding for ethnic support. One of the reasons in fact for Dewey's repeated emphasis in the campaign on the role of the small nations in a future international organization was the support that such an emphasis promised among American voters with ethnic ties to those nations. From their mutual platform-planning days, moreover, Dewey also adopted Vandenberg's rhetoric as well as his advice in arguing that any peace to be approved must in the end be "just."[118]

What developed in the presidential wing of the party, then, during the campaign of 1944, was essentially the strategy worked out in the congressional wing earlier that year. It called for associating the G.O.P. with the administration on the popular issue of international organization while at the same time preserving Republican options in that and other areas of foreign policy. The strategy aimed at neutralizing these areas as issues in the campaign, carrying the fight to the administration on domestic grounds, and awaiting control of the White House before making any final commitments. Political considerations of party, personal leadership and, above all, potential power undergirded these objectives. As Vandenberg himself explained, "the whole strategy of the Dewey campaign has been to soft-pedal questions of foreign policy so as not to renew the old cleavage between Western 'isolationists' and Eastern 'interventionists.' "[119]

This strategy, which soon came to be known as "bipartisan foreign policy," was one which Vandenberg, perhaps more consistently than any other Republican leader, had advocated since Pearl Harbor. In passing out credit for it, he himself noted that in "practical operation the Dewey-Dulles-Hull arrangement in the campaign of 1944 was undoubtedly the first formal. . . exercise of this policy." But he also correctly observed that "of course it was preceded . . . by many expressions of purpose on my own part."[120]

To the contention that Dulles converted Vandenberg from isolationism to internationalism during and after the campaign, one might reply that Vandenberg converted Dulles from internationalism to politics, provided there was any converting left to do. Vandenberg, in his

exchanges with Dulles during the campaign, did come to realize that
his wish to know "pretty definitely" the nature of the peace before
being called upon "to accept obligations under a 'league' which must
enforce the 'peace' " was "probably not practical. I certainly am in
favor of developing the *machinery* for the 'league' at once," he wrote
Dulles.

> The particular point I want to make, however, is that *if* the use of
> military force in major situations is to come back to Congress for
> approval, there is far less need for us to know the nature of the
> "peace" before we join the "league." But if we are to accept an
> obligation to the "league" under which the President can take us
> into any foreign war without Congressional approval, *then* it seems
> to me it becomes far *more* necessary that we should know precisely
> what kind of a "peace" we are underwriting before we underwrite
> it with a blank check. In other words, I think we "kill several birds
> with one stone" if we can start out with a formula under which we
> are not taken into major foreign wars without Congressional ap-
> proval.[121]

Despite his own doubts about the validity or desirability of such congressional approval, Dulles "realized the difficult position" that Vandenberg and other congressional Republicans were in. He hoped as they
did, he reassured Vandenberg, that, in line with his original understanding with Hull and accepted campaign strategy, "this issue can be postponed" until after the election.[122]

The most accurate interpretation of their relationship, therefore, would
seem to be that Vandenberg, the acknowledged leader of the congressional
wing of the party on foreign policy, and Dulles and Dewey, the obvious
leaders of the presidential wing, were by 1944 pursuing a commonly agreed-
upon strategy. This "bipartisan foreign policy," as all three leaders preferred
to call it, was more a response to the necessities of the party's political
situation as they perceived it than a movement dictated by overriding principle or conviction. In the end, Republican bipartisanship was a product of
political compromise and calculation, not conversion, and of the search
for "common ground" which was an overriding concern of these three
leaders.

During the 1944 campaign, however, the bipartisan strategy was not allowed to run its expected course. Despite the efforts at Mackinac and the
convention to write off the old Republican image as the party of isolationism and opposition to the League, the G.O.P. was still plagued by it in the
1944 campaign. Dewey was regularly referred to as a second Harding. Dulles
came under attack from Democrats in Congress and from columnist Drew

Pearson in the press for some of his prewar isolationist associations and views.[123] The party in general, including its congressional wing, was charged by Democratic opponents with promising a return to isolationism and to the kind of prewar policies that had resulted in a lack of preparedness for the conflict. One of the most persistent of those opponents, internationalist Senator Claude Pepper, put the charges succinctly in a printed debate with Senator Taft: "The Republican party is the party of big business and isolation. The Democratic party is the party of the people and international collaboration."[124]

Greatly distressed by such renewals of the isolationist issue, Vandenberg and others were obliged to treat wounds that had been closed since 1942. All the talk about "isolationists" was "sheer bunk," he complained; every measure "for our *own* national defense for the last twelve years has passed by the practically unanimous vote of Congress." In defense of the prewar record of Republicans like himself, Vandenberg pointed the finger of blame elsewhere:

> Mr. Roosevelt was the greatest "isolationist" among us until Pearl Harbor. He was an "isolationist" in 1932 when he said that we never again would have anything to do with the League of Nations. He was an "isolationist" in 1933 when he dynamited the London Economic Conference. He was an "isolationist" in 1935 when he said that only war profiteers could ever take us into another conflict. He was an "isolationist" in 1939 when he told Governor Dewey that anybody who talked about a two-ocean Navy was a chump. He was an "isolationist" when he made that 1940 Boston speech [in which he promised repeatedly that American boys would not be sent into any foreign wars]. He was a *complete* "isolationist" in all of his secret diplomacy which pointed straight toward war for many months preceding Pearl Harbor. At any rate, he "isolated" the Congress and the country from any conscious knowledge about the inevitable war which he *knew* was on the way.[125]

Taft expressed the same view. [126] Again, however, Vandenberg, Taft, and the other Republican leaders generally confined themselves to such counterattacks in private. They were reluctant to add the light of further public exposure to the heat of anti-isolationist endeavors and thus jeopardize a struggling bipartisanship even more.

Opposition from Republicans, however, ultimately frustrated the development of the bipartisan strategy. Not surprisingly, Willkie became the first and most prominent Republican to object to it. Prior to meeting with Hull in Washington to conclude their celebrated campaign agreement, Dulles had consulted with Willkie in New York but had failed to satisfy his qualms about Dewey's stand on the issue of who should commit American troops to battle under the new world organization, the United States representative, as Willkie believed, or the Congress. Having already condemned the Republican platform for the weakness of its stand on foreign policy, Willkie now pointedly refrained from endorsing the party's nominee for president. He dangled his approval in front of both major candidates, challenging each to obtain it by taking a stronger stand than the other in favor of effective international organization.[127] In what was proving to be a closer presidential contest than originally anticipated, Willkie's endorsement might have been crucial. He did not have the opportunity to make one, however. On October 8, 1944, one month before the election, Wendell Willkie died without having announced his choice for president.

Willkie was followed into the position of offering an endorsement in exchange for a stronger stand by Senator Joseph Ball. On September 29, Ball announced that his support, like Willkie's, was being reserved for the presidential candidate who promised the fullest possible commitment by the United States to effective postwar organization.[128] One of the original sponsors of the $B_2 H_2$ resolution with its distinctive emphasis on the need for an international police force to control future aggression, Ball opposed removing such issues from the public forum during the election, as the principal Republican leaders, Secretary Hull, and presumably President Roosevelt had agreed to do. In the end, the commitment that Ball wanted for his endorsement also related to the question of sending American troops into action for the new world organization without the specific approval of the United States Congress.

Although he had seconded Dewey's nomination at the Republican convention in June, Ball had apparently begun to fear by late September that Dewey's campaign had been taken over by isolationists within the party.[129] Dewey had not yet convinced him, Ball said in a public statement, that "he would fight for a foreign policy which will offer real hope of preventing World War Three. . . . That being the case, I would violate my own deepest convictions if I were at this time to try to campaign for Governor Dewey."[130] Senator Harold Burton, a fellow Republican internationalist and a cosponsor with Ball of the $B_2 H_2$ resolution, pleaded that the latter's position would be "used effectively as ammunition by the Roosevelt supporters" and that the president's reelection itself might impede Senate approval of an effective world organization.[131] Ball, however, stuck to his position. He appreciated Burton's point, he replied, but was convinced that the ultimate fight in the Senate could not be won unless the really controversial issues, like the question of American participation in the organization's armed force, were brought out in the open and discussed in the campaign.[132] In combination with Willkie, therefore, and perhaps more effectively than the Democrats, Ball resurrected the dreaded image of isolationism for Republicans and propelled it to the forefront of the 1944 campaign.

Following Willkie's death, Ball challenged both Roosevelt and Dewey to answer three questions concerning a future world organization: should the United States enter it; should crippling reservations to that entry be opposed; and should the vote of the American representative to the body be able to commit American forces to action without prior congressional approval? Dewey answered yes to the first two questions but refused to address himself to the third, maintaining that his prior agreement with the Democrats precluded public discussion of such subjects. His and Dulles's previous understandings with Republican leaders in Congress and the campaign's strategy, which dictated avoidance of controversial issues in foreign policy, undoubtedly determined Dewey's stand as much as the agreement with Hull. Roosevelt, however, following Dewey's reply, seized the opportunity thus presented to him, and in a speech delivered on October 21 to the Foreign Policy Association in New York he appeared at least to answer all three questions in the affirmative.[133]

Dewey himself contended later that Roosevelt violated their understanding during the campaign. Both he and the president, Dewey claimed, agreed not to discuss "the very thorny issue of whether there should be a United Nations army." In the final week before the election, however, "Roosevelt broke his commitment and said in a very deft way that the town hall didn't have any power unless it had a policeman, thereby satisfying a great many people who felt that there should be a United Nations army, about which I had a good many reservations."[134] Whether or not Roosevelt's statement was a violation of that agreement, Ball was convinced by it. Although Dewey, in a last-minute departure from his campaign strategy, made known his intention not to insist on specific congressional approval for every deployment of American troops in the future and lashed out at Roosevelt's ability to conduct foreign policy, it was too late. Ball threw his support to the president, and other internationalists followed his lead. Despite the strategy of bipartisanship, Dewey was·effectively portrayed in the end as just another Harding.[135]

In the elections held on November 7, with the world war still raging on all fronts, the Republican candidate went down to defeat (for the fourth consecutive time) to the incumbent president. It is difficult to say whether Ball's actions or a general disenchantment with Dewey's positions on international organization in the closing days of the campaign were decisive factors in the outcome. The election was much closer than expected, given the president's impressive position as the successful commander-in-chief; not since Wilson's victory in 1916 had the margin of victory been so slim. Though Dewey lost, he polled more votes than any previous Republican candidate in history. On the other hand, a host of prominent Republican isolationists in the congressional wing of the party—Hamilton Fish and Stephen Day in the House, for example, and Gerald Nye, Stephen Danaher, and James Davis in the Senate—were everywhere defeated and the trend of the 1942 elections was definitely reversed. This development should indicate something, one would think, of the significance of the foreign policy issue in the campaign. For Republicans it was to indicate that any further association with isolationism meant political death and that the strategy of bipartisanship developed by Vandenberg, Dulles, and Dewey merited further consideration.

8 A POSTSCRIPT ON BIPARTISANSHIP

When Republicans began to contemplate results after the elections of 1944, they were impressed with the two most obvious ones: the size and closeness of the presidential vote and the political decimation of congressional isolationists. Not only was attention focused on the record number of ballots cast for their presidential candidate, but it was also drawn to the realization that a shift of approximately 300,000 votes in fifteen states outside the South, as National Chairman Herbert Brownell reported in a postelection analysis, would have given Thomas E. Dewey a victory.[1]

Elsewhere, of course, the G.O.P. had not come nearly so close. It had lost thirty seats in the House and had gained only one in the Senate—and that one just barely, as Senator Robert A. Taft was reelected in Ohio by a scant 17,740 votes.[2] The trend toward Republican congressional growth that had seemed inevitable in 1942 appeared to have been dramatically halted. Internationalists campaigning to rewrite the aftermath of World War I—to convince Americans this time of the necessity for postwar international organization—and the Democrats in league with them had apparently won the day.

In terms of the strategy of bipartisanship in foreign policy, the combination of these results had important positive ramifications. Given Dewey's strong showing, his loss was interpreted as a near success rather than as a failure. Thus, he maintained his strong position of leadership in the presidential wing of the party after the election instead of losing it to leaders of the congressional wing, as Wendell Willkie had after his defeat in 1940. Herbert Brownell, installed by Dewey as Republican national chairman following the 1944 convention, retained the office after the election and was confirmed in his position at a meeting in December between Dewey and various congressional leaders in New York.

Dewey's continued prominence in the presidential wing of the party, his cooperative attitude toward Republicans in Congress, and the widespread defeat of isolationist candidates for office virtually assured that the bipartisan approach to foreign policy elaborated in the campaign would be continued.[3]

The Republicans could hardly abandon bipartisanship. They could not readily return to strategies of partisan opposition on foreign policy, particularly on issues of postwar order, given the congressional results and the difficulties that Dewey himself had encountered on that subject in the campaign. Nor were they likely to go forward and try to outdistance the administration in foreign policy. Willkie's results in the 1944 primaries provided a vivid example of the futility of that strategy. Furthermore, pressures on Republicans like Senator Vandenberg, whose constituencies and past political beliefs dictated that they exercise extreme caution on issues involving postwar relations with the Allies, especially the Russians, militated against the party's taking a too advanced position. Continuation of the bipartisan strategy, originally embarked on as a middle path between these two extremes, was therefore deemed essential.

At the top of the Republican presidential wing, Dulles and Dewey remained personally dissatisfied with many of the foreign policies of the administration after the election. They continued to have qualms about the Russians and Roosevelt's dealings with them, most immediately at Yalta. Dulles, moreover, objected to the doctrine of unconditional surrender, particularly as applied to Japan, for he believed that it might unnecessarily prolong the war and cost a good many lives.[4] Nevertheless, the Republican leaders continued to follow the road to bipartisanship which they had staked out in the campaign. Writing to his brother Allen in December, John Foster Dulles revealed that the new secretary of state, Edward Stettinius, had asked him "to come down to Washington" and go over the administration's current approach to international organization. "I think we may find a basis," Dulles confided, "for continuing to work in contact with each other in relation to that particular matter."[5] Although he still retained a good many reservations about Dumbarton Oaks, Dulles now decided to support that plan for international organization as a realistic alternative to world chaos.[6]

In the congressional wing of the party, Vandenberg likewise retained his doubts about the administration's foreign policies, including its proposal for an international organization. Following the elections, he declared:

> I too fear that we are once more headed for tragic disillusionment.
> I too wish that the high spokesmen for our own America would always be as loyal to our own indispensable self-interest as Mr. Churchill

is to Britain's and as Mr. Stalin is to Russia's. I think there is *more* need
for an effective postwar peace organization following *this* war than was
the case following World War No. One—chiefly because the awful ad-
vances which science is making in the arts of mass destruction seems
[sic] to promise that World War No. Three would be the end of civilization. But certainly we must be eternally and courageously vigilant in
the constant protection of the rights and interests of our own United
States. Furthermore, I have the deep conviction that the peace terms
themselves must be *just* to all concerned (despite the appetites of Mr.
Churchill and Mr. Stalin) if there is to be any hope that an international
peace organization can succeed.[7]

On January 10, 1945, moreover, the eve of President Roosevelt's departure for the Yalta conference, Vandenberg delivered a famous speech in
the Senate to this effect. The speech contained the same distinctive themes
mentioned above. Apprehension of the Allies, references to "justice," and
fears of World War III were all present. The tone of the talk, however, was
remarkably conciliatory, considering the outburst against Soviet designs
on Eastern European territory that the administration, for one, had been
expecting from the senator. There was also a new proposal amidst the
characteristic Vandenberg rhetoric. He declared his opinion that prior
congressional approval would not be necessary for the United States to
act militarily in helping to enforce disarmament upon Germany and Japan
after the war. Such action, contended Vandenberg, together with a treaty
guaranteeing it, ought to alleviate the Russians' fears of postwar insecu-
rity along their borders, thus making them more amenable to the causes
of the smaller European states situated there.[8]

Much to his own amazement, Vandenberg's speech was considered at
the time symbolic of his conversion from isolationism to internationalism
and indicative of a widespread sentiment for approval of the new international organization in the Senate as a whole.[9] In truth, the sentiments of
the speech, including the point about enforcing disarmament, were not
much different from those that Vandenberg had been expressing in private discussions for some months. The speech itself was merely an elaboration of these views in public for the first time and a minimal extension
of the strategy of bipartisanship. Indeed, Dewey's comment some years
later on Vandenberg's address characterized it most succinctly: "He made
a speech which happened to make big news."[10] The overwhelmingly favorable response to that speech, however, certainly reinforced Republican
belief in the inherent advantages of bipartisanship.

The next important step in the development of this bipartisanship for
Republicans was taken by Vandenberg and Dulles together. It was highly

symbolic also, given the party's past history. Both men participated in the San Francisco Conference of 1945 which established the United Nations. Vandenberg was at first reluctant to attend the conference as a member of the United States delegation, exhibiting the same caution he had demonstrated earlier in agreeing to join Secretary Hull's Committee of Eight. Before agreeing to go to San Francisco, he demanded assurances from President Roosevelt in writing that he (Vandenberg) would be considered a "free agent" at the conference and guaranteed the right to present his own views to the American delegation and to reserve judgment upon the final result. In addition to such "untrammeled freedom," Vandenberg also requested that Dulles be permitted to accompany him to the conference.[11] Anxious to maintain the trappings of bipartisanship and insure Republican acceptance of the proposed international organization, the administration in the end assented to Vandenberg's requests. Both he and Dulles attended the San Francisco conference, took highly active roles in its deliberations, and associated themselves later with the Senate's approval of United States participation in the United Nations organization.[12]

The successful collaboration on bipartisanship between Vandenberg in the congressional wing of the party and Dulles in the presidential continued throughout the 1940s. As Republican members of American delegations, the two regularly attended conferences of the United Nations and of foreign ministers. In their persons, speeches, and activities, moreover, they further symbolized and justified for Republicans the bipartisan approach to foreign policy, especially after the G.O.P. won control of both houses of Congress in 1946 and Vandenberg became chairman of the Senate Foreign Relations Committee. Following Dewey's unexpected loss to Harry S. Truman in 1948, the fall of Chiang Kai-shek in China, the Korean War, and Vandenberg's illness and subsequent death, bipartisan foreign policy fell victim, temporarily at least, to Senator Taft and his reemergent strategy of public, partisan opposition. However, Republican presidential and congressional victories in 1952, Dulles' appointment as Secretary of State, and the party's return to more or less permanent minority status in Congress two years later facilitated the resurrection and enthronement of bipartisanship. It became the preferred strategy of both parties in foreign policy for the remainder of the decade, and of most Republicans even after that.

The collaboration of Vandenberg and Dulles on the bipartisan approach to foreign policy was strikingly close, personal, and full of mutual appreciation. The two men saw a good deal of each other socially as well as politically.[13] Dulles was reportedly amazed that a lifelong politician could be as idealistic as Vandenberg.[14] Vandenberg, for his part, commented after the election of 1944:

I really think it is little short of amazing that our views on foreign policy should have proved to be so emphatically harmonious. One of the most interesting and significant things *thus* demonstrated is the fact that so-called "isolationists" and so-called "internationalists" are not *necessarily* very far apart and really may be "brothers under the skin."[15]

Some, of course, would not consider this brotherhood so amazing. Revisionist historians, for example, have argued that a basic concensus, or agreement on ends, underlies the making of foreign policy in the United States; that any differences therein arise over means, not ends; and that distinctions between isolationists and internationalists are superficial. When Americans like Vandenberg and Dulles disagree, therefore, they do so over form, not substance. Conversely, when they realize agreement, as Vandenberg did in the passage quoted above, they are returning to a kind of natural state of rest.[16] Other analysts, as mentioned earlier, have concluded from the closeness of their association and views that Dulles was responsible for Vandenberg's conversion from isolationism to internationalism.[17]

While acknowledging the presence of strong personal and even ideological elements in the Vandenberg-Dulles alliance, one can nevertheless conclude that after the elections of 1944, as before, the "brotherhood" of the two which Vandenberg acclaimed resulted less from any conversion experience or basic identity of views on foreign policy than from political calculation. This is not to say that Vandenberg was unconcerned about the prospect of another world war or unaware of the serious implications that technological change and advanced weaponry posed for the future security of the United States. Nor is it to deny that John Foster Dulles was deeply committed to a new, more rational form of international organization. The gamut of individual motivations for action is always extremely wide and complex.

Nevertheless, it remains that "under the skin" both Vandenberg and Dulles were blood brothers in politics, sharing an appreciation of and a commitment to their own and their party's requirements in the political arena. Each man could disagree with the other's views on foreign policy yet find in the political situation enough common ground upon which to stand. Vandenberg never shared Dulles's degree of interest in and commitment to matters of international trade and finance. He was skeptical of the Bretton Woods agreements, for example, where Dulles was sure.[18] Dulles, on the other hand, could never summon up Vandenberg's enthusiasm for affirmations of national sovereignty in party and governmental pronouncements on foreign policy. Both men, however, could agree on the political necessity of supporting each other's posi-

tions, as they had in the Republican platform plank on foreign policy
in 1944.

For Vandenberg, the political motive for bipartisan action in foreign
policy was immediate. With the question of his reelection to the Senate
due to be decided again in 1946, he stood confronted with the ominous
precedent of the mass elimination of former isolationists from Congress
in 1944. Perhaps too, in 1945, he had not entirely given up the idea of
running for president that he had entertained in 1940. In either event,
Vandenberg depended on the bipartisan approach to foreign policy to
keep not only his party's political hopes alive but also his own. To
Dulles, who was to speak in Detroit early in 1945 and asked him for
advice on what to say, Vandenberg replied:

> I frankly (and probably selfishly) hope that you can refer to *our*
> relationship as a fine example of the fact that there is a sound mid-
> dle ground (between extremists at the right and left) upon which we
> can hope to proceed in organizing the postwar world for peace. Fur-
> thermore, it is the best example I know of that we must clear our minds
> of old "labels" in searching for this common ground. You were *supposed*,
> out our way, to have been a so-called "internationalist". I was supposed,
> out our way, to be a so-called "isolationist". But after we had been to-
> gether for half an hour in our initial discussion, we discovered that we
> believed substantially in precisely the same theme. I think the substantial
> nature of this agreement has been demonstrated upon many subsequent
> occasions.
>
> Selfishly, I should like to have my Michigan constituents know from
> someone like you that I am highly placed on the small special Senate
> Committee which is cooperating with the State Department in respect
> to this whole problem and that I am trying to take a thoroughly con-
> structive viewpoint in respect to it.[19]

Vandenberg was confronted with a difficult political dilemma in 1945.
On the one hand, he did not want to appear to be assaying the role of Senator Henry Cabot Lodge in 1920 and leading a return to isolationism, so
thoroughly had that position been discredited in the public mind by the
wartime campaign for internationalism. To critics of his pursuit of the bipartisan image for Republicans in foreign policy, Vandenberg remarked
that he did not know what the effect of the San Francisco Conference on
the party would be, but was "deeply convinced that if representatives of
the Republican Party had declined the President's invitation, it would have
been just about equivalent to committing suicide in public." Contending
that at least 90 percent of the American people were pinning their hopes
for future peace on a successful outcome of the deliberations at San Fran-

cisco, he expressed an "equally profound conviction that these people will not forgive *anybody* who needlessly handicaps this aspiration."[20]

On the other hand, given the pressures of Vandenberg's heavily ethnic constituency, he could not afford to be identified too closely in bipartisanship with decisions made at Yalta concerning the fate of Eastern Europe. His solution, therefore, was to focus on the word "justice," as he did in his speech on January 10, 1945, and to insist that his cooperation with the administration on foreign policy was intended to insure the maintenance of "justice" in that area. He had set himself a definite objective at San Francisco, Vandenberg announced:

> The word "justice" does not once appear in Dumbarton Oaks (except briefly in the World Court chapter). This omission is equally evident in the mechanism itself. I propose to *try* to put "justice" in the cornerstone. . . . I have proposed nine specific amendments along this line to the State Department and to the American delegation. I am happy to say that Mr. John Foster Dulles has endorsed them. I am also happy to say that the State Department thus far seems to be receptive. If we are to think of this adventure in terms of politics, I would like to identify our Republicanism with "justice."[21]

Once again, a demonstrably political solution (notice Vandenberg's fixation upon the word "justice" itself) was tailored by the Republican congressional leader to fit a particular political problem.

This is not to say that Vandenberg was oblivious to the effects of bipartisanship on the American political system as a whole. Far from it. In a most interesting and revealing letter which he wrote to the chairman of the Democratic National Committee, Robert E. Hannegan, in 1946, a little more than a week before the elections that year, Vandenberg himself raised the key questions: "Is bipartisan foreign policy permanently possible? . . . Does this necessity irrevocably collide with our two-party political system (which is equally necessary)?" The people of this country, he acknowledged, "certainly are entitled to control 'foreign policy' with their ballots—and any moratorium which stops discussion of these problems at the water[']s edge smacks of cloture." Nevertheless, the immediate question for him remained "whether—and if so, how—bi-partisan, united, American foreign policy can live under the two-party political system in the United States."[22]

More specifically, Vandenberg contended in two passages of this letter, which deserve to be quoted at length, that

> During my foreign policy collaboration with President Truman and Secretary Byrnes (Democrats) I have flatly refused to make *any* speeches on a partisan (Republican) basis because I have considered that this would tend to destroy bi-partisan (which is to say, *United American)* foreign pol-

icy. I have been severely criticized in some sectors of my own Party as
a result. It has been argued that this trend toward the *"one party system"*
which would spell the negation of American political liberties, transfer
the infirmities of totalitarian elections to the United States, and thus defeat (for us) the achievement of what Secretary Byrnes calls a "peoples'
peace." It has been argued that this helps the "ins" to keep the "outs"
out. Unquestionably there is a powerful argument to be made along
these lines—*particularly if and when the majority party takes "foreign
policy" into election politics.* It is, of course, off-set by considerations
of *national interest* (which ought to be paramount)—and I hesitate to
think what might have happened to our foreign relations and to peace
if we Republicans had not patriotically thus subordinated partisan politics to the national interest. But again we find ourselves plagued by
the fact that the "national interest" *also* requires the maintenance of
the two-party political system.

This immediately poses an equally embarrassing (and perhaps imponderable) question for the *political majority*—the Administration in
power. Having been the beneficiary of minority cooperation (without which it might have been in a grave dilemma), what is *its* ethical
and essential attitude when election time rolls round? Shall *it* keep
"foreign policy" out of its campaign appeal? Shall *it* forego the
partisan capitalization of its leadership in what, for the sake of
argument, is a successful "foreign policy" (even though this "success"
stems from bi-partisan cooperation)? If so, what does it do—as a practical matter—in respect to the candidates of *minority* leaders whose indispensable cooperation has made this successful "foreign policy"
possible? Does a Democratic Administration *endorse* these Republicans—or visa versa? [*sic*] Is that fair to the two-party system? Does
not that immediately transfer all the *political* advantage of a bipartisan "foreign policy" to the minority?"[23]

In these two passages, Vandenberg had both thoroughly and effectively
defined for opposition and majority alike in the United States the central dilemma of the country's political system in dealing with foreign
policy. With his references to "considerations of national interest,"
moreover, he had even touched on questions of closed versus open diplomacy that had been central to the debate on American participation
in World War I and the Treaty of Versailles and on questions of presidential prerogative that came to dominate discussion of foreign policy
in the 1960s.

True to form, however, Vandenberg was not content to allow his
analysis to remain on this high "academic level," as he put it. Offer-

ing himself as a "guinea pig" in the analysis, he observed that for
eighteen months he had spent most of his time "cooperating with two
Democratic Presidents and three Democratic Secretaries of State—at
their solicitation—in developing a bi-partisan, American foreign policy.
All five of them have been kind enough to express their gratitude and
appreciation," he added. Then, after reminding the Democratic chairman
that he was "a candidate for re-election on the *Republican* ticket on
November 5th," Vandenberg let fly with a complaint which, one sus-
pects, he had been harboring all along:

> On the same day that I received President Truman's commission as
> an American Delegate to the second session of the General Assembly
> of the United Nations—a commission which says that he "reposes
> special trust and confidence in my integrity and ability"—his Party's
> National Committee, at the request of his Party's State Committee,
> sends two of its most prominent orators (whom I shall not name be-
> cause this is a purely impersonal inquiry) into Michigan to seek *my*
> Party's defeat in general and *my* defeat in particular. Bang! "Foreign
> policy" is back in politics! Do I *still* keep still (which I *am* doing)?
> Or do I shove "foreign policy" still further into politics—and probably
> for keeps?[24]

Indeed, Vandenberg had kept relatively "still" with his complaint.
He had, after all, told Hannegan at the outset of the letter to put it
aside "for post-election answer" and had acknowledged later that perhaps it was "impossible" for the latter "to generalize in answering." But
Vandenberg had not failed to point out that "many Democrats have
answered, in their *personal* capacities, by generously supporting me"
and that "Secretaries of State Hull and Stettinius and Byrnes have answered by never making partisan, political speeches." Furthermore, he
warned the Democratic chairman to take heed: "if *I* am defeated it is
the *Administration's* 'foreign policy' which really takes the licking because I am so closely identified with it. Yet if I *win*, I may contribute
to a major *political* defeat for the Administration. So the Administration loses in *either* event." Despite a professed desire in his letter to
Hannegan to keep discussion of bipartisanship "at the academic
level," Vandenberg could not resist—doubtless intended—pointing his
remarks in the direction of his personal political situation.[25]

For John Foster Dulles in the presidential wing, the political promise
of a bipartisan approach to foreign policy after the election of 1944 was
a little more remote but nonetheless as real as it was for Vandenberg. By
virtually all accounts, Dulles wanted to become, like his grandfather and
uncle before him, secretary of state.[26] One does not have to go as far as

Wendell Willkie reportedly did, and charge that Dulles's State Department ambitions led him to make Dewey a presidential candidate in the first place, to admit the essential validity of the point.[27]

The background of Dulles's appointment in 1953 as Secretary of State lay not only in his prominence among presidential Republicans but also in his connections with members of the party's congressional wing. According to House Republican leader Martin, Dulles went out of his way to assist G.O.P. congressmen and was known more as a party than as a Dewey man in Republican circles.[28] While associating with Vandenberg in the development of bipartisanship, Dulles always kept open his lines of communication with Senator Taft. In the presidential contest of 1952 between Dwight D. Eisenhower and Taft, therefore, Dulles proved once again to be acceptable to both sides, much as he had to both Taft and Willkie in 1944. Drawing upon his experience with Vandenberg in that earlier election year, Dulles prepared a foreign policy plank for the Republican platform in 1952 and saw it unanimously accepted, largely because he had obtained Taft's approval of it in advance. Because of such efforts and associations, moreover, Dulles himself remained confident, according to his contemporaries, that he would have been secretary of state in the new Republican administration even if the party had nominated and elected Taft instead of Eisenhower.[29]

In response to the questions raised at the outset of this work, therefore, one might reasonably conclude that the bipartisan approach to foreign policy developed by the Republican party during World War II represented less of a conversion in basic attitudes toward foreign affairs (as is commonly supposed) and more of a strategic response to a hazardous situation in American politics. The party's image of former isolationism, particularly in connection with the defeat of the League of Nations in the United States, threatened disaster at the polls on a number of occasions between 1941 and 1945. Only by ridding themselves of that image completely could Republicans hope to survive World War II as a viable party of opposition and, ultimately, to regain the White House.

Several remedies for this situation were advanced during the period. Wendell Willkie and the internationalists, drawing support mainly from the presidential wing of the party, proposed getting rid of the onus of isolationism by publicly admitting such past "mistakes" and atoning for them with programs for future world order more advanced, in some cases, than those of the Democrats. Republican isolationists, their strength centered primarily in Congress, wanted to ignore the problem of their prewar image as completely as possible and attack the administration's wartime foreign policy instead. Both factions, as well as both wings of the party initially, appeared set on a collision course for ultimate political disaster.

To avert this disaster, Vandenberg in the congressional wing of the party and Dulles in the presidential fashioned a compromise: the bipartisan approach to foreign policy. Its aim officially, according to the Hull-Dulles agreement during the 1944 campaign, was to remove questions of postwar international organization from "destructive political criticism." The destructiveness of such criticism, Dulles and Vandenberg believed, was more likely to harm Republicans than it was the international organization. Their bipartisan approach worked. It ultimately removed the threat of the party's old image in foreign policy. At the same time, it coaxed the isolationist factions within the party, as well as the congressional and presidential wings, into suspending for the most part their habitual competition for power and dominance.

As practiced during the war, however, the bipartisan strategy *was* a way of preserving rather than stifling Republican opposition. It applied largely to the issue of international organization and even there, as defined by Vandenberg and Dulles, did not necessarily commit party members in advance to specific administration policies. Association with the publicly popular issue of international organization freed Republican energies for dissent in other areas of domestic and foreign policy. It may, indeed, have eventually put the party "in a position to alter basic public attitudes, especially with respect to Russia, labor, and government controls," as Donald R. McCoy has argued. It may even have made it clear "as a result of demands by Vandenberg and others . . . that the United States must begin to stand up to Soviet demands."[30]

Within the party itself, bipartisanship allowed such persistent critics of the administration as Senator Taft to maintain their opposition to specific policies in comparative political safety from hostile public reaction.[31] Thus, that opposition could easily burst forth again in full partisan array during the Korean War in the early 1950s. When, at that time, bipartisanship came under heavy attack from the partisans, Vandenberg himself defended it as follows: "Bipartisan cooperation in Foreign Policy (which involves no remote suggestion of withholding vigorous and vigilant criticism when and where deserved) is not only 'good patriotism' in my book; it is also the best kind of *Republican politics.*"[32]

In the long run, as McCoy has suggested, "the most important contribution of Republican opposition during the war" may have been "that it showed partisan politics could be conducted without damaging the war effort," a subject of some concern at the war's outset. Moreover, the "covert weapon of opposition" (bipartisanship) did continue "as a way by which many of the tough problems of the postwar period could be tackled with

a modicum of effectiveness and a maximum of national unity."[33] Contrary
to McCoy's view, however, the weapon was as much offered by the administration, in hopes of coopting Republican support, as "wrung from"
it, and the important question still remains: Just how effective was that
weapon in the long run?

Bipartisanship in foreign policy may have preserved formal opposition
in the United States during World War II, but as time went on, form seems
to have substituted for function. Republicans like Senator Taft may have
renewed direct opposition in foreign policy from 1948 to 1953. But that
was just about the last time anyone in government attempted to do so until the late 1960s. When Eisenhower and Dulles after 1952 reunited their
party and opposition Democrats (themselves no strangers to policies which
they had previously urged on Republicans) along bipartisan and anti communist lines, the remnants of opposition on foreign policy disappeared
from the citadels of government in the United States for more than a decade.

In retrospect, it seems clear that since World War II, opposition on
foreign policy, particularly in Congress, has been surrendered, in part for
the sake of increasing power, influence, and interest in domestic affairs.
Bipartisanship always extended more to foreign policy than to domestic.
Opposition efforts, begun in the late 1930s, to halt and dismantle the
New Deal gained impetus during the war; they succeeded then in abolish-
ing the Civilian Conservation Corps, the Works Progress Administration,
the National Youth Administration, and the National Resources Planning
Board; and they continued afterwards. However, nothing like the degree
or intensity of opposition on foreign policy existing among Republicans
before the war remained. Even such opposition as there was during the
war, operating under the cloak of bipartisanship, was limited, especially
in comparison to prewar standards. The pattern from the beginning of
World War II to the mid-1960s at least is consistent: real opposition may
exist in domestic matters, but bipartisanship reigns supreme in the area
of foreign policy. The Executive has steadily amassed more and more
power in that area, invariably at the expense of the Legislature and presumably, too, of the American people.

Neither World War II itself nor the development of a bipartisan strategy during the war appears to have altered prewar Republican attitudes
on foreign policy either fundamentally or extensively. The American
public's reaction to these and future events perhaps worked such changes
later on; perhaps Republican attitudes helped condition this public reaction. For the moment, however, congressional Republicans like Vandenberg were still, essentially, isolationists, believing ultimately in the
security of a better-armed and fortified America first and of an interna-

tional organization second; presidential Republicans like Dulles remained internationalists, but ultimately they came to believe in the same thing. Thus the thesis of James MacGregor Burns discussed and qualified in Chapter 1, that members of a party's presidential wing are in general more internationalist than their relatively isolationist congressional counterparts, would seem to be, if not exactly verified, at least not contradicted by the case of the Republican party during World War II.

Most congressional Republicans at that time, it seems fair to conclude, had no "grand vision" of a new world order for which they were willing to exert themselves or their party. And those who may have had such a vision—like Joseph Ball, for example, in the Senate—often became estranged from their colleagues as a result. Most of these congressional Republicans looked to the past, and then only to defend themselves against charges that they, or their party, had lacked such vision at critical times. Among presidential Republicans during the war, those who propagated their views on future world order either isolated themselves from the mainstream of party thinking, like Wendell Willkie, or, like John Foster Dulles, sacrificed these views on occasion to the claims of political, and sometimes personal, expediency.

In sum, the Republicans were faced with a difficult political problem after Pearl Harbor, one to which they finally applied a distinctively political solution. The strategy of bipartisan foreign policy ultimately removed from the party and some of its more prominent leaders the discredited image of isolationism, providing them at the same time with one that was more appealing. Bipartisanship also averted a potential split between the presidential and congressional wings of the G.O.P. at the outset of World War II and drew them closer together by the end. Finally, it permitted Republicans, in the 1940s at least, to maintain a diversity of views on foreign policy within the context of a single and still politically viable opposition party, though at some cost, undoubtedly, to other institutions of American government, like the Congress, where opposition on foreign policy in the past had been more openly expressed.

NOTES

CHAPTER 1

1. In his many writings on the subject since the end of World War II, Hans J. Morgenthau has alerted scholars to this dimension of the war's effects. For a recent statement of Morgenthau's views, see his essay in Lloyd C. Gardner, Arthur Schlessinger, Jr., and Hans J. Morgenthau, *The Origins of the Cold War* (Waltham, Mass.: Ginn-Blaisdell, 1970), 79-102. For an example among historians of the United States of a work displaying an awareness of the war's ramifications in terms of global power, as well as its social revolutionary aspects, see Gabriel Kolko, *The Politics of War: The World and United States Foreign Policy, 1943-1945* (New York: Random House, 1968).

2. Richard Polenberg, *War and Society: The United States, 1941-1945* (Philadelphia: J.B. Lippincott Company, 1972), 4.

3. See James T. Patterson, "A Conservative Coalition Forms in Congress, 1933-1939," *Journal of American History* 52 (March 1966), 757-772, for a concise analysis of the role of Congress in domestic policy from the start of the New Deal to the outbreak of World War II in Europe; see Patterson's full-length study, *Congressional Conservatism and the New Deal: The Growth of the Conservative Coalition in Congress, 1933-1939* (Lexington: University of Kentucky Press, 1967), 337, for the conclusion that "foreign policy considerations, strange though it may seem now, had not been divisive congressional issues before 1939, mainly because the President, concentrating upon meeting the domestic emergency, declined to defy congressional sentiment for neutrality legislation." For a particularly striking example of Roosevelt surrendering on foreign policy (on repeal of the arms embargo) only a matter of weeks before the war in Europe began, see Robert A. Divine, *The Reluctant Belligerent: American Entry into World War II* (New York: John Wiley & Sons, Inc., 1965), 62-63. Political scientist James A. Robinson in *Congress and Foreign Policy-Making:*

A Study in Legislative Influence and Initiative (Homewood, Ill.: The Dorsey Press, 1967), 26-27, 213, confirms the notion of a congressional initiative on neutrality legislation from 1935 to 1939 while at the same time concluding that the trend during the period 1933-1961 finds Congress foregoing initiatives and losing effective power to the president in decision-making on foreign policy.

4. Charles O. Jones, *The Minority Party in Congress* (Boston: Little, Brown & Co., 1970), 1. The reference to Dahl is from Robert A. Dahl, "The American Oppositions: Affirmation and Denial," in Robert A. Dahl (ed.), *Political Oppositions in Western Democracies* (New Haven: Yale University Press, 1966), 196.

5. H. Bradford Westerfield, *Foreign Policy and Party Politics: Pearl Harbor to Korea* (New Haven: Yale University Press, 1955), 410.

6. James MacGregor Burns, "Bipartisanship and the Weakness of the Party System," *American Perspective* 4 (Spring 1950), 169-174, reprinted in Harold Karan Jacobson (ed.), *America's Foreign Policy* (New York: Random House, 1965), 48-52.

7. Norman A. Graebner, *The New Isolationism: A Study In Politics and Foreign Policy since 1950* (New York: The Ronald Press Company, 1956), 4.

8. James MacGregor Burns, *The Deadlock of Democracy: Four-Party Politics in America* (Englewood Cliffs, N.J.: Prentice-Hall, Inc., 1967), 196.

9. James MacGregor Burns, "White House vs. Congress," *The Atlantic* 205 (March 1960), 65, as quoted in Ronald J. Caridi, *The Korean War and American Politics: The Republican Party as a Case Study* (Philadelphia: University of Pennsylvania Press, 1968), 19. I am indebted to Caridi's work for first calling my attention to Burns's line of thought on the structure of political parties.

10. Burns, *The Deadlock of Democracy*, 263.

11. Burns, "White House vs. Congress," 65.

12. Burns, *The Deadlock of Democracy*, 200.

13. For examples of such definitions by historians, embodied in works covering different chronological periods, see Felix Gilbert, *To the Farewell Address: Ideas of Early American Foreign Policy* (Princeton: Princeton University Press, 1961); Selig Adler, *The Isolationist Impulse: Its Twentieth-Century Reaction* (New York: The Free Press, 1957); and Manfred Jonas, *tionism in America, 1935-1941* (Ithaca, N.Y.: Cornell University Press, 1966).

14. See Arthur S. Link, *Wilson The Diplomatist: A Look at His Major Foreign Policies* (Chicago: Quadrangle Books, 1965), 127-156.

15. See George H. Mayer, *The Republican Party, 1854-1966* (New York: Oxford University Press, 1967), 450-452; and Robert A. Dahl,

Congress and Foreign Policy (New York: Harcourt, Brace and Company, Inc., 1950), 188-190, 292, 294. Opposition to Lend-Lease, to repeal of neutrality legislation, and to establishment and, later, extension of selective service have regularly been taken as touchstones of congressional isolationism in both contemporary and historical accounts of this period. See, for example, the lead editorial in the *New York Times*, August 14, 1941, and Adler, *The Isolationist Impulse*, 282-288.

16. See Link, *Wilson the Diplomatist*, 127-156.

17. George L. Grassmuck, *Sectional Biases in Congress on Foreign Policy*, The John Hopkins University Studies in Historical and Political Science LXVIII, 3 (Baltimore: John Hopkins Press, 1951), 104,412.

18. Burns, *The Deadlock of Democracy*, 198.

19. Ibid.

20. The presidential wing of a party, with its national, state, and local organizations and their various officers, may possess more of the trappings of an institution or a "party" than the congressional, which is noticeably deficient in such structures, particularly in the period under consideration here. Nevertheless, members of a party's presidential wing depend primarily on the party's national leadership to formulate and represent for them party positions on pressing national issues, such as those of foreign policy were during this period. For the lack of structures in Congress comparable to those in the presidential wing of the party during the early 1940s, and one recently elected congressional Republican's surprise at that lack, see the Diary of Harold H. Burton, March 6, 1941, in the Papers of Harold H. Burton, Library of Congress (hereinafter cited as the Burton Diary). See also James T. Patterson, *Mr. Republican: A Biography of Robert A. Taft* (Boston: Houghton Mifflin Company, 1972), 267, for Senator Taft's efforts in 1944 to bring a greater degree of institutional organization to Republicans in Congress by establishing a steering committee to formulate Republican policy.

21. Burns, *The Deadlock of Democracy*, 255.

22. Charles D. Hilles to Werner W. Schroeder, December 9, 1942, in the Papers of Charles D. Hilles, Yale University Library (hereinafter cited as the Hilles Papers).

23. Burns, *The Deadlock of Democracy*, 202.

24. Gabriel A. Almond, *The American People and Foreign Policy* (New York: Frederick A. Praeger, Inc., 1960), 70-80.

25. A staple of textbook and other interpretations of this period, the notion that both the United States and the Republican party underwent a conversion experience in foreign policy during World War II has long been familiar in American historiography. For an interesting yet succinct account of this view, see Robert Freeman Smith, "Amer-

ican Foreign Relations, 1920-1942," in Barton J. Bernstein (ed.), *Towards a New Past: Dissenting Essays in American History* (New York: Random House, 1967), 232-237.

26. Donald R. McCoy, "Republican Opposition During Wartime, 1941-1945," *Mid America: An Historical Review* 49 (July 1967), 184.

CHAPTER 2

1. Diary of Harold H. Burton, December 7, 1941, Burton Papers.

2. Arthur H. Vandenberg, Jr., and Joe Alex Morris (eds.), *The Private Papers of Senator Vandenberg* (Cambridge, Mass.: Houghton Mifflin Company, 1952), 1, 16.

3. See p. 18 of this book.

4. The papers of senators Burton, White, La Follette, Taft, and McNary are in the Library of Congress. The papers of Senator Austin are in the Library of the University of Vermont; the papers of Senator Vandenberg, in the William L. Clements Library of the University of Michigan. All have been consulted in the preparation of this study. The best available account of Senator Ball's ideas and activities in this period is contained in Robert A. Divine, *Second Chance: The Triumph of Internationalism in America During World War II* (New York: Atheneum, 1967); Divine benefited from access to Ball's papers and from interviews with the former senator. Reliable accounts of Senator Nye and Representative Fish in the prewar period may be found in Wayne S. Cole, *Senator Gerald P. Nye and American Foreign Relations* (Minneapolis: The University of Minnesota Press, 1962), and Jonas, *Isolationism in America.*

5. *New York Times*, January 4, 1942. See also John Callan O'Laughlin to Herbert Hoover, February 28 and June 6, 1942, the Papers of John Callan O'Laughlin, Library of Congress (hereinafter cited as the O'Laughlin Papers). Editor of the *Army and Navy Journal*, O'Laughlin was a frequent correspondent of former President Hoover, Charles D. Hilles (a former chairman of the Republican National Committee), and General John J. Pershing. O'Laughlin endeavored to keep them thoroughly and regularly informed of events transpiring in the nation's capitol, where he resided, by means of a private weekly newsletter in which he reported recent developments in politics and military affairs.

6. Joseph F. Guffey, *New York Times*, December 29, 1941. Guffey was a Democratic senator from Pennsylvania at this time.

7. Walter Littlefield to the editor, *New York Times*, January 4, 1942.

8. Address by Oscar R. Ewing, February 23, 1942, in M. H. McIntyre to Oscar R. Ewing, March 30, 1942, PPF 1820 (Correspondence, Box 8), the Papers of Franklin D. Roosevelt, Roosevelt Library, Hyde Park, New York (hereinafter cited as the Roosevelt Papers).

9. Austin, "Memorandum . . . regarding White House Conference of Sunday, December 7, 1941," in the Papers of Warren R. Austin, University of Vermont Library, Burlington, Vermont (hereinafter cited as the Austin Papers).

10. *New York Times*, December 8, 1941.

11. *Congressional Record*, 77th Cong., 1st sess., 9505 (December 8, 1941).

12. Ibid., 9506, 9536-9537,

13. *New York Times*, December 9, 1941.

14. Burton Diary, December 11, 1941; *New York Times*, December 12, 1941; *Congressional Record*, 77th Cong., 1st sess., 9650 (December 11, 1941).

15. *Congressional Record*, 77th Cong., 1st sess., 9650-9653, 9665-9667 (December 11, 1941); *New York Times*, December 12, 1941.

16. Arthur H. Vandenberg to John H. Schouten, December 15, 1941, the Papers of Arthur H. Vandenberg, William L. Clements Library, University of Michigan, Ann Arbor (hereinafter cited as the Vandenberg Papers).

17. *New York Times*, January 7, 1942.

18. Ibid., January 6, 1942.

19. Ibid., December 8, 1941; Vandenberg to Patrick H. Walsh, January 2, 1942, Vandenberg Papers.

20. *New York Times*, December 8, 1941.

21. Joseph H. Ball, "This Month in Congress," *The Republican* 7 (February 1942), 17.

22. *New York Times*, December 8, 1941.

23. Ibid., December 12, 1941; *Congressional Record*, 77th Cong., 1st sess., 9656-9659 (December 11, 1941).

24. *Congressional Record*, 77th Cong. 1st sess., 9542 (December 9, 1941).

25. *Current Biography*, 1941, 862.

26. *Congressional Record*, 77 Cong., 1st sess., 9658, 9659 (December 11, 1941); *New York Times*, December 12, 1941.

27. *Congressional Record*, 77th Cong., 1st sess., 9563 (December 9, 1941); *New York Times*, December 12, 1941.

28. *New York Times*, December 12, 1941.

29. *Congressional Record*, 77th Cong., 1st sess., 9659 (December 11, 1941); see also the *New York Times*, December 12, 1941.

30. Ball, "This Month in Congress," 17.

31. Vandenberg to Howard Ellis, February 12, 1942, Vandenberg Papers. For further comments of this sort by Vandenberg, see C. David Tompkins, *Senator Arthur H. Vandenberg: The Evolution of a Modern Republican, 1884-1945* (East Lansing: Michigan State University Press, 1970), 189. Elements of support for the noninterventionist position later appeared in historical accounts of United States-Japanese diplomacy prior to Pearl Harbor. See the memoirs of the U.S. Ambassador to Japan at the time, Joseph C. Grew, *Turbulent Era: A Diplomatic Record of Forty Years, 1904-1945*, 2 vols. (Boston: Houghton Mifflin Company, 1952), II, 1244-1375, edited by Walter Johnson, and Paul W. Schroeder, *The Axis Alliance and Japanese-American Relations* (Ithaca, N.Y.: Cornell University Press, 1958).

32. Vandenberg to H. I. Walker, September 4, 1942, Vandenberg Papers.

33. Vandenberg to Leo C. Lillie, January 7, 1942, Vandenberg Papers.

34. Vandenberg to Walker, September 4, 1942, Vandenberg Papers.

35. *Congressional Record*, 77th Cong., 2nd sess., A442 (February 9, 1942).

36. O'Laughlin to Herbert Hoover, February 21, 1942, O'Laughlin Papers.

37. *Vital Speeches* 8 (December 19, 1941), 169-173.

38. Ibid., 169.

39. Ibid.

40. Ball, "This Month in Congress," 17.

41. Vandenberg to Charles McBride, January 12, 1942, Vandenberg Papers.

42. O'Laughlin to Hoover, February 21, February 28, March 7, 1942, O'Laughlin Papers.

43. As quoted in Tompkins, *Senator Arthur H. Vandenberg*, 190.

44. *Congressional Record*, 77th Cong., 1st sess., 9543 (December 9, 1941).

45. For an account of the role of the Committee on the Conduct of the war during the Civil War, which also devotes attention to the Vandenberg proposal, see Louis Smith, *American Democracy and Military Power* (Chicago: University of Chicago Press, 1951), 203, 211-212.

46. Vandenberg to Henry Hazlitt, February 20, 1942, Vandenberg Papers.

47. Vandenberg, *Private Papers*, 25.

48. Vandenberg to Henry Hazlitt, February 20, 1942, Vandenberg Papers.

49. Donald H. Riddle, *The Truman Committee: A Study in Congres-*

sional Responsibility (New Brunswick, N.J.: Rutgers University Press, 1964), 9.

50. *New York Times,* December 17, 1941; *Congressional Record,* 77th Cong., 1st. sess., 9543 (December 9, 1941).

51. See the *New York Times,* December 28, 1941, for an example of editorial support for a joint congressional-executive committee with power to oversee the war's conduct; see also Vandenberg to Hazlitt, February 20, 1942, Vandenberg Papers.

52. Vandenberg to Hazlitt, February 20, 1942, Vandenberg Papers.

53. *New York Times,* January 14, 1942.

54. *Chicago Daily Tribune,* January 14, 1942.

55. O'Laughlin to Hoover, January 17 and 31, 1942, O'Laughlin Papers; Burton Diary, January 26, 1942. The willingness of American isolationists to make an exception of Asia in their foreign policies is a difficult phenomenon to comprehend, let alone explain. Perhaps historical and ideological antipathies to Europe (and particularly Great Britain) left over from colonial days and exacerbated in modern times by imperial rivalries and the experience of World War I provide the best starting point for an explanation.

56. *New York Times,* January 16, 1942.

57. O'Laughlin to Hoover, January 24, 1942, O'Laughlin Papers.

58. *New York Times,* January 3, 1942; O'Laughlin to Hoover, February 14, 1942, O'Laughlin Papers.

59. *Congressional Record,* 77th Cong., 2nd sess., 3645 (April 23, 1942), 4705 (May 23, 1942), 4926 (June 5, 1942).

60. O'Laughlin to Hoover, February 14, 1942, O'Laughlin Papers.

61. O'Laughlin to Hoover, February 7, 1942, O'Laughlin Papers.

62. O'Laughlin to Hoover, February 14, 1942, O'Laughlin Papers.

63. Robert A. Taft to Charles D. Hilles, January 27, 1943, Hilles Papers.

64. As quoted by Representative Hamilton Fish in the *Congressional Record,* 77th Cong., 2nd sess., A1465 (April 21, 1942).

65. Hoover to O'Laughlin, February 23, 1942, O'Laughlin Papers.

66. *Vital Speeches* 8 (December 19, 1941), 172; *New York Times,* March 11, 1942; O'Laughlin to Hoover, February 14, 1942, O'Laughlin Papers.

67. *New York Times,* April 20 and 21, 1942.

68. Raymond Moley, "War and the New Deal," *Newsweek* 20. (September 7, 1942), 45.

69. *Newsweek* 19 (April 20, 1942), 28.

70. As quoted in Patterson, *Mr. Republican,* 247.

CHAPTER 3

1. *New York Times,* December 20, 1941.

2. Ibid., December 9, 1941.

3. *Chicago Daily Tribune,* December 8, 1941. The *Tribune* in a front page editorial declared:

> War has been forced on America by an insane clique of Japanese militarists who apparently see the desperate conflict into which they have led their country as the only thing that can prolong their power.
>
> Thus the thing that we all feared, that so many of us worked with all our hearts to avert, has happened. That is all that counts. It has happened. America faces war thru no volition of any American.
>
> Recriminations are useless and we doubt that they will be indulged in. Certainly not by us. All that matters today is that we are in the war and the nation must face that simple fact. All of us, from this day forth, have only one task. That is to strike with all our might to protect and preserve the American freedom that we all hold dear.

4. *New York Times,* December 11,1941.

5. Ibid., December 12, 1941.

6. See p. 13 of this book for a discussion of the role of leadership in the presidential wing of the party. See also Robert A. Taft to Colby Chester, August 12, 1942, Taft Papers, for a similar, contemporary appraisal of leadership's formative role in the national party: "A party headquarters cannot make party policy, in any event. That must be made by the leaders of the party, elected or nominated by the voters of the party. But a wise Chairman can keep these leaders in touch with each other, and see that there is no fundamental division. Apart from that, a national headquarters should have two purposes: publicity and organization."

7. *The Republican* 6 (December 1941), 14-15.

8. Ibid.

9. Wendell Willkie, as quoted in Francis Brown, "National Unity— A Willkie Formula," *New York Times Magazine* (December 14, 1941), 11.

10. Ibid.

11. As quoted in Donald Bruce Johnson, *The Republican Party and Wendell Willkie* (Urbana, Ill.: University of Illinois Press, 1960), 166.

12. Willkie, in Brown, "National Unity—A Willkie Formula," 11.

13. *New York Times*, January 7, 1942.

14. Ibid., January 15, 1942. See also Robert E. Sherwood, *Roosevelt and Hopkins: An Intimate History*, 2 vols. (New York: Harper & Brothers, 1950), II, 44, for White House discussion of a job for Willkie in the war effort.

15. *New York Times*, December 22, 1941.

16. Ibid., January 5, 1942.

17. Willkie, in Brown, "National Unity—a Willkie Formula," 11.

18. Jay G. Hayden, *Detroit News*, February 24, 1942.

19. *New York Times*, January 9, 1942.

20. *Newsweek* 19 (February 23, 1942), 23.

21. *New York Times*, February 7, 1942. See also John Callan O'Laughlin to Herbert Hoover, February 7, 1942, O'Laughlin Papers.

22. *New York Times*, February 12 and 24, 1942.

23. Ibid., February 12, 1942.

24. Raymond Moley, "Perspective: Formula for Wartime Politics," *Newsweek* 19 (February 16, 1942), 80.

25. For a contemporary discussion of the implications of the Illinois primary, see Jay G. Hayden, *Detroit News*, February 11 and 24, 1942.

26. Walter Littlefield to the editor, *New York Times*, December 29, 1941. The United Nations Declaration, signed in Washington, pledged that the twenty-six anti-Axis nations which signed it would adhere to the principles of the Atlantic Charter, employ their full military and economic resources in the war effort, and refuse to make a separate armistice or peace.

27. Wendell Willkie, "Let's Look Ahead," *New York Times Magazine* (February 15, 1942), 5ff; *New York Times*, January 3, 1942.

28. *New York Times*, April 19, 1942.

29. *Newsweek* 19 (April 27, 1942), 38.

30. *New York Times*, April 21, 1942.

31. *Newsweek* 19 (April 27, 1942), 38.

32. For a discussion of general press and public reaction to the declaration, see *Newsweek* 19 (April 27, 1942), 38.

33. *New York Times*, April 23, 1942.

34. Vandenberg, *Private Papers*, 30.

35. Hoover to O'Laughlin, April 22, 1942, O'Laughlin Papers.

36. "Letter to the Editor," *New York Times*, April 26, 1942.

37. Memorandum of correspondence with David K. Niles, March 18, 1942, OF 3855, Roosevelt Papers.

38. *Newsweek* 19 (May 4, 1942), 26.

39. Hoover to O'Laughlin, May 10, 1942, O'Laughlin Papers.

40. Hoover to O'Laughlin, April 10, 1942, O'Laughlin Papers.

41. Landon to Taft, February 21, 1942, Taft Papers.

42. As quoted in James MacGregor Burns, *Roosevelt: The Soldier of Freedom, 1940-1945* (New York: Harcourt Brace Jovanovich, Inc., 1970), 290.

43. Ernest K. Lindley, "Political Pressure and War Strategy," *Newsweek* 20 (August 10, 1942), 35.

44. Vandenberg to H. I. Walker, September 4, 1942, Vandenberg Papers.

45. Raymond Moley, "Political Roundup," *Newsweek* 19 (May 18, 1942), 64.

46. See Polenberg, *War and Society*, 189, for discussion of the effects of military enlistments and worker mobility on registration and voting in 1942; see Charles D. Hilles to Ezra R. Whitla, September 12, 1942, O'Laughlin Papers, for a sample of Republican reaction to the primaries.

47. *New York Times*, April 19, and July 13, 1942.

48. See *Chicago Daily Tribune*, June 4, 1942; see also *Newsweek* 20 (August 17, 1942), 37, and 20 (August 24, 1942), 33.

49. *Chicago Daily Tribune*, June 9, 1942; see also Johnson, *The Republican Party and Wendell Willkie*, 213.

50. *Chicago Daily Tribune*, June 19, 1942.

51. *The Republican* 6 (December 1941), 14; *New York Times*, May 20, 1942.

52. *New York Times*, June 20, 1942.

53. Johnson, *The Republican Party and Wendell Willkie*, 208.

54. *New York Times*, July 2, 1942.

55. Robert A. Divine, *Second Chance: The Triumph of Internationalism in America During World War II* (New York: Atheneum, 1967), 68-70.

56. *New York Times*, August 4, 1942.

57. Taft to Colby Chester, August 12, 1942, Taft Papers; see also Chester's memorandum, "The Republican Party," Taft Papers.

58. Herbert Hoover and Hugh Gibson, *The Problems of Lasting Peace* (Garden City, N.Y.: Doubleday, Doran and Co., Inc., 1942).

59. Ibid., 257-268, 283.

60. The following account of Willkie's trip is taken largely from a personal memoir written by one of his traveling companions, Joseph Barnes, which is contained in Barnes's later biography, *Willkie* (New York: Simon and Schuster, 1952).

61. See Johnson, *The Republican Party and Wendell Willkie*, 215.

62. Barnes, *Willkie*, 299.

63. Ibid., 283.

64. Ibid., 299.

65. Ibid., 308.

66. Ibid., 303.

67. Franklin D. Roosevelt, *Complete Presidential Press Conferences of Franklin D. Roosevelt*, 25 vols. (New York: Da Capo Press, Inc., 1972), XX, 131.

68. Barnes, *Willkie*, 307.

69. Ibid., 296.

70. Johnson, *The Republican Party and Wendell Willkie*, 220.

71. Wendell L. Willkie, *One World* (New York: Simon & Schuster, 1943); for a discussion of the impact of the book itself, see p. 94 of this book.

72. Johnson, *The Republican Party and Wendell Willkie*, 221-222; see also p. 88 of this book.

73. Burns, *Roosevelt: The Soldier of Freedom*, 277; see also O'Laughlin to Hoover, July 18, 1942, O'Laughlin Papers; and Polenberg, *War and Society*, 190.

74. Hilles to Joe R. Hanley, August 31, 1942, Hilles Papers.

75. See Hilles to Robert A. Taft, July 27, 1942, Hilles Papers.

76. Arthur Krock, *New York Times*, August 16, 1942.

77. *New York Times*, September 23, 1942, quoted in Divine, *Second Chance*, 71.

78. *New York Times*, September 24, 1942.

79. Ibid., September 23, 1942.

80. See Polenberg, *War and Society*, 189-190.

81. See Burns, *Roosevelt: The Soldier of Freedom*, 280-281.

82. Memorandum of Edwin W. Pauley to Roosevelt, December 14, 1942, PPF 1820 (Correspondence, Box 8), Roosevelt Papers.

83. Burns, *Roosevelt: The Soldier of Freedom*, 291.

84. Pauley Memorandum, Roosevelt papers.

85. L. G. Lenhardt to Blair Moody, November 10, 1942, the Papers of Blair Moody, Michigan Historical Collections, University of Michigan; see also Henry A. Wallace to Roosevelt, December 1942, PPF 1820 (Correspondence Box 8), Roosevelt Papers.

86. See, for example, Nicholas Murray Butler to Hilles, November 5, 1942, Hilles Papers.

87. C. M. Oehler, "The Meaning of the 1942 Elections," *The Republican* 7 (November 1942), 24.

88. Ibid.

89. Ibid.

CHAPTER 4

1. C. M. Oehler, "The Meaning of the 1942 Elections," *The Republican* 7 (November 1942), 10.

2. *The Republican* 8 (March 1943), 8; *Washington Post*, February 9, 1943; Polenberg, *War and Society*, 192.

3. *New York Times*, October 20 and 23, 1942.

4. Arthur H. Vandenberg to Major George Fielding Eliot, February 10, 1943, Vandenberg Papers.

5. *New York Times*, November 6, 8, and 10, 1942.

6. Alexander Wiley to Cordell Hull, September 16, 1942, 711.00/ 1614, the Records of the State Department, Record Group 59, in the National Archives (hereinafter cited as RG 59, National Archives). See also Wiley's article, "Foreign Relations Advisory Council," *The Republican* 7 (November 1942), 4-5, 19-20.

7. Wiley to Hull, October 23, 1942, 711.00/1616, RG 59, National Archives.

8. *New York Times*, November 6, 1942.

9. Ibid., November 11, 1942.

10. See John M. Vorys to Hull, January 26, 1943; Hull to Vorys, January 30, 1943; and Breckinridge Long to Vorys, February 1, 1943; all in 711.00/1621, RG 59, National Archives. See also Roland Young, *Congressional Politics in the Second World War* (New York: Columbia University Press, 1956), 18.

11. *New York Times*, January 10, 1943; for Flynn's statement, see p. 42 of this book.

12. See John Callan O'Laughlin to Herbert Hoover, January 16, 1943, O'Laughlin Papers.

13. Vandenberg, *Private Papers*, 33.

14. Warren R. Austin, "The Republican Conference," January 8-21, 1943, a memorandum, Austin Papers.

15. *Christian Science Monitor*, December 31, 1942.

16. Austin Memorandum, January 8, 1943, Austin Papers.

17. Roscoe Drummond, *Christian Science Monitor*, December 28, 1942; *Washington Post*, December 28, 1942.

18. Roscoe Drummond, *Christian Science Monitor*, December 28, 1942; Gould Lincoln, *Washington Evening Star*, December 27, 1942; *New York Herald Tribune*, December 25, 1942.

19. Roscoe Drummond, *Christian Science Monitor*, December 28, 1942.

20. *New York Herald Tribune*, December 25, 1942.

21. *Washington Post*, December 28, 1942; Gould Lincoln, *Washington Evening Star*, December 27, 1942.

22. Austin Memorandum, January 8, 1943, Austin Papers; Gould Lincoln, *Washington Evening Star*, December 27, 1942.

23. *Washington Post*, December 28, 1942.

24. Austin to Howard C. Rice, December 31, 1942, and Austin Memorandum, January 8, 1943, Austin Papers.

25. *Washington Post*, January 9, 1943.

26. Austin, Memorandum of February 1, 1943, Austin Papers.

27. Burlington, Vermont, *Burlington Free Press and Times*, March 22, 1943; Robert De Vore, *Washington Post*, February 28, 1943.

28. Austin Memorandum, January 8, 1943, Austin Papers.

29. Ibid.

30. Austin Memorandum, January 19-21, 1943, Austin Papers.

31. Austin to J.P.H. Adams, January 6, 1943, Austin Papers.

32. Memorandum of February 1, 1943, Austin Papers.

33. George C. Herring, Jr., "Experiment in Foreign Aid: Lend-Lease, 1941-1945" (unpublished Ph.D. dissertation, University of Virginia, 1965), 388 ff. I am indebted to Herring's work for an account of the debate over renewal of Lend-Lease in 1943.

34. *Congressional Record*, 78th Cong., 1st sess., 1846 (March 11, 1943).

35. Hugh Butler, "Lend-Lease for War Only?" *The Nation's Business* 31 (May 1943), 34 ff.

36. See Herring, "Experiment in Foreign Aid," 381-422.

37. *Congressional Record*, 78th Cong., 1st sess., 1804 (March 10, 1943).

38. Ibid., 1641 (March 7, 1943).

39. George C. Herring, Jr., *Aid to Russia, 1941-1946: Strategy, Diplomacy, the Origins of the Cold War* (New York: Columbia University Press, 1973), 93.

40. *Congressional Record*, 78th Cong., 1st sess., 1815 (March 10, 1943), 1853 (March 11, 1943).

41. Ibid., 76th Cong., 3rd sess., 1936 (February 23, 1940), 4105 (April 5, 1940); see also Charles J. Graham, "The Republican Party and Foreign Policy, 1939-1952" (unpublished Ph.D. dissertation, University of Illinois, 1955), 285-303, for a summary of the history of Republicans and tariff issues.

42. U.S. Congress, House, Committee on Ways and Means, *Extension of Reciprocal Trade Agreement Act*, H. Report 409 to accompany H.J. Res. 111, 2 pts., *Pt. 2: Minority Views*, 78th Cong., 1st sess., *House*

Miscellaneous Reports, II (Washington, D. C., 1943). See also "Recent Indications of Republican Thinking on Post-War Foreign Policy," June 12, 1943, Leo Pasvolsky Office Files, RG 59, National Archives.

43. Quoted in "Recent Indications of Republican Thinking," June 12, 1943, Pasvolsky Office Files, RG 59, National Archives.

44. Ibid.

45. Karl E. Mundt, "This Month in Congress," *The Republican* 8 (May 1943), 25.

46. *Congressional Record*, 78th Cong., 1st sess., 4378 (May 13, 1943), 5203 (June 2, 1943); see also Robert A. Taft to Jack Kennon, May 31, 1943, Taft Papers.

47. "Recent Indications of Republican Thinking," June 12, 1943, Pasvolsky Office Files, RG 59, National Archives.

48. Austin to B. L. Byington, August 14, 1943, Austin Papers.

49. Taft to Jack Kennon, May 31, 1943, Taft Papers.

50. Vandenberg to H.M. Taliaferro, May 14, 1943, Vandenberg Papers.

51. Quoted in "Recent Indications of Republican Thinking," June 12, 1943, Pasvolsky Office Files, RG 59, National Archives; see also *New York Times*, May 25, 1943.

52. *Congressional Record*, 77th Cong., 2nd sess., 9267 (December 3, 1942); see also Richard Nowinson to Harold H. Burton, January 5, 1943, and Burton to Nowinson, January 26, 1943, Burton Papers.

53. Vandenberg to James Kennedy, February 11, 1943, Vandenberg Papers.

54. Vandenberg, *Private Papers*, 34.

55. Divine, *Second Chance*, 85.

56. Austin, "Memorandum re Senator Ball's Dinner for Governor Stassen," January 28, 1943, Austin Papers.

57. *Congressional Record*, 78th Cong., 1st sess., 2031 (March 16, 1943).

58. Joseph H. Ball, "Our Post-War Domestic Problems," *The Republican* 7 (September 1943), 4, 5.

59. "American Foreign Policy and the Senate," a radio discussion by Senator Ralph O. Brewster over N.B.C., March 23, 1943, 111.11 Hull, Cordell/1475, RG 59, National Archives.

60. Divine, *Second Chance*, 91.

61. Vandenberg to Major George Fielding Eliot, March 26, 1943, Vandenberg Papers.

62. Quoted in "Recent Indications of Republican Thinking," June 12, 1943, Pasvolsky Office Files, RG 59, National Archives.

63. Ibid.; see also Taft's debate with Ball on the resolution in *The Republican* 8 (April 1943), 6-8, 25.

64. *New York Times,* April 16, 1943, quoted in Divine, *Second Chance,* 110.

65. Vandenberg to Eliot, March 26, 1943, Vandenberg Papers.

66. Vandenberg to Harold Titus, April 23, 1943, Vandenberg Papers.

67. Vandenberg to Eliot, March 26, 1943, Vandenberg Papers.

68. Vandenberg to Rev. Paul Wengel, March 29, 1943, Vandenberg Papers.

69. Vandenberg to Titus, April 23, 1943, and also Vandenberg to George H. Moses, April 21, 1943, both in Vandenberg Papers. Vandenberg to Z. C. Dickinson, March 22, 1943, in the Papers of the Unviersity Committee on Post-War International Problems, Michigan Historical Collections, University of Michigan.

70. Vandenberg, *Private Papers,* 40-41.

71. *Congressional Record,* 78th Cong., 1st sess., 4503-4504 (May 17, 1943).

72. Ibid., 4507 (May 17, 1943).

73. Ibid.

74. Vandenberg to Chandler, April 17, 1943, Vandenberg Papers.

75. Cordell Hull to Warren Robinson Austin, May 27, 1942, 111 Advisory Committee/7A, RG 59, National Archives.

76. Divine, *Second Chance,* 83.

77. Ibid., 95.

78. Vandenberg, *Private Papers,* 33; for more about the deal with Darlan, see pp. 89-90 of this book.

79. Young, *Congressional Politics,* 46.

80. Vandenberg to Titus, April 23, 1943, Vandenberg Papers.

81. Vandenberg, *Private Papers,* 33; also see pp. 89-90 of this book.

82. See John M. Vorys's favorable comments on Stettinius in *Congressional Record,* 78th Cong., 1st sess., 1652 (March 8, 1943), and Arthur Krock in the *New York Times,* March 12, 1943.

83. Henry Cabot Lodge, Jr., "Why an Army of 7½ Million Men?" *The Republican* 8 (February 1943), 4.

84. *New York Times,* December 18, 1942.

85. Jay G. Hayden, *Detroit News,* July 5, 1943.

86. See the memorandum for Dorothy Brady from Samuel I. Rosenman, March 4, 1943, and Lewis B. Schwellenback to Joseph Guffey, January 14, 1943, PPF 1820 (Correspondence, Box 9) Roosevelt Papers.

87. Divine, *Second Chance,* 116.

88. Karl E. Mundt, "This Month in Congress," *The Republican* 8 (May 1943), 14.

89. *Congressional Record*, 78th Cong., 1st sess., 5168 (June 1, 1943), A3168 (June 2, 1943); see also O'Laughlin to Charles D. Hilles, June 28, 1943, O'Laughlin Papers.

90. *New York Times*, December 23, 1942; O'Laughlin to Harrison E. Spangler, June 17, 1943, O'Laughlin Papers.

91. Mundt, "This Month in Congress," 14; Dean Acheson, *Present at the Creation: My Years in the State Department* (New York: W. W. Norton & Co., 1969), 74-75.

92. Acheson, *Present at the Creation*, 71.

93. Vandenberg to Hull, June 22, 1943, 800.48/75, RG 59, National Archives.

94. Ibid., Hackworth's comment is attached.

95. Hull to Vandenberg, July 7, 1943, as quoted in Vandenberg to Charles McNary, July 15, 1943, Vandenberg Papers, and in Vandenberg, *Private Papers*, 67. See also Acheson, *Present at the Creation*, 71, for the judgment in retrospect that the department "should have answered Senator Vandenberg that of course everything would and must be submitted to the Congress since American participation would be wholly dependent upon Congress to both authorize and appropriate the funds with which to do so."

96. Vandenberg to McNary, July 7, 1943, the Papers of Charles L. McNary, Library of Congress (hereinafter cited as the McNary Papers).

97. Vandenberg to Edward R. Stettinius, Jr., June 15, 1943, Vandenberg Papers.

98. *New York Times*, July 9 and 13, 1943.

99. Vandenberg to McNary, July 7, 1943, Vandenberg Papers.

100. Ibid.

101. Vandenberg to McNary, July 15, 1943, Vandenberg Papers.

102. McNary to Vandenberg, July 14, 1943, McNary Papers.

103. Vandenberg to McNary, July 7, 1943, Vandenberg Papers; Vandenberg, *Private Papers*, 68.

104. Tom Connally and Alfred Steinberg, *My Name is Tom Connally* (New York: Thomas Y. Crowell Co., 1954), 262.

105. Vandenberg to McNary, July 15, 1943, Vandenberg Papers; see also Cordell Hull, *Memoirs*, 2 vols. (New York: The Macmillan Company, 1948), II, 1637.

106. See Vandenberg to Acheson, August 6, 1943, 111.64/51; Acheson to Vandenberg, August 13, 1943, 111.12 Acheson, Dean/33A; Vandenberg to Acheson, 840.50/697; Memorandum of Francis B. Sayre to Michael J. McDermott, August 26, 1943, FW 840.50/2697; and Acheson to Vandenberg, September 11, 1943, 840.50/2697, RG 59, National Archives.

107. *New York Times*, August 18, 1943.

108. Vandenberg to the editor of the Grand Rapids, Michigan *Herald*, August 25, 1943, Vandenberg Papers.

109. Vandenberg to John T. Flynn, August 24, 1943, Vandenberg Papers.

110. Vandenberg to Gerald L. K. Smith, August 27, 1943, Vandenberg Papers.

111. Vandenberg to Flynn, August 24, 1943, Vandenberg Papers.

112. Ibid.

113. For Roosevelt's suspicion of Vandenberg, see Burns, *Roosevelt: The Soldier of Freedom*, 361, and Vandenberg, *Private Papers*, 5. See also the memorandum of Dean Acheson to Breckinridge Long, June 4, 1943, 800.24/1028, RG 59, National Archives, for a further example of the State Department's approach to Vandenberg.

114. For a synopsis of Taft's position and views on foreign policy in this period, see James T. Patterson, "Alternatives to Globalism: Robert A. Taft and American Foreign Policy, 1939-1945," *Historian* 36 (August 1974), 670-688; for an account of his activities in domestic affairs, see Patterson's *Mr. Republican*, 251-267.

115. Vandenberg to Eliot, March 26, 1943, Vandenberg Papers; excerpted in Vandenberg, *Private Papers*, 35.

116. Vandenberg, *Private Papers*, 43, 53.

117. Ibid., 42.

118. Vandenberg to Walter George, March 27, 1943, and Vandenberg to Hull, March 24, 1943, Vandenberg Papers.

119. *Congressional Record*, 78th Cong., 1st sess., 5943, 5971 (June 16, 1943); see also *New York Times*, October 4, 1943.

120. Westerfield, *Foreign Policy and Party Politics*, 149.

121. J. W. Fulbright to Franklin D. Roosevelt, June 26, 1943, FW 711.00/1659 2/3, RG 59, National Archives.

122. Roosevelt to Hull, June 28, 1943, and Hull to Roosevelt, June 28, 1943, 711.00/1659 1/3, RG 59, National Archives.

123. Vandenberg, *Private Papers*, 54.

124. Austin to White, July 22, 1943, Austin Papers.

125. White to Austin, July 19, 1943, Austin Papers.

126. Ibid.

127. Austin to White, July 22, 1943, Austin Papers.

128. Ibid.

129. Vandenberg to Warren R. Austin, June 29, 1943, Vandenberg Papers.

130. Vandenberg to Thomas W. Lamont, August 4, 1943, Vandenberg Papers.

131. Vandenberg to Henry K. DeHaan, July 8, 1943, Vandenberg Papers.

132. Ibid.; see also Vandenberg to Nellie M. Hayes, August 3, 1943, Vandenberg Papers.

133.Vandenberg to Lamont, August 4, 1943, Vandenberg Papers.

134. Jay G. Hayden, *Detroit News*, July 8, 1943.

CHAPTER 5

1. Clarence Buddington Kelland, "Lincoln Dinner Speech," February 15, 1943, Taft Papers.

2. *New York Times*, November 29, 1942; see also the *New York Times*, November 8, 1942.

3. Ibid., December 6, 1942.

4. Vandenberg to Roy E. Brownell, January 8, 1943, Vandenberg Papers; see also the *New York Times*, December 15, 1942.

5. Henry L. Stimson and McGeorge Bundy, *On Active Service in Peace and War* (New York: Harper & Brothers, 1947), 543.

6. Barnes, *Willkie*, 312.

7. Johnson, *The Republican Party and Wendell Willkie*, 227.

8. *New York Times*, December 16, 1942; see also pp. 74-75 of this book.

9. Joseph Martin, Jr., and Robert J. Donovan, *My First Fifty Years in Politics* (New York: McGraw-Hill Book Co., 1960), 132.

10. Ibid., 134.

11. Ibid., 133.

12. Ibid., 135.

13. *New York Times*, December 8, 1942.

14. *Chicago Daily Tribune*, December 7, 1942.

15. See Harrison E. Spangler to Robert A. Taft, November 23, 1942, Charles D. Hilles to Werner W. Schroeder, December 9, 1942, the memorandum of December 9, 1942 attached, and the undated memorandum of Hilles to Taft, all in Box 694, Taft Papers.

16. See T.R.B., "Washington Notes," *New Republic* 109 (August 16, 1943), 223.

17. Charles D. Hilles to John Callan O'Laughlin, August 17, 1943, O'Laughlin Papers.

18. *New York Times*, December 9, 1942.

19. Divine, *Second Chance*, 89.

20. Ibid., 86-89.

21. John Maynard Keynes, *Economic Consequences of the Peace* (New York and London: Macmillan Co., 1920).

22. See Richard D. Challener and John Fenton, "Which Way America? Dulles Always Knew," *American Heritage* 22 (June 1971), 13 and 84-93, for a sketch of Dulles's early career based directly on materials in the Papers of John Foster Dulles and the Dulles Oral History Collection, Princeton University Library. For more substantial biographies of Dulles, see Michael A. Guhin, *John Foster Dulles, A Statesman and His Times* (New York: Columbia University Press, 1972), 11-50, a topically organized account, and Townsend Hoopes, *The Devil and John Foster Dulles* (Boston: Little, Brown and Co., 1973), 3-61, a penetrating chronological interpretation.

23. John Foster Dulles to Lieutenant-Colonel C. Stanton Babcock, January 21, 1943, in the Papers of John Foster Dulles, Princeton University Library (hereinafter cited as the Dulles Papers).

24. "A Just and Durable Peace" [March 19, 1943], Dulles Papers.

25. Johnson, *The Republican Party and Wendell Willkie*, 234-235.

26. Divine, *Second Chance*, 105.

27. William Bradford Huie, "Stassen Challenges the Republican Party," *American Mercury* 56 (March 1943), 263-272.

28. See the *New York Times*, April 11, 1943, for Stassen's review of *One World*. Willkie's reaction to that review is reported in Johnson, *The Republican Party and Wendell Willkie*, 236, n. 16.

29. *The Republican* 8 (May 1943), 10; see also Watson to Austin, June 11, 1943, the copy of Watson's remarks of May 3 enclosed, and the Republican Postwar Policy Association to Members and Republican Leaders [no date, 1943], Austin Papers.

30. *The Republican* 8 (May 1943), 10. Also see "Recent Indications of Republican Thinking," June 12, 1943, Pasvolsky Office Files, RG 59, National Archives, and *Newsweek* 22 (July 19, 1943), 42, for accounts of the Chicago meeting.

31. *Washington Daily News*, July 19, 1943; Divine, *Second Chance*, 106.

32. Hilles to John E. Jackson, August 24, 1943, O'Laughlin Papers.

33. Sevellon Brown III, Providence, Rhode Island *Journal*, July 4, 1943.

34. Hilles to John E. Jackson, August 24, 1943, O'Laughlin Papers; *New York Times*, March 7, 1943.

35. Barry Keith Beyer, "Thomas E. Dewey, 1937-1942: A Study in Political Leadership" (unpublished Ph.D. dissertation, University of Rochester, 1962), 419-427.

36. *New York Times*, June 21, 1943.

37. Ibid., June 27, 1943.

38. Herbert Hoover and Hugh Gibson, "New Approaches to Lasting Peace," *Collier's* 111 (June 5, 1943), 11-12 ff.; ibid. (June 12, 1943), 15 ff.; ibid. (June 19, 1943), 28 ff.; ibid. (June 26, 1943), 33-36. See also Hoover to O'Laughlin, January 3, 1943, O'Laughlin Papers.

39. *New York Times*, August 17, 1943; Divine, *Second Chance*, 123-124.

40. Hilles to Medley G. B. Whelpley, June 21, 1943, O'Laughlin Papers.

41. Hoover to O'Laughlin, January 3, 1943, O'Laughlin Papers.

42. Hilles to J. Harvie Williams, June 7, 1943, O'Laughlin Papers.

43. Ibid.; see also in this general connection Lawrence Dennis to Robert E. Wood, June 12, 1943, Taft Papers.

44. "Republican Revival Meeting . . . Program," May 20, 1943, Austin Papers.

45. Republican Nationalist Revival Committee, "Proposed Declaration of Principles and Purposes" [no date, 1943], Austin Papers.

46. See *Chicago Daily Tribune*, March 31, 1943; *New Republic* (June 21, 1943), 814; Johnson, *The Republican Party and Wendell Willkie*, 235 and 238.

47. Taft to Jack Kennon, June 8, 1943, Taft Papers. For a view similar to Taft's from an equally important Republican, see Thomas E. Dewey to Mrs. Albert [Ruth H.] Simms, November 9, 1942, in the Papers of Thomas E. Dewey, University of Rochester Library, Rochester, New York (hereinafter cited as the Dewey Papers).

48. See O'Laughlin to Hilles, August 10, 1943, O'Laughlin Papers; and [Daniel O. Hastings] to [Hilles], August 16, 1943, Hilles Papers.

49. See *Congressional Record*, 78th Cong., 1st sess., A2811 (May 27, 1943).

50. *New York Times*, August 12, 1943.

51. See Spangler to Taft, January 20, 1943, Taft Papers, and Spangler to McNary, January 20, 1943, in the Papers of Charles W. Tobey, Dartmouth College Library, Hanover, New Hampshire (hereinafter cited as the Tobey Papers).

52. Quoted in Johnson, *The Republican Party and Wendell Willkie*, 241, and based on an interview of Johnson with Spangler.

53. Ibid., 241; Spangler to Austin, July 8, 1943, Austin Papers. For views of the Watson association similar to Spangler's, see Hilles to John E. Jackson, August 24, 1943, Hilles and Dewey Papers, and Arthur Sears Henning, *Washington* [D.C.] *Times-Herald*, July 22, 1943.

54. Statement of Harrison E. Spangler, May 31, 1943, Burton Papers. See also Republican National Committee Press Release, July 24, 1943, Burton Papers, and Taft to Spangler, July 17, 1943, Taft Papers.

55. Statement of Harrison E. Spangler, May 31, 1943, Burton Papers. The senators were Charles L. McNary of Oregon, John G. Townsend, Jr., of Delaware, Arthur H. Vandenberg of Michigan, Albert W. Hawkes of New Jersey, Robert A. Taft of Ohio, and Warren R. Austin of Vermont.

The representatives were Joseph W. Martin, Jr., of Massachusetts, Albert E. Carter of California, Everett M. Dirksen of Illinois, Charles A. Halleck of Indiana, Clifford R. Hope of Kansas, Edith Nourse Rogers of Massachusetts, Roy O. Woodruff of Michigan, August H. Andresen of Minnesota, Louis E. Miller of Missouri, Daniel A. Reed of New York, Frances P. Bolton of Ohio, J. William Ditter of Pennsylvania, and Carroll Reece of Tennessee.

The governors were Earl Warren of California, John Vivian of Colorado, Raymond E. Baldwin of Connecticut, Walter W. Bacon of Delaware, C. A. Bottolfsen of Idaho, Dwight H. Green of Illinois, Bourke B. Hickenlooper of Iowa, Andrew Schoeppel of Iowa, Sumner Sewall of Maine, Leverett Saltonstall of Massachusetts, Harry F. Kelly of Michigan, Ed Thye of Minnesota, Forrest C. Donnel of Missouri, Sam C. Ford of Montana, Dwight Griswold of Nebraska, Robert O. Blood of New Hampshire, Thomas E. Dewey of New York, John W. Bricker of Ohio, Earl Snell of Oregon, Edward Martin of Pennsylvania, M.Q. Sharpe of South Dakota, William H. Willis of Vermont, Arthur B. Langlie of Washington, and Walter S. Goodland of Wisconsin.

The National Committee members were Clarence Buddington Kelland of Arizona, Henry Leonard of Colorado, Mrs. Bertha Baur of Illinois, Mrs. Dudley C. Hay of Michigan, Dan Whetstone of Montana, and H. Alexander Smith of New Jersey.

A fiftieth Republican, Representative Charles A. Eaton of New Jersey, ranking minority member of the House Foreign Affairs Committee, was later made an "advisor" to the council. Spangler had mistakenly overlooked him in the original announcement of the council but had not wanted to appoint him directly afterwards as that might have set a precedent for others to demand appointment as well. See Johnson, *The Republican Party and Wendell Willkie*, 243, n. 34.

For an example of the geographical consciousness involved in selecting council members, see Spangler to Taft, January 20, 1943, Taft Papers.

56. Statement of Harrison E. Spangler, May 31, 1943, Burton Papers.

57. Ibid.

58. Spangler interview, in Johnson, *The Republican Party and Wendell Willkie*, 243, n. 35.

59. *Chicago Daily Tribune*, June 2, 1943.

60. Republican National Committee Press Release, July 24, 1943, Burton Papers.

61. Divine, *Second Chance*, 106-107. For examples of the pressure by Watson's association which was troubling Spangler at this time see Warren A. Seavey to Spangler, and Seavey to Austin, July 22, 1943; Austin to Seavey, July 27, 1943; and Harold W. Mason to Austin, July 21, 1943, Austin Papers.

62. As quoted in "Recent Indications of Republican Thinking," June 12, 1943, Pasvolsky Office Files, RG 59, National Archives.

63. Divine, *Second Chance*, 129-131.

64. *Washington Daily News*, July 19, 1943; Spangler to Austin, July 8, 1943, Austin Papers.

65. Spangler to Austin, July 8, 1943, and Austin to Spangler, July 12, 1943, Austin Papers. See also Leo Casey to Austin, June 23, 1943, and Austin to Casey, June 25, 1943, Austin Papers, for the Republican Postwar Policy Association's invitation to Austin to speak and his acceptance of it.

66. Austin to Harold W. Mason, July 22, 1943, Austin Papers.

67. Spangler to Austin, July 22, and July 31, 1943; Harold W. Mason to Austin, July 21, 1943, Austin Papers.

68. Statement by Representative Charles A. Eaton of New Jersey, July 28, 1943, Austin Papers; see also H. Alexander Smith to Austin, July 30, 1943, and Spangler to Austin, July 31, 1943, Austin Papers.

69. John Foster Dulles to Mrs. Albert G. Simms, June 29, 1943, 1971 Supplement, Dulles Papers.

70. Dulles to Dewey, June 9, 1943, and Dulles to Ruth H. Simms, June 15, 1943, 1971 Supplement, Dulles Papers.

71. Dulles to Dewey, July 19, 1943, 1971 Supplement, Dulles Papers; see also Dulles to Dewey, June 9, 1943, 1971 Supplement, Dulles Papers.

72. See Ruth Simms to Dulles, July 13, 1943, Dulles to Ruth H. Simms, June 15, 1943, and Dulles to Ruth H. Simms, July 23, 1943, 1971 Supplement, Dulles Papers.

73. Dulles to Dewey, June 9, 1943, 1971 Supplement, Dulles Papers.

74. Dulles to Dewey, July 30, 1943, 1971 Supplement, Dulles Papers.

75. Dulles to Henry J. Taylor, August 13, 1943, 1971 Supplement, Dulles Papers.

76. H. Alexander Smith to Dulles, August 7, 1943, 1971 Supplement, Dulles Papers.

77. Dulles to Smith, August 10, 1943, 1971 Supplement, Dulles Papers.

78. Smith to Dulles, August 13, 1943, 1971 Supplement, Dulles Papers.

79. Spangler to Austin, July 8, and July 15, 1943, Austin Papers.

80. See pp. 83-84 of this book, and Austin to White, July 22, 1943, Austin Papers.

81. *Washington Daily News*, July 19, 1943; Spangler to Austin, July 22, 1943, and Smith to Austin, July 30, 1943, Austin Papers.

82. Smith to Austin, August 5, 1943, Austin Papers.

83. Ibid.; Austin to Fred. H. Howland, August 7, 1943, Austin Papers.

84. "Advice by Republican Postwar Advisory Council to Republican National Committee," Draft of August 16, 1943, and Draft of August 30, 1943, Austin Papers.

85. Vandenberg to Charles W. Tobey, August 9, 1943, Tobey Papers; Vandenberg to Dewey, August 13, 1943, Vandenberg Papers.

86. Vandenberg to Dewey, August 13, 1943, Vandenberg Papers.

87. *New York Times*, September 6, 1943.

88. Turner Catledge, *New York Times*, September 6, 1943.

89. *Chicago Daily Tribune*, September 6, 1943.

90. *New York Times*, September 7, 1943.

91. Ibid. For a later view of Dewey's statement by one of its early critics (a view similar to that expressed in the text), see Taft to Margaret Hopkins Worrell, January 25, 1944, Taft Papers; see also the extensive correspondence on the subject in Box 2, Political Correspondence, 1971 Supplement, Dulles Papers.

92. For Austin's comment and Baldwin's statement, see the memorandum [no date, 1943] and the transcript "covering the executive session of the Committee on Foreign Policy wherein plans were presented by various people," September 6, 1943, Austin Papers; see also the *New York Times*, September 9, 1943.

93. Transcript, September 6, 1943, Austin Papers.

94. "Resolution on Foreign Policy and International Relations Adopted Unanimously by the Republican Post-War Advisory Council," September 7, 1943, Burton Papers. See also the "Mackinac Declaration of *Foreign* Policy," September 7, 1943, enclosed with Austin to Roy L. Patrick, April 3, 1944, and Austin to Walter M. Higgins, November 29, 1943, Austin Papers.

95. Austin to Roy L. Patrick, April 3, 1944, Austin Papers; see also Austin to Boyd Edwards, September 14, 1943, Austin Papers.

96. Austin to Boyd Edwards, Austin Papers. See the *Tennessee Republican Age* 1 (February and March 1944), 10, 46, for Vandenberg's continued use of term "postwar cooperation."

97. For the Baldwin-Vandenberg exchange, see the "Record of executive session which Foreign Policy Committee had with whole Council" [September 7, 1943], Austin Papers.

98. Ibid.

99. "Mackinac Declaration of *Foreign* Policy," September 7, 1943,

Austin Papers.

100. "Advice . . . ," Draft of August 30, 1943, Austin Papers.

101. "Mackinac Declaration of *Foreign* Policy," September 7, 1943, Austin Papers.

102. *Tennessee Republican Age* 1 (February and March 1944), 10.

103. Ibid., 46.

104. Austin to Spangler, September 14, 1943, Austin Papers; Austin to Dewey, September 20, 1943, Dewey Papers.

105. Dewey to Austin, September 16, 1943, Dewey Papers. See also Vandenberg, *Private Papers*, 59.

106. Quoted in "Public Attitudes on Foreign Policy," September 25, 1943, Pasvolsky Office Files, RG 59, National Archives.

107. *New York Times*, September 9, 1943.

108. Taft to Arthur Krock, September 16, 1943, Taft Papers.

109. "Record of executive session" [September 7, 1943], Austin Papers; *New York Times*, September 9, 1943.

110. *Chicago Daily Tribune*, September 10, 1943.

111. "Public Attitudes on Foreign Policy," September 25, 1943, Pasvolsky Office Files, RG 59, National Archives.

112. Divine, *Second Chance*, 132; *New Republic* 109 (September 20, 1943), 376.

113. Hull, *Memoirs*, II, 1258-1259; see also Divine, *Second Chance*, 132.

114. "Public Attitudes on Foreign Policy," September 25, 1943, Pasvolsky Office Files, RG 59, National Archives.

115. Divine, *Second Chance*, 131.

116. *Christian Science Monitor*, September 17, 1943.

117. Ibid., as quoted and concluded by Roscoe Drummond.

118. *The Republican* 8 (October 1943), 25.

119. Ibid. (September 1943), 22.

120. See pp. 118-123 and 143 of this book.

121. *The Republican* 8 (October 1943), 25; *Tennessee Republican Age* 1 (February and March 1944), 10.

122. *The Republican* 8 (September 1943), 22.

123. *Tennessee Republican Age* 1 (February and March 1944), 10.

124. Vandenberg, *Private Papers*, 57.

125. Vandenberg to Harry A. Jung, September 17, 1943, Vandenberg Papers. See also Jung to Vandenberg, September 15, 1943, Vandenberg Papers, and Vandenberg, *Private Papers*, 60.

126. Vandenberg to Martin J. Gillen, September 14, 1943, Vandenberg Papers.

127. *The Republican* 8 (September 1943), 2.

128. Dewey to Austin, September 16, 1943, Dewey Papers; Taft to Krock, September 16, 1943, Taft Papers; Vandenberg, *Private Papers*, 59.

129. Vandenberg to Henry R. Luce, September 24, 1943, Vandenberg Papers.

130. "Record of executive session" [September 7, 1943], Austin Papers.

CHAPTER 6

1. See the Burton Diary, September 16, 1943, Burton Papers.

2. See "Public Attitudes on Foreign Policy," September 25, 1943, Pasvolsky Office Files, RG 59, National Archives.

3. Ibid.; see also Divine, *Second Chance*, 140.

4. See "Public Attitudes on Foreign Policy," September 25, 1943, Pasvolsky Office Files, RG 59, National Archives.

5. As quoted in "Public Attitudes on Foreign Policy," September 25, 1943, Pasvolsky Office Files, RG 59, National Archives.

6. Ibid.

7. *Congressional Record*, 78th Cong., 1st sess., 7646-7747 (September 20, 1943).

8. Ibid., 7662 (September 20, 1943).

9. Ibid., 7681 (September 20, 1943).

10. Ibid., 7668 (September 20, 1943).

11. Ibid., 7655 (September 20, 1943).

12. See Norman M. Clapp to Robert A. LaFollette, Jr., October 6, 1943, LaFollette Papers, for the report of Vandenberg's and Martin's efforts in regard to the Fulbright resolution.

13. *Congressional Record*, 78th Cong., 1st sess., 7659 (September 20, 1943).

14. Ibid., 5943 (June 16, 1943).

15. Ibid., 7723 (September 21, 1943).

16. Ibid., 7728-7729 (September 21, 1943).

17. *New York Times*, June 30, 1943.

18. Connally, *My Name Is Tom Connally*, 263-264; Clapp to LaFollette, October 6, 1943, LaFollette Papers.

19. *Congressional Record*, 78th Cong., 1st sess., 8294 (October 14, 1943); see also Divine, *Second Chance*, 146.

20. Vandenberg, *Private Papers*, 63; *Congressional Record*, 78th Cong.,

1st sess., 8650-8651 (October 25, 1943), 8854 (October 28, 1943). See also Philip J. Briggs, "Congress and Collective Security: The Resolutions of 1943," *World Affairs* 132 (March 1970), 332-344.

21. *Congressional Record*, 78th Cong., 1st sess., 8665-8670 (October 25, 1943), 9042, 9061-9062, and 9066 (November 3, 1943), 9186-9187, 9211, and 9222 (November 5, 1943).

22. Ibid., 9106 (November 4, 1943).

23. Ibid., 9096 (November 4, 1943).

24. Quoted in Divine, *Second Chance*, 153.

25. "Public Attitudes on Foreign Policy," November 18, 1943, 711.00 Public Attitudes/4, RG 59, National Archives; *ibid.*, December 4, 1943, Pasvolsky Office Files, RG 59, National Archives.

26. *New York Herald Tribune*, January 21, 1944; *Christian Science Monitor*, January 18, 1944.

27. "Committee Report," February 21, 1944, Austin Papers.

28. *Congressional Record*, 78th Cong., 1st sess., 8951-8953 and 8956-8957 (October 28, 1943), 8993 and 9012-9013 (October 29, 1943), 9168-9178 (November 3, 1943).

29. Austin to Nye, February 10, 1944, and Austin, "Confidential Memoranda Apropos State Department Postwar Meetings," April 26, 1944, Austin Papers.

30. The quotation is from Representative Jessie Sumner of Illinois, *Congressional Record*, 78th Cong., 1st sess., 7682 (September 20, 1943); for the speculation about Marshall, see Stimson and Bundy, *On Active Service*, 440-443.

31. *Congressional Record*, 78th Cong., 1st sess., 7585-7586 (September 17, 1943).

32. Ibid., 10535-10536 (December 9, 1943).

33. See Henry Cabot Lodge, Jr., to Charles L. McNary, August 23, 1943, McNary Papers; "Public Attitudes on Foreign Policy," November 1, 1943, 711.00 Public Attitudes/3 Office of Special Consultant, RG 59, National Archives; *New York Times*, October 9 and 29, 1943; and Karl E. Mundt, "This Month in Washington," *The Republican* 8 (November 1943), 16.

34. *Congressional Record*, 78th Cong., 2nd sess., 3581-3582 (April 19, 1944) and 4106 (May 8, 1944); Patterson, "Alternatives to Globalism," 686.

35. See Vandenberg to Dr. A. Haapanen, June 20, 1944, Vandenberg Papers.

36. Vandenberg to Frank Januszewski, November 6, 1943, Vandenberg Papers.

37. LaFollette to Vandenberg, October 6, 1943, LaFollette Papers.

38. Clapp to LaFollette, October 6, 1943, LaFollette Papers.

39. "Public Attitudes on Foreign Policy," November 18, 1943, 711.00 Public Attitudes/4, RG 59, National Archives.

40. Vandenberg to Januszewski, November 19, 1943, Vandenberg Papers.

41. Divine, *Second Chance*, 159-160.

42. Taft, "A 1944 Program for the Republicans," *The Saturday Evening Post* 215 (December 11, 1943), 17.

43. See *Congressional Record*, 78th Cong., 1st sess., 9096 (November 4, 1943); "Public Attitudes on Foreign Policy," November 1, 1943, 711.00 Public Attitudes/3, RG 59, National Archives; and pp. 35-37, 43-45 of this book.

44. "Recent Indications of Republican Thinking," June 12, 1943, Pasvolsky Office Files, RG 59, National Archives; Patterson, "Alternatives to Globalism," 676-677.

45. Taft to Robert E. Wood, April 11, 1944, Taft Papers.

46. Acheson, *Present at the Creation*, 107; *Congressional Record*, 78th Cong., 2nd sess., 2608 (March 14, 1944); see also "Public Attitudes on Foreign Policy," November 18, 1943, 711.00 Public Attitudes/4, RG 59, National Archives.

47. *Congressional Record*, 78th Cong., 2nd sess., 2204 (March 3, 1944).

48. Ibid., 2594 (March 14, 1944).

49. Ibid., 78th Cong., 1st sess., 10320 (December 6, 1943); 78th Cong., 2nd sess., 4529 (May 16, 1944).

50. Ibid., 78th Cong., 2nd sess., 5414 (June 6, 1944) and 5476 (June 7, 1944).

51. See John Callan O'Laughlin to William Allen White, October 12, 1943, O'Laughlin Papers.

52. Taft to Roger Faherty, April 6, 1944, Taft Papers.

53. Vandenberg to Monroe Shakespeare, March 18, 1944, Vandenberg Papers.

54. Vandenberg to John W. Blodgett, Jr., May 1, 1944, Vandenberg Papers.

55. Vandenberg to Acheson, September 25, 1943, 711.00/1739, RG 59, National Archives.

56. *Congressional Record*, 78th Cong., 2nd sess., 471-472 (January 20, 1944), 1826-1828 (February 17, 1944); "Public Attitudes on Foreign Policy," February 5, 1944, 711.00 Public Attitudes/7, RG 59, National Archives.

57. *Congressional Record*, 78th Cong., 2nd sess., 1739 (February 16, 1944); see also "Public Attitudes on Foreign Policy," October 11, 1943, Pasvolsky Office Files, RG 59, National Archives.

58. Vandenberg to Warren Austin, April 4, 1944, Vandenberg Papers.

59. Vandenberg to Raymond L. Buell, March 11, 1944, Vandenberg Papers.

60. Ibid.

61. *Congressional Record,* 78th Cong., 2nd sess., 694-695 (January 25, 1944), 1826, 1828, and 1829 (February 17, 1944), 2803-2804 (March 21, 1944), 2938 (March 22, 1944); see also Dahl, *Congress and Foreign Policy,* 292-293.

62. *Congressional Record,* 78th Cong., 2nd sess., 1815 (February 17, 1944).

63. Acheson to Vandenberg, February 19, 1944, 840.50 UNRRA/318A, RG 59, National Archives.

64. Vandenberg to Acheson, February 22, 1944, 840.50 UNRRA/355, RG 59, National Archives.

65. "Public Attitudes on Foreign Policy," September 25, 1943, Pasvolsky Office Files, RG 59, National Archives. See also Robert A. Divine, *Foreign Policy and U.S. Presidential Elections, 1940-1948* (New York: Franklin Watts, Inc., 1974), 101.

66. See Divine, *Second Chance,* 192-194.

67. Connally, *My Name is Tom Connally,* 264-265; Vandenberg, *Private Papers,* 93-95.

68. Taft to Vandenberg, March 29, 1944, Vandenberg Papers; see also Vandenberg, *Private Papers,* 93-94.

69. Vandenberg, *Private Papers,* 94-95; Connally to Hull, April 15, 1944, Sen 78A-F11, RG 46, National Archives.

70. Vandenberg, *Private Papers,* 95.

71. Ibid., 96, 98.

72. Ibid., 98.

73. Vandenberg to Hull, May 3, 1944, Vandenberg Papers; see also Vandenberg to LaFollette, May 3, 1944, LaFollette Papers.

74. Vandenberg, *Private Papers,* 96; for various drafts of letters proposed for the committee to send Hull, see Connally to Hull, May 19, May 23, and May 26, 1944, Austin Papers.

75. Vandenberg, *Private Papers,* 102.

76. Forrest Davis, "What Really Happened at Teheran," *Saturday Evening Post* 216 (May 13, 1944), 12-13 ff.; ibid. (May 20, 1944), 22-23 ff.; see also Divine, *Second Chance,* 199.

77. Vandenberg, *Private Papers,* 102-107; Hull, *Memoirs,* II, 1667-1669.

78. Patterson, "Alternatives to Globalism," 684.

79. *The Republican* 9 (June 1944), 13-14.

80. Tobey to Mr. and Mrs. Joseph E. Desmond, November 14, 1941, Tobey Papers; also see p. 25 of this book.

81. Tobey to Mrs. H. H. Amsden, July 25, 1944, Tobey Papers.

82. Tobey to Henry C. Arwe, June 30, 1943, Tobey Papers.

83. Tobey to Wallace E. Mason, June 26, 1943, Tobey Papers.

84. Tobey to Vandenberg, August 9, 1943, Tobey to John R. McLane, June 21, 1943, Tobey to Mr. and Mrs. Henry Arwe, November 4, 1943, Tobey Papers.

85. Acheson, *Present at the Creation*, 82; see also Vandenberg, *Private Papers*, 109-110.

86. Tobey to Thomas E. Elder, September 29, 1944, Tobey Papers.

87. Vandenberg, *Private Papers*, 109-110.

88. Vandenberg to Wilbur Forest, May 23, 1944, Vandenberg Papers.

89. Vandenberg, *Private Papers*, 118.

90. See Hull, *Memoirs*, II, 1697-1699.

91. *Congressional Record*, 78th Cong., 2nd sess., 7522-7528 (September 5, 1944).

92. Vandenberg to Dewey, May 10, 1944, Vandenberg Papers.

CHAPTER 7

1. Wendell Willkie, "How the Republican Party Can Win in 1944," *Look*, October 5, 1943, 25-31, in *Congressional Record*, 78th Cong., 1st sess., A3953-A3954 (September 22, 1943).

2. *New York Times*, November 12, 1943.

3. Taft to Louis E. Melvin, February 16, 1944, Taft to Mr. and Mrs. Elton Chapman, October 6, 1943, Taft Papers; see also Taft to J. B. Doan, February 24, 1944, Taft Papers, and O'Laughlin to Hilles, August 10, 1943, O'Laughlin Papers. For Roosevelt's attempts to interest Willkie later in a possible political alliance, see Divine, *Foreign Policy*, 134-135.

4. Quoted from Divine, *Second Chance*, 186.

5. Johnson, *The Republican Party and Wendell Willkie*, 239.

6. Hilles to Thomas L. Anderson, March 13, 1944, Hilles Papers; see also Kelland to Taft, June 7, 1943, Taft Papers.

7. For the Hamilton trip see Johnson, *The Republican Party and Wendell Willkie*, 255-257; for examples of Republican congressional reactions to the former nominee, see *Congressional Record*, 78th Cong., 1st sess., 8203-8206 (October 11, 1943), A4320-A4321 (October 14, 1943).

8. *New York Times*, December 7 and 13, 1943.

9. Johnson, *The Republican Party and Wendell Willkie*, 258.

10. *The Republican* 9 (February 1944), 2; *Newsweek* 23 (January 10, 1944), 40.

11. *The Republican* 9 (January 1944), 2.

12. Ibid.

13. Spangler interview, in Johnson, *The Republican Party and Wendell Willkie*, 252.

14. *New York Times*, March 12, 1944; see also Hilles to Anderson, March 13, 1944, Hilles Papers.

15. Dulles to Mrs. Albert G. Simms, September 15, 1943, 1971 Supplement, Dulles Papers.

16. Dulles to Simms, September 21, 1943, 1971 Supplement, Dulles Papers.

17. See Divine, *Second Chance*, 163.

18. Dulles to Simms, October 20, 1943, 1971 Supplement, and Dulles to Morris L. Ernst, October 5, 1943, Dulles Papers.

19. Dulles to Simms, September 21, October 20, 1943, 1971 Supplement, Dulles Papers; interview with John Coleman Bennett, in the Dulles Oral History Collection, Princeton University Library (hereinafter cited as Dulles Oral History Project).

20. John Coleman Bennett interview, Dulles Oral History Project; also, see p. 92 of this book.

21. See Divine, *Second Chance*, 163.

22. Dulles to Joseph H. Willits, January 3, 1944, Dulles Papers.

23. See Divine, *Second Chance*, 163.

24. *New York Times*, November 8, 1943, and "Public Attitudes on Foreign Policy," December 4, 1943, 711.00 Public Affairs/5, RG 59, National Archives.

25. For a sketch of Sullivan and Cromwell's clientele and interests (including the office it maintained in Berlin before the war) as well as of Dulles's career and significance within the firm, see Hoopes, *The Devil and John Foster Dulles*, 25-47.

26. Dulles to Whitney H. Shepardson, April 28, 1942, Dulles Papers. For the reference to Keynes, see p. 92 of this book.

27. Dulles to Lord McGowan, September 15, 1943, Dulles Papers.

28. Dulles to Shepardson, April 28, 1942, Dulles Papers.

29. Dulles to McGowan, September 15, 1943, Dulles Papers.

30. Dulles to John Dickinson, November 3, 1943, Dulles Papers.

31. Guhin, *John Foster Dulles*, 51; Graham, "Republican Foreign Policy," 293-297.

32. Dulles to S.L.W. Mellen, January 6, 1942, Dulles Papers.

33. Dulles to Sophia Dulles, August 10, 1943, Dulles Papers.

34. Dulles to W. Randolph Burgess, June 23, 1943, Dulles Papers.

35. Dulles to Dewey, December 10, 1943, 1971 Supplement, Dulles Papers.

36. Dulles to Simms, September 21, 1943, 1971 Supplement, Dulles Papers.

37. Divine, *Second Chance*, 187-189.

38. See Johnson, *The Republican Party and Wendell Willkie*, 271-280; see also Hilles to Edward C. Stone, April 7, 1944, and Hilles to R. B. Creager, April 7, 1944, O'Laughlin Papers.

39. Quoted in Vandenberg, *Private Papers*, 84.

40. *New York Times*, October 26 and 29, 1942.

41. Vandenberg to A.B. Chandler, April 17, 1943, Vandenberg Papers.

42. See O'Laughlin to Hilles, February 11, 1943, O'Laughlin Papers, and *Congressional Record*, 78th Cong., 1st sess., 3102,3128 (April 8, 1943); see also *New York Times*, December 13 and 20, 1943.

43. See Vandenberg, *Private Papers*, 75-79.

44. Vandenberg to Wood, September 15, 1943, Vandenberg Papers.

45. Arthur Capper to McNary, January 8, 1944, McNary Papers; Taft to Fred Schluter, February 5, 1944, Taft Papers.

46. Dulles to Simms, September 21, 1943, 1971 Supplement, Dulles Papers.

47. Vandenberg, *Private Papers*, 84. For more on the MacArthur-Miller exchange, see O'Laughlin to Hilles, April 15, 1944, and O'Laughlin to Hoover, April 14, 1944, O'Laughlin Papers; also see *Congressional Record*, 78th Cong., 2nd sess., 3548-3550 (April 18, 1944).

48. Vandenberg to A. L. Miller, May 5, 1944, Vandenberg Papers.

49. Vandenberg to Wood, May 1, 1944, and Vandenberg to G.W. MacNurlen, April 21, 1944, Vandenberg Papers.

50. Taft to John Bricker, April 7, 1944, and Taft to R. B. Creager, April 10, 1944, Taft Papers.

51. *New York Times*, February 13, 1944.

52. See Divine, *Second Chance*, 187.

53. Address of April 27, 1944, Dewey Papers; see also *Vital Speeches* 10 (May 15, 1944), 451.

54. *Time* 43 (May 8, 1944), 15-16.

55. Wood to Vandenberg, May 2, 1944, and Edmund E. Lincoln to

Joseph W. Martin, Jr., May 3, 1944, Taft Papers.
    56. Quoted in *Time* 41 (March 29, 1943), 13.
    57. See Taft to C. Emory Glander, April 12, 1944, and Bricker,
"America's Place in World Affairs," April 25, 1944, Taft Papers. Taft
believed that Bricker had made a critical political error in not entering
the Wisconsin primary and establishing himself there as the anti-Willkie
candidate in place of Dewey, who had not yet formally entered the
race; see Taft to Lester Bradshaw, May 30, 1944, Taft Papers.
    58. Wood to Vandenberg, March 29 and April 13, 1944, Vandenberg
Papers.
    59. Vandenberg to Wood, April 15, 1944, Vandenberg Papers.
    60. Vandenberg to Frank E. Gannett, April 11, 1944, Vandenberg
Papers.
    61. Hilles to O'Laughlin, April 20, 1944, O'Laughlin Papers.
    62. Vandenberg to Warren Austin, March 8, 1944, Vandenberg
Papers.
    63. Vandenberg to Dewey, March 30, 1944, Vandenberg Papers.
    64. Vandenberg to Dewey, March 30, 1944, Vandenberg Papers.
    65. Dewey to Vandenberg, March 31, 1944, Vandenberg Papers.
    66. Austin to Vandenberg, March 10, 1944, Vandenberg Papers.
    67. Austin to Vandenberg, May 5, 1944, Vandenberg Papers.
    68. Vandenberg to Austin, May 8, 1944, Vandenberg Papers.
    69. Vandenberg to Dewey, May 10, 1944, Vandenberg Papers.
    70. Vandenberg to Austin, May 8, 1944, Vandenberg Papers.
    71. Vandenberg to Dewey, May 22, 1944, Vandenberg Papers.
    72. Ibid.; see also Vandenberg to Austin, May 22, 1944, Austin
Papers.
    73. Vandenberg to Charles A. Eaton, May 22, 1944, Vandenberg
Papers.
    74. Vandenberg to Dulles, May 29, 1944, 1971 Supplement,
Dulles Papers; Vandenberg to Austin, May 27, 1944, Austin Papers;
Dulles to Vandenberg, June 12, 1944, Vandenberg Papers.
    75. Vandenberg to Eaton, June 10, 1944, and Vandenberg to
Edward Martin, June 10, 1944, Vandenberg Papers.
    76. O'Laughlin to Hilles, April 20, 1944, O'Laughlin Papers; Taft to
R. B. Creager, May 30, 1944, Taft Papers.
    77. Vandenberg to Dewey, May 10, 1944, Vandenberg Papers.
    78. Fred L. Israel (ed.), *The War Diary of Breckinridge Long,
Selections from the Years 1939-1944* (Lincoln, Neb.: University
of Nebraska Press, 1966), 356-358; see also Hull, *Memoirs*, II, 1670.
    79. Barnes, *Willkie*, 364.
    80. *New York Times*, June 18, 1944; see the *New York Times*,

June 12, 13, 14, 15, 16, 17, and 18, 1944, for Willkie's seven articles.

81. Vandenberg to Dulles, June 14, 1944, Vandenberg Papers.

82. Quoted in Johnson, *The Republican Party and Wendell Willkie*, 291.

83. Arthur Krock, *Memoirs: Sixty Years on the Firing Line* (New York: Funk & Wagnalls, 1968), 196; *New York Times*, June 27, 1944; Johnson, *The Republican Party and Wendell Willkie*, 293.

84. *New York Times*, June 27 and 28, 1944; Divine, *Foreign Policy*, 115; Robert E. Wood to Taft, April 19, 1944, and Gerald L. K. Smith to Taft, June 24, 1944, Taft Papers.

85. "Statement by Senator Vandenberg to Resolutions Committee," June 23, 1944, Austin Papers.

86. Republican National Committee, "Republican Platform 1944, Adopted by Republican National Convention, June 27, 1944, Chicago, Illinois," Austin Papers.

87. *Chicago Daily Tribune*, June 27, 1944.

88. *New York Times*, June 29, 1944.

89. Ibid., June 30, 1944.

90. See Beyer, "Thomas E. Dewey," 363-364, for an analysis of the Dewey campaign strategy.

91. Taft, "Two Senators State the Campaign Issues," *New York Times Magazine*, September 3, 1944, 12; see also the memorandum to Stanley High from Governor Dewey, September 5, 1944, Dewey Papers.

92. Taft to Mrs. Ed Ruth, May 19, 1944, Taft Papers.

93. Johnson, *The Republican Party and Wendell Willkie*, 295.

94. Taft to Lester Bradshaw, May 30, 1944, Taft to Alf M. Landon, August 11, 1944, and Taft to Roger Faherty, July 25, 1944, Taft Papers.

95. *New York Times*, August 31, 1944; August 17, 1944.

96. Hull, *Memoirs*, II, 1689; see also Divine, *Second Chance*, 216-217.

97. Elliot V. Bell interview, Dulles Oral History Project.

98. Hull, *Memoirs*, II, 1690-1693.

99. Ibid., 1694.

100. *New York Times*, September 8, 1944.

101. Ibid.; see also Hull, *Memoirs*, II, 1694.

102. See O'Laughlin to Hilles, August 30, 1944, O'Laughlin Papers; Divine, *Second Chance*, 218.

103. John M. Hightower interview, Dulles Oral History Project.

104. See O'Laughlin to Hilles, August 30, 1944, O'Laughlin Papers.

105. Hull, *Memoirs*, II, 1695; see also Wilson to Dulles, September 18, 1944, 1971 Supplement, Dulles Papers.

106. Hull, *Memoirs*, II, 1698; O. Frederick Nolde and Roswell P. Barnes interviews, Dulles Oral History Project; Dulles to Hugh R. Wilson,

September 21 and September 25, 1944, 1971 Supplement, Dulles Papers.

107. See Herbert Brownell interview, Dulles Oral History Project; H. G. McCarthy to Dulles, July 13, 1944, Dulles Papers; and *Congressional Record*, 78th Cong., 2nd sess., 7648-7651 (September 11, 1944), 8110-8112 (September 21, 1944). See also Divine, *Foreign Policy*, 145-147.

108. Thomas E. Dewey interview, Dulles Oral History Project.

109. See O'Laughlin to Roger W. Straus, October 11, 1944, O'Laughlin Papers; Vandenberg to George M. Montross, August 2, 1944, Vandenberg Papers.

110. Herbert Brownell interview, Dulles Oral History Project.

111. Dewey interview, Dulles Oral History Project.

112. Brooks Emeny interview, Dulles Oral History Project.

113. James Reston interview, Dulles Oral History Project.

114. For a comparable analysis by the administration at the time, see Divine, *Foreign Relations*, 127.

115. Dulles to Shipstead, September 8, 1944, 1971 Supplement, Dulles Papers; see also Dulles to Nye, September 7, 1944, 1971 Supplement, Dulles Papers.

116. Vandenberg, *Private Papers*, 117.

117. Vandenberg to Milton Carmichael, April 29, 1944, Vandenberg Papers.

118. See Divine, *Foreign Relations*, 138-144, for a comparative analysis of Democratic and Republican appeals to various ethnic voters.

119. Vandenberg to B. E. Hutchinson, October 28, 1944, Vandenberg Papers.

120. Vandenberg, *Private Papers*, 112.

121. Vandenberg to Dulles, September 11, 1944, 1971 Supplement, Dulles Papers.

122. Dulles to Vandenberg, September 14, 1944, 1971 Supplement, Dulles Papers.

123. See Joseph Dillinger to Dulles, November 20, 1945, Dulles Papers; Vandenberg to Dulles, November 11, 1944, Vandenberg Papers. See also Guhin, *John Foster Dulles*, 53-54.

124. Pepper, "Two Senators State the Campaign Issues," *New York Times Magazine*, September 3, 1944, 12. See also Divine, *Foreign Policy*, 133-134.

125. Vandenberg to B. E. Hutchinson, October 28, 1944, Vandenberg Papers.

126. Taft to George F. Stanley, September 8, 1944, Taft Papers.

127. Johnson, *The Republican Party and Wendell Willkie*, 296-297.

128. *New York Times*, October 23, 1944.

129. Divine, *Second Chance*, 237.

130. Speech by Senator Joseph H. Ball, in Ball to Harold Burton, October 6, 1944, Burton Papers.

131. Burton to Ball, October 3, 1943, Burton Papers.

132. Ball to Burton, October 6, 1944, Burton Papers.

133. See Divine, *Second Chance*, 238-240.

134. Thomas E. Dewey interview, Dulles Oral History Project; for reports of a similar statement by Dewey, see Vandenberg, *Private Papers*, 112-113 and Walter Millis (ed.), *The Forrestal Diaries* (New York: Viking Press, 1951), 348.

135. See Divine, *Foreign Policy*, 149-154, 156.

CHAPTER 8

1. See Johnson, *The Republican Party and Wendell Willkie*, 314, n. 9.

2. Patterson, *Mr. Republican*, 278.

3. Vandenberg, *Private Papers*, 126-127; Hilles to O'Laughlin, December 26, 1944, O'Laughlin Papers; Taft to Dewey, December 13, 1944 and Taft to Roy Dunn, January 18, 1945, Taft Papers.

4. Herbert Brownell interview, Dulles Oral History Project.

5. John Foster Dulles to Allen W. Dulles, December 20, 1944, Dulles Papers.

6. See O. Frederick Nolde interview, Dulles Oral History Project; and Divine, *Second Chance*, 230-231.

7. Vandenberg to Henry D. Hatfield, December 29, 1944, Vandenberg Papers.

8. *Congressional Record*, 79th Cong., 1st sess., 164-167 (January 10, 1945).

9. See Vandenberg, *Private Papers*, 138-145.

10. Dewey interview, Dulles Oral History Project.

11. Vandenberg, *Private Papers*, 152; Vandenberg to Dulles, February 17, 1945, Vandenberg Papers.

12. Dulles, however, attended the conference as a private citizen (in his role as a churchman) rather than as Vandenberg's chief aide; see Divine, *Second Chance*, 273.

13. W. Randolph Burgess and Douglas G. Mode interviews, Dulles Oral History Project.

14. Robert Thayer interview, Dulles Oral History Project.

15. Vandenberg to Dulles, November 11, 1944, Vandenberg Papers.

16. For a brief but cogent presentation of this revisionist point of view, see Robert Freeman Smith, "American Foreign Relations, 1920-1942," in Barton J. Bernstein (ed.), *Towards a New Past: Dissenting Essays in American History* (New York: Random House, 1967), 232-262, especially 248.

17. See p. 165 of this book.

18. See Vandenberg, *Private Papers*, 108-110; Vandenberg to Jesse P. Wolcott, July 27, 1944, Vandenberg Papers; Vandenberg to Taft, July 8, 1944, Taft Papers.

19. Vandenberg to Dulles, January 4, 1945, Dulles Papers.

20. Vandenberg to Harry G. Hogan, March 26, 1945, Vandenberg Papers.

21. Ibid.

22. Vandenberg to Robert E. Hannegan, October 28, 1946, in the Papers of James F. Byrnes, Robert Muldrow Cooper Library, Clemson University, Clemson, South Carolina.

23. Ibid.

24. Ibid.

25. Ibid.

26. See, for example, the Marquis Childs, Ferdinand Eberstadt, and Richard Rovere interviews, Dulles Oral History Project.

27. Rovere interview, Dulles Oral History Project.

28. Joseph Martin, Jr., interview, Dulles Oral History Project.

29. Brownell interview, Dulles Oral History Project.

30. McCoy, "Republican Opposition During Wartime," 188-189, 185.

31. See Taft to Dewey, February 26, 1945, Taft Papers, for the following statement by Taft: "I don't think much of the Yalta results, but I am inclined to go along with any international organization that is set up, after presenting the objections for the record."

32. Vandenberg, *Private Papers*, 555.

33. McCoy, "Republican Opposition During Wartime," 189.

BIBLIOGRAPHY

The following is a list of unpublished sources and published works either cited in this study or consulted in its preparation.

MANUSCRIPTS AND ORAL HISTORIES

In the Library of Congress:

The Papers of Harold H. Burton.
The Papers of John D. M. Hamilton.
The Papers of Frank Knox.
The Papers of Robert M. LaFollette, Jr.
The Papers of Charles L. McNary.
The Papers of George W. Norris.
The Papers of John Callan O'Laughlin.
The Papers of Gifford Pinchot.
The Papers of Helen Rogers Reid.
The Papers of Robert A. Taft.
The Papers of Wallace H. White.

In the Robert Muldrow Cooper Library, Clemson University, Clemson, South Carolina:

The Papers of James F. Byrnes.

In the Dartmouth College Library, Hanover, New Hampshire:

The Papers of Charles W. Tobey.

In the William L. Clements Library, University of Michigan, Ann Arbor:

The Papers of Arthur H. Vandenberg.

In the Michigan Historical Collections, University of Michigan, Ann Arbor:

The Papers of the Ann Arbor, Michigan National Defense Committee.
The Papers of Blair Moody.

The Papers of Albert Joseph Engel.
The Papers of Jay G. Hayden.
The Papers of Clare E. Hoffman.
The Papers of Earl Cory Michener.
The Papers of Ralph Lawes Smith.
The Records of the Universities Committee on Post-war International Problems, Ann Arbor Branch.

In the New England College Library, Henniker, New Hampshire:

The Papers of Styles Bridges.

In the National Archives:

The Leo Pasvolsky Office Files in the Records of the Department of State, Record Group 59.
The Papers of the Senate Foreign Relations Committee, Record Group 46.
The Records of the Department of State, Record Group 59.

In the Princeton University Library:

The Papers of John Foster Dulles.
The Dulles Oral History Collection.
The Papers of H. Alexander Smith.

In the University of Rochester Library, Rochester, New York:

The Papers of Thomas E. Dewey.

In the Franklin D. Roosevelt Library, Hyde Park, New York:

The Papers of Franklin D. Roosevelt.

In the University of Vermont Library, Burlington, Vermont:

The Papers of Warren R. Austin.

In the Yale University Library:

The Papers of Charles Dewey Hilles.
The Papers of George H. E. Smith.
The Papers of Henry L. Stimson.

PUBLIC DOCUMENTS

Congressional Record, 77th Cong., 1st sess., through 79th Cong., 1st sess. Washington, D.C., 1941-1945.

Roosevelt, Franklin D. *Complete Presidential Press Conferences of Franklin D. Roosevelt.* 25 vols. New York: Da Capo Press, Inc., 1972.

U.S. Congress. House. Committee on Ways and Means. *Extension of Reciprocal Trade Agreements Act.* H. Report 409 to accompany

H. J. Res. 111, 78th Cong., 1st sess. 2 pts. *House Miscellaneous Reports*, II. Washington, D.C., 1943.

MEMOIRS, AUTOBIOGRAPHIES, AND PUBLISHED PAPERS

Acheson, Dean. *Present At the Creation: My Years in the State Department.* New York: W. W. Norton & Co., Inc., 1969.

Bloom, Sol. *The Autobiography of Sol Bloom.* New York: G. P. Putnam's Sons, 1948.

Connally, Tom, and Steinberg, Alfred. *My Name is Tom Connally.* New York: Thomas Y. Crowell Co., 1954.

Drury, Allen. *A Senate Journal, 1943-1945.* New York: McGraw-Hill Book Co., 1963.

Hoover, Herbert C. *Addresses Upon the American Road: World War II, 1941-1945.* New York: D. Van Nostrand Co., Inc., 1946.

Hull, Cordell. *The Memoirs of Cordell Hull.* 2 vols. New York: The Macmillan Co., 1948.

Israel, Fred L., ed. *The War Diary of Breckinridge Long.* Lincoln, Neb.: University of Nebraska Press, 1966.

Martin, Joseph W., and Donovan, Robert J. *My First Fifty Years in Politics.* New York: McGraw-Hill Book Co., 1960.

Stimson, Henry L., and Bundy, McGeorge. *On Active Service in Peace and War.* New York: Harper & Brothers, 1947.

Young, Donald, ed. *Adventure in Politics: The Memoirs of Philip LaFollette.* New York: Holt, Rinehart and Winston, 1970.

Vandenberg, Arthur H., ed. *The Private Papers of Senator Vandenberg.* Edited with Joe Alex Morris. Cambridge, Mass.: Houghton Mifflin Co., 1952.

CONTEMPORARY BOOKS AND PAMPHLETS

Commission on a Just and Durable Peace of the Federal Council of Churches *A Just and Durable Peace: Statement of Political Propositions.* New York: By the Author, 1943.

———. *A Message from the National Study Conference on the Churches and a Just and Durable Peace.* New York: By the Author, 1942 and 1945.

———. *World Organization: Curative and Creative.* New York: By the Author, 1944.

Dulles, John Foster. *War or Peace*. New York: Macmillan Co., 1950.

Hoover, Herbert, and Gibson, Hugh. *The Problems of Lasting Peace.*
   Garden City, N.Y.: Doubleday, Doran and Co., 1943.

Republican National Committee. *What to Talk About*. New York:
   By the Author, 1944.

Willkie, Wendell. *One World*. New York: Simon & Schuster, 1943.

NEWSPAPERS AND PERIODICALS
(Specific articles are cited in full in the text)

American Mercury
Chicago Daily Tribune
Christian Science Monitor
Current Biography
Life
Nation
New Republic
New York Herald-Tribune
New York Times
New York Times Book Review
New York Times Magazine
Newsweek
Republican
Saturday Evening Post
Time
Vital Speeches
Washington Evening Star
Washington Post

SECONDARY SOURCES

Adler, Selig. *The Isolationist Impulse: Its Twentieth Century Reaction.*
   New York: The Free Press, 1957.

Almond, Gabriel A. *The American People and Foreign Policy*. New York:
   Frederick A. Praeger, Inc., 1960.

Armstrong, John Paul. "Senator Taft and American Foreign Policy, The
   Period of Opposition." Unpublished Ph.D. dissertation, University
   of Chicago, 1953.

Bankson, Marjory Zoet. "The Isolationism of Senator Charles W. Tobey."
   Unpublished Master's Thesis, University of Alaska, 1971.

Barnes, Joseph. *Willkie: The Events He Was Part Of—The Ideas He Fought
   For*. New York: Simon & Schuster, 1952.

Beale, Howard K. *Theodore Roosevelt and the Rise of America to World Power.* Baltimore: Johns Hopkins Press, 1956.

Bernstein, Barton J., ed. *Towards a New Past: Dissenting Essays in American History.* New York: Random House, 1967.

Beyer, Barry Keith. "Thomas E. Dewey, 1937-1947: A Study in Political Leadership." Unpublished Ph.D. dissertation, University of Rochester, 1962.

Blum, John M. "The Limits of American Internationalism: 1941-45." *The Responsibility of Power: Historical Essays in Honor of Hajo Holborn,* 387-401. Edited by Leonard Krieger and Fritz Stern. Garden City, N.Y.: Doubleday & Co., Inc., 1967.

Briggs, Philip J., ed. *Politics in America: Readings and Documents.* New York: MSS Information Corp., 1972.

Burns, James MacGregor. "Bipartisanship and the Weakness of the Party System." *American Perspective* 4 (Spring 1950), 169-174. Reprinted in *America's Foreign Policy.* Edited by Harold Karan Jacobson. New York: Ramdom House, 1965.

——. *The Deadlock of Democracy: Four-Party Politics in America.* Englewood Cliffs, N.J.: Prentice-Hall, Inc., 1967.

——. *Presidential Government: The Crucible of Leadership.* Boston: Houghton Mifflin Co., 1973.

——. *Roosevelt: The Soldier of Freedom.* New York: Harcourt, Brace, Jovanovich, Inc., 1970.

——. "White House vs. Congress." *The Atlantic* 205 (March 1960), 65-69.

Caridi, Ronald J. *The Korean War and American Politics: The Republican Party as a Case Study.* Philadelphia: University of Pennsylvania Press, 1968.

Chadwin, Mark Lincoln. *The Warhawks: American Interventionists before Pearl Harbor.* New York: W. W. Norton & Co., Inc., 1970.

Challener, Richard D., and Fenton, John. "Which Way America? Dulles Always Knew." *American Heritage* 22 (June 1971), 13 and 84-89.

Cole, Wayne S. *America First: The Battle Against Intervention, 1940-1941.* Madison: University of Wisconsin Press, 1953.

——. *Senator Gerald P. Nye and American Foreign Relations.* Minneapolis: University of Minnesota Press, 1962.

Crabb, Cecil V., Jr. *Bipartisan Foreign Policy, Myth or Reality?* Evanston, Illinois: Row, Peterson, 1957.

Dahl, Robert A. *Congress and Foreign Policy.* New York: W. W. Norton & Co., Inc., 1964.

———. ed. *Political Oppositions in Western Democracies.* New Haven and New London, Conn.: Yale University Press, 1966.

Dillon, Mary Earhart. *Wendell Willkie, 1892-1944.* New York: J. B. Lippincott Co., 1952.

Divine, Robert A. *Foreign Policy and U.S. Presidential Elections, 1940-1948.* New York: Franklin Watts, Inc., 1974.

———. *The Reluctant Belligerent: American Entry into World War II.* New York: John Wiley & Sons, Inc., 1965.

———. *Roosevelt and World War II.* Baltimore, Md.: Johns Hopkins Press, 1969.

———. *Second Chance: The Triumph of Internationalism in America During World War II.* New York: Atheneum, 1967.

Feis, Herbert. *Churchill, Roosevelt, Stalin: The War They Waged and the Peace They Sought.* Princeton, N.J.: Princeton University Press, 1957.

———. *The Diplomacy of the Dollar, 1919-1932.* New York: W. W. Norton & Co., Inc., 1966.

Ferrell, Robert H. *American Diplomacy in the Great Depression: Hoover-Stimson Foreign Policy, 1929-1933.* New York: W. W. Norton & Co., Inc., 1970.

———. *Peace in Their Time: The Origins of the Kellogg-Briand Pact.* New York: W. W. Norton & Co., Inc., 1969.

Gaddis, John Lewis. *The United States and the Origins of the Cold War, 1941-1947.* New York: Columbia University Press, 1972.

Gardner, Lloyd C., Schlesinger, Arthur, Jr., and Morgenthau, Hans J. *The Origins of the Cold War.* Waltham, Mass.: Ginn-Blaisdell, 1970.

Gardner, Lloyd C. *Economic Aspects of New Deal Diplomacy.* Madison, Wis.: University of Wisconsin Press, 1964.

Gilbert, Felix. *To the Farewell Address: Ideas of Early American Foreign Policy.* Princeton, N.J.: Princeton University Press, 1961.

Graebner, Norman A. *The New Isolationism: A Study in Politics and Foreign Policy Since 1950.* New York: The Ronald Press Co., 1956.

Graham, Charles John. "The Republican Party and Foreign Policy, 1939-1952." Unpublished Ph.D. dissertation, University of Illinois, 1955.

Grande, Joseph A. "Republican Wartime Politics, 1941-1945." Unpublished Master's Thesis, University of Buffalo, 1955.

Grassmuck, George L. *Sectional Biases in Congress on Foreign Policy.* The Johns Hopkins University Studies in Historical and Political Science LXVIII, 3. Baltimore: Johns Hopkins Press, 1951.

Grew, Joseph C. *Turbulent Era: A Diplomatic Record of Forty Years, 1904-1945.* 2 vols. Boston: Houghton Mifflin Co., 1952.

Guhin, Michael A. *John Foster Dulles: A Statesman and His Times.* New York: Columbia University Press, 1972.

Gustafson, Milton Odell. "Congress and Foreign Aid: The First Phase, UNRRA, 1943-1947." Unpublished Ph.D. dissertation, University of Nebraska, 1966.

————. "Senator Vandenberg and State Department Decision-Making." Paper presented at the 84th Annual Meeting of the American Historical Association, Washington, D.C., December 30, 1969.

Herring, George C., Jr. *Aid to Russia, 1941-1946: Strategy, Diplomacy, the Origins of the Cold War.* New York: Columbia University Press, 1973.

————. "Experiment in Foreign Aid: Lend Lease, 1941-1945." Unpublished Ph.D. dissertation, University of Virginia, 1965.

Hofstadter, Richard. *The American Political Tradition and the Men Who Made It.* New York: Alfred A. Knopf, Inc., 1948.

Hoopes, Townsend. *The Devil and John Foster Dulles.* Boston: Little, Brown and Co., 1973.

Johnson, Curtiss S. *Raymond E. Baldwin, Connecticut Statesman.* Chester, Conn.: Pequot Press, 1972.

Johnson, Donald Bruce. *The Republican Party and Wendell Willkie.* Urbana, Ill.: University of Illinois Press, 1960.

Jonas, Manfred. *Isolationism in America, 1935-1941.* Ithaca, N.Y.: Cornell University Press, 1969.

Jones, Charles O. *The Minority Party in Congress.* Boston: Little, Brown and Co., 1970.

Kissinger, Henry A. *American Foreign Policy: Three Essays.* New York: W. W. Norton & Co., Inc., 1969.

Kolko, Gabriel. *The Politics of War: The World and United States Foreign Policy, 1943-1945.* New York: Random House, 1968.

Krock, Arthur. *Memoirs: Sicty Years on the Firing Line.* New York: Funk & Wagnalls, 1968.

LaFeber, Walter. *The New Empire: An Interpretation of American Expansion, 1860-1898.* Ithaca, N.Y.: Cornell University Press, 1963.

Leary, William M., Jr. "Smith of New Jersey: A Biography of H. Alexander Smith, United States Senator from New Jersey 1944-1959." Unpublished Ph.D. dissertation, Princeton University, 1966.

Levin, N. Gordon, Jr. *Woodrow Wilson and World Politics: America's*

Response to War and Revolution. New York: Oxford University Press, 1968.

Link, Arthur S. *Wilson the Diplomatist: A Look at His Major Foreign Policies.* Chicago: Quadrangle Books, 1965.

McCormick, Thomas J. *China Market: America's Quest for Informal Empire, 1893-1901.* Chicago: Quadrangle Books, 1967.

McCoy, Donald R. *Landon of Kansas.* Lincoln: University of Nebraska Press, 1966.

——. "Republican Opposition During Wartime, 1941-1945." *Mid America: An Historical Review* 49 (July 1967), 174-189.

McNeill, William Hardy. *America, Britain and Russia: Their Cooperation and Conflict, 1941-1946.* III, *Survey of International Affairs.* London: Royal Institute of International Affairs, 1953.

Mayer, George H. *The Republican Party, 1854-1966.* New York: Oxford University Press, 1967.

——. "The Republican Party, 1932-1952." Vol. 3, *History of U.S. Political Parties.* 4 vols. Chelsea House Publishers and R. R. Bowker Co., 1973. Edited by Arthur M. Schlesinger, Jr.

Moore, John Robert. "The Conservative Coalition in the United States Senate, 1942-1945." *Journal of Southern History* 33 (August 1967), 368-376.

Moore, Newell S. "The Role of Senator Arthur H. Vandenberg in American Foreign Affairs." Unpublished Ph.D. dissertation, George Peabody College, 1954.

Patterson, James T. "Alternatives to Globalism: Robert A. Taft and American Foreign Policy, 1939-1945." *The Historian: A Journal of History* 36 (August 1974), 670-688.

——. *Congressional Conservatism and the New Deal: The Growth of the Conservative Coalition in Congress, 1933-1939.* Lexington: University of Kentucky Press, 1967.

——. "A Conservative Coalition Forms in Congress, 1933-1939." *Journal of American History* 52 (March 1966), 757-772.

——. *Mr. Republican, A Biography of Robert A. Taft.* Boston: Houghton Mifflin Co., 1972.

Philipose, Thomas. "The 'Loyal Opposition': Republican Leaders and Foreign Policy, 1943-1946." Unpublished Ph.D. dissertation, University of Denver, 1972.

Polenberg, Richard. *War and Society: The United States, 1941-1945.* Philadelphia: J. B. Lippincott Co., 1972.

Poole, Walter Sloan. "The Quest for a Republican Foreign Policy: 1941-1951." Unpublished Ph.D. dissertation, University of Pennsylvania, 1968.

Riddle, Donald H. *The Truman Committee: A Study in Congressional Responsibility.* New Brunswick, N.J.: Rutgers University Press, 1964.

Rieselbach, Leroy N. *The Roots of Isolationism: Congressional Voting and Presidential Leadership in Foreign Policy.* Indianapolis: The Bobbs-Merrill Co., Inc., 1966.

Robinson, James A. *Congress and Foreign Policy-Making: A Study in Legislative Influence and Initiative.* Homewood, Ill.: The Dorsey Press, 1967.

Salter, J. T., ed. *Public Men In and Out of Office.* Chapel Hill, N.C.: University of North Carolina Press, 1946.

Schroeder, Paul W. *The Axis Alliance and Japanese-American Relations.* Ithaca, N.Y.: Cornell University Press, 1958.

Sherwood, Robert E. *Roosevelt and Hopkins, an Intimate History.* 2 vols. New York: Harper & Brothers, 1950.

Smith, Gaddis. *American Diplomacy During the Second World War, 1941-1945.* New York: John Wiley and Sons, Inc., 1965.

Tompkins, C. David. *Senator Arthur H. Vandenberg: The Evolution of a Modern Republican, 1884-1945.* East Lansing, Mich.: Michigan State University Press, 1970.

Van Alstyne, Richard W. *The Rising American Empire.* New York: Oxford University Press, 1960.

Waltz, Kenneth N. *Foreign Policy and Democratic Politics: The American and British Experience.* Boston: Little, Brown and Co., 1967.

Westerfield, H. Bradford. *Foreign Policy and Party Politics: Pearl Harbor to Korea.* New Haven: Yale University Press, 1955.

White, William S. *The Taft Story.* New York: Harper & Row, 1954.

Williams, William Appleman. *The Tragedy of American Diplomacy.* New York: Dell Publishing Co., Inc., 1962.

Wiltz, John E. *From Isolation to War, 1931-1941.* New York: Thomas Y. Crowell Co., 1968.

Young, Roland. *Congressional Politics in the Second World War.* New York: Columbia University Press, 1956.

INDEX

About the Author

Richard E. Darilek received his A.B. from Rice University in 1967, his M.A. from Princeton University in 1969, and his Ph.D. from Princeton in 1973. He is assistant professor of history at Lehman College.